Stay the Distance

Marshal of the Royal Air Force
Sir Michael Beetham GCB CBE DFC AFC

Stay the Distance

The Life and Times of
Marshal of the Royal Air Force
Sir Michael Beetham

Peter Jacobs

Foreword by Sebastian Cox

FRONTLINE BOOKS, LONDON

FRONTLINE BOOKS, LONDON

Stay the Distance:
The Life and Times of Marshal of the Royal Air Force Sir Michael Beetham

This edition published in 2011 by Frontline Books, an imprint of
Pen & Sword Books Limited, 47 Church Street, Barnsley, S. Yorkshire, S70 2AS
www.frontline-books.com

ISBN: 978-1-84832-552-4

CIP data records for this title are available from the British Library

For more information on our books, please visit
www.frontline-books.com,
email info@frontline-books.com
or write to us at the above address.

Typeset by JCS Publishing Services Ltd, www.jcs-publishing.co.uk,
in palatino font (11pt on 13.2pt)

Printed in Great Britain by CPI Antony Rowe

Contents

Illustrations

COLOUR PLATES
(between pages 172 and 173)

Foreword

It is both a pleasure and an honour to have been asked to contribute a foreword to this biography of a truly distinguished airman. Sir Michael Beetham's career spans some forty years of the Royal Air Force and encompasses a period when air power truly came of age. Here, encapsulated in the service of one individual, is the story of the rapid advance and revolutionary impact of air power on military operations and the wider world. It is entirely fitting that Sir Michael's career should span the years from the piston-engined Lancaster through the dawn of the jet age and on to the modern era in the shape of the Tornado. He joined an Air Force that was moulded by the visionary ideas of Lord Trenchard concerning the potential strategic effect of air power and he helped to turn those ideas into reality in the skies over Germany. There can be few more fearsome cauldrons in which to forge one's character than the winter of 1943–4 and the Battle of Berlin, arguably the fiercest battle that the RAF has ever fought. He enjoyed his fair share of luck, as any who survived that battle did, but it is also clear from these pages that even at the age of twenty his powers of leadership were combined with an intense professionalism. The fact that he and his crew, if not the aircraft, came through their operational tour unscathed owed as much to the skills honed in the crew by the young captain as it did to good fortune.

Sir Michael's post-war career reflects precisely the practical application of those qualities of character and professionalism forged in the cockpit of a Lancaster over Germany, culminating in the longest tenure of any CAS since Lord Trenchard himself. That too seems entirely fitting, since the two men have two particular qualities in common. First, their capacity to operate successfully in the highly politicised world that Service Chiefs must *ipso facto* inhabit, and to steer their service through a time of retrenchment. And second, their ability to combine such political skills with the successful application of air power in war. As the following chapters show, at nearly every stage of his career he has made a significant contribution to the task he was given. It would be too easy to assume, for example, that there was no great difficulty involved in developing something so commonplace in the modern world as air-to-air refuelling but that would be to underestimate both the technical and the philosophical challenges it posed. Here too there is a symmetry to Sir Michael's career in that the young pioneer of aerial tanking would, as CAS, not only see aerial refuelling prove vital to the successful conduct of the Falklands campaign, but would also oversee the purchase of more VC10s and Tristar tankers, strategic assets that were to prove of immeasurable value in later conflicts.

Similarly, in both RAF Germany and NATO he showed himself to be capable of dealing with the inherent complexities of inter-alliance and inter-service relationships. Whilst no one could be in any doubt about his commitment to the RAF and air power he showed himself capable of understanding and appreciating the problems and perspectives of others. His recognition that a truly joint approach to warfare was essential but that this also required careful explanation of the role that air power could play to the other services still has resonance today. It is perhaps unfortunate that at the time of the Falklands he could not persuade some naval officers, still embittered by the carrier controversies of the 1960s, to concede that the RAF voice on air power was worth a hearing.

It is a sad fact that too few of the RAF's post-war leaders have been the subject of biographies or penned their own stories. Of the post-1945 Chiefs of Air Staff only the giant wartime figures of Sir Arthur Tedder and Sir John Slessor have full biographies and both men restricted their autobiographies to their wartime and not their post-war service. Sir Dermot Boyle wrote a short privately published memoir, but no other post-war CAS has his story in print. Sir Michael Beetham is undoubtedly a worthy addition to this august company and the story laid out in these pages is therefore doubly to be welcomed. It will fascinate and inspire the reader in equal measure, and I thoroughly commend it to anyone with an interest in the RAF or defence.

Sebastian Cox
Head of Air Historical Branch (RAF)

Acknowledgements

First and foremost I am indebted to Sebastian Cox, the head of the Air Historical Branch, and his staff. For so many years the AHB has proved invaluable, not just for me but for all authors of RAF history, and so I say a big thank you once again.

In addition to the AHB, there have been many individuals who have helped me compile the most important years, from a historical point of view, of Sir Michael's career, most notably when he was Commander-in-Chief RAF Germany and Commander of the Second Allied Tactical Air Force and then, of course, during the five years when he led the Royal Air Force as the Chief of the Air Staff. I would, therefore, like to publicly acknowledge the contributions of: Air Chief Marshal Sir David Cousins (PSO to Sir Michael 1981–2), Air Chief Marshal Sir Michael Stear (PSO 1977–9), Air Marshal Ian Macfadyen (PSO 1976–7), Air Vice-Marshal Nigel Baldwin (RAF Historical Society), Air Vice-Marshal Peter Harding (PSO 1976), Dr Michael Fopp (RAF Museum), David Bonner (PS 1981–2), Andrew Ward (PS 1977–8), Mike Winning (ADC 1975–8), Jeremy Brown (air attaché in Brazil 1981) and Peter Walker (214 Squadron Association). I would also like to thank two members of Sir Michael's wartime crew, Les Bartlett and Reg Payne. I have now known them both for twenty years and they have provided me with much information over the years. Each time I have seen the crew back together again I find it a most special moment. I am also indebted to Sir Michael's son, Alex, for his personal interest and contribution to this work; I know that Sir Michael is extremely grateful too.

My opportunity to write Sir Michael's story only came about because of the sudden death of Air Commodore Henry Probert, the highly respected former head of the Air Historical Branch, who had originally intended to write the book, and so I would like to thank Michael Leventhal at Frontline Books for giving me the opportunity to step in and tell this most remarkable story; I only hope I have done the subject justice and that Henry would have approved.

The photographs used in the book have come from a number of sources. Most are from official RAF sources, and I must again thank the AHB for giving permission for their use, but others were kindly given to Sir Michael over the years – from other air forces, industry or friends – and, where possible, I have acknowledged these accordingly.

My final thanks go to Lady Beetham, for so many wonderful lunches and welcome cups of coffee over the past two and a half years, and to my wife, Claire, for her patience and understanding. I have written a number of books over the years and each one has taken a considerable amount of time but this one, above all others, has taken the most.

Abbreviations

AAFCE	Allied Air Forces Central Europe
ACAS	Assistant Chief of the Air Staff
ACDS	Assistant Chief of the Defence Staff
ACOS	Assistant Chief of Staff
ACRC	Air Crew Reception Centre
ADC	Aide-de-Camp
ADGE	Air Defence Ground Environment
ADV	Air Defence Variant
AEW	Airborne Early Warning
AFCENT	Allied Forces Central Europe
AFNORTH	Allied Forces Northern Europe
AFPRB	Air Force Pay Review Body
AFSOUTH	Allied Forces Southern Europe
AFU	Advanced Flying Unit
AHQ	Air Headquarters
AOC	Air Officer Commanding
AOC-in-C	Air Officer Commanding-in-Chief
ATAF	Allied Tactical Air Force
AWACS	Airborne Warning and Control System
BAOR	British Army of the Rhine
BFAP	British Forces Arabian Peninsula
BOAC	British Overseas Airways Corporation
BRITANZ	British Australian and New Zealand
BRIXMIS	British Commanders'-in-Chief Mission to the Soviet Forces in Germany
CAS	Chief of the Air Staff
CDS	Chief of the Defence Staff
CGS	Chief of the General Staff
C-in-C	Commander-in-Chief
CINCENT	Commander-in-Chief Central
CINCUKAIR	Commander-in-Chief United Kingdom Air
CNS	Chief of the Naval Staff

COBR	Cabinet Office Briefing Room
COMAAFCE	Commander Allied Air Forces Central Europe
COS	Chief of Staff
COS(I)	Chief of Staff (Informal)
CTTO	Central Trials and Tactics Organisation
DCDS	Deputy Chief of the Defence Staff
DCINCSTC	Deputy Commander-in-Chief Strike Command
DCOS	Deputy Chief of Staff
DEFCON	Defence Readiness Condition
DFC	Distinguished Flying Cross
DFM	Distinguished Flying Medal
DOR	Director Operational Requirements
DSACEUR	Deputy Supreme Allied Commander Europe
DSO	Distinguished Service Order
EAP	Experimental Aircraft Programme
EFTS	Elementary Flying Training School
FAB	Força Aerea Brasileira (Brazilian air force)
FCO	Foreign and Commonwealth Office
FIDO	Fog Intense Dispersal Operation
FRL	Flight Refuelling Limited
GEC	General Electric Company
GMT	Greenwich Mean Time
HCU	Heavy Conversion Unit
HDU	Hose Drum Unit
IAF	Indian Air Force
IDC	Imperial Defence College
IDS	Interdictor/Strike
ILS	Instrument Landing System
IRA	Irish Republican Army
IRBM	Intermediate Range Ballistic Missile
ITW	Initial Training Wing
JHQ	Joint Headquarters
LAC	Leading Aircraftman
LDV	Local Defence Volunteers
LFS	Lancaster Finishing School
LTC	Long-Term Costing
MEAF	Middle East Air Force
MISREP	Mission Report
MOD	Ministry of Defence
MRCA	Multi-Role Combat Aircraft
MRR	Maritime Radar Reconnaissance

MRT	Medium-Range Transport
MT	Motor Transport
NAAFI	Navy Army and Air Force Institutes
NATO	North Atlantic Treaty Organisation
NFT	Night-Flying Test
NORTHAG	Northern Army Group
OATS	Officer Advanced Training School
OCU	Operational Conversion Unit
OR	Operational Requirement
ORD	Optional Retirement Date
ORP	Operational Readiness Platform
OTU	Operational Training Unit
PS	Private Secretary
PSO	Personal Staff Officer
PUS	Permanent Under-Secretary
QRA	Quick Reaction Alert
RAAF	Royal Australian Air Force
RAFG	Royal Air Force Germany
RAFVR	Royal Air Force Volunteer Reserve
RNZAF	Royal New Zealand Air Force
RSAF	Royal Saudi Air Force
RV	Rendezvous
SACEUR	Supreme Allied Commander Europe
SALT	Strategic Arms Limitation Talks
SAM	Surface-to-Air Missile
SASO	Senior Air Staff Officer
SHAPE	Supreme Headquarters Allied Powers Europe
SLAF	Sri Lankan Air Force
SO	Staff Officer
SOC	Sector Operations Centre
SRT	Short-Range Transport
SSBN	Ship Submersible Ballistic Nuclear
TACEVAL	Tactical Evaluation
TTTE	Tri-National Tornado Training Establishment
USAAF	United States Army Air Forces
VE	Victory in Europe
WAAF	Women's Auxiliary Air Force

Introduction

Rarely does an opportunity like this come along. To be asked to tell the story of one of the Royal Air Force's greatest post-war leaders, and the longest-serving Chief of the Air Staff since Lord Trenchard, is an immense privilege, particularly because it was Sir Michael who asked me to write it.

When I joined the Royal Air Force as an apprentice in 1977, Sir Michael Beetham had just been appointed as the Chief of the Air Staff. At that point in time, we could not have been any further apart; me at the very bottom of the ladder and wondering if I had made the right decision after leaving school, and Sir Michael at the very top of the service I had just joined. Much has happened since then, and thirty-three years later I feel enormously privileged to have come to know Sir Michael very well over many years.

Our first meeting was in 1989 when I started writing and was living in Lincoln. As the president of the 50 and 61 Squadrons' Association, Sir Michael had just unveiled a memorial to the two former Bomber Command squadrons on the site of the former airfield of RAF Skellingthorpe in Lincoln, where both squadrons had operated together during the Second World War. The airfield had long gone and had become a housing estate, and I had come across the ceremony by chance. It was a pleasant Sunday morning in June and I was out to buy a newspaper when the Lancaster of the Battle of Britain Memorial Flight passed low overhead. Curious to find out what was going on, I went to see why a crowd had gathered nearby. I started talking to one of the veterans, who happened to be Les Bartlett. We soon found that we had so much in common, mainly because of our RAF aircrew connection but also because we were both from Southampton. I soon discovered that Les had been Sir Michael's wartime bomb aimer and so began my interest in the Beetham crew, and it was also the start of my long involvement with the Squadrons' Association.

While I did not meet Sir Michael on that day in June, I did end up producing the Casualty Roll of Honour for the association and I also wrote an article for the local newspaper about the wartime experiences of the Beetham crew when they flew from the airfield of Skellingthorpe during the Second World War. Both of these projects took me directly to Sir Michael, and I met him for the first time in November that year. I still have the 'Dear Jacobs' letter inviting me to his home in Norfolk and I vividly remember arriving in the area about an hour and a half early, for fear of being late.

That was over twenty years ago and things have moved on significantly since then. First, Sir Michael kindly agreed to write the foreword to my book *The Lancaster Story* and since then I have become the chairman of the 50 and 61 Squadrons' Association. This brought me into more frequent contact with Sir Michael and we became quite well acquainted. Then, following the untimely death of Henry Probert, who had originally intended to write Sir Michael's story, and the success of my own book *Bomb Aimer Over Berlin*, based on the wartime memoirs of Sir Michael's bomb aimer, Les Bartlett, I felt honoured when Sir Michael asked me to write this book.

Of all the books I have written, this has been by far the most fascinating and I have been enormously privileged to visit Sir Michael regularly in the comfort of his own home in Norfolk during the past two and a half years, spending countless hours talking to him in detail about his life. And what a fascinating life he has lived. Before he was twenty-one years old he had completed a tour of operations as a Lancaster pilot with Bomber Command and he had been awarded the Distinguished Flying Cross. He then went on to enjoy a most distinguished career in the Royal Air Force, ending up as the Chief of the Air Staff during the Falklands conflict of 1982; his career had both begun and ended in warfare on the world stage.

From the way his career unfolded, I can see why Sir Michael reached the very top. This might seem a flippant remark to make, but there were some defining moments throughout his career and I have pointed these out along the way. He certainly had no early advantages in his career. He was not born the son of an air marshal and so the name 'Beetham' would have been quite unknown during the early years. Furthermore, it was never his intention during those first years after the Second World War to forge a career; he simply wanted to stay flying and he even took a reduction in rank in order to do so. But there were certainly times in his early career when he was doing something quite different from the norm and this took my research into areas that I previously knew little about, such as aerial surveying of Africa during the post-war years, the nuclear tests at Maralinga in 1956, the pioneering days of air-to-air refuelling in the late 1950s and the near disaster of the Cuban Missile Crisis of 1962.

Sir Michael soon found himself advancing through the ranks at some pace; he was a wing commander for less than four years and a group captain less than five. Then, having reached air rank at the age of forty-three, more senior appointments came his way until he reached the very top. He then served as the Chief of the Air Staff for more than five years, making him the second-longest-serving Chief since Trenchard, and he is now just one of four men to hold the rank of marshal of the Royal Air Force.

In addition to his personal memories of events, Sir Michael has kept several boxes containing his memoirs, as well as many photograph albums, which has ensured that an accurate record of his life can be told, in particular of those years when he held the most senior appointments. It is a remarkable story of a truly remarkable man and the title of the book takes its name from the Beetham family motto: 'Stay the Distance'.

Finally, the book rightly focuses on Sir Michael's career in the Royal Air Force as there is neither the space nor the appetite to examine his personal life, although passing references to his family are made. From my perspective, I am delighted. The 'Dear Jacobs' letters of twenty years ago have now been replaced by those beginning 'Dear Peter'. Enjoy the book!

Peter Jacobs

CHAPTER 1

Southern Skies

———

In life and death, timing is everything, and no date is more fundamental than the era of one's birth. For example, young men born from around 1927 onwards were fortunate enough to be just too young for war service and they inherited a secure peacetime Britain soon to be at the epicentre of the swinging sixties. But for those born even five years earlier fate offered a very different prospect. Their generation was called upon, quite literally, to save the world in a total war unleashed by Nazi Germany. Michael Beetham was one of this latter cadre. Born in 1923, he had flown thirty missions as a Lancaster bomber pilot, an officer in RAF Bomber Command, against some of the heaviest-defended German targets before he had reached the age of twenty-one, indeed before he had even learned to drive a car.

Nearly four decades later, as Air Chief Marshal Sir Michael Beetham, and the most senior officer in the RAF, he masterminded the astonishing Vulcan raid on Stanley in the Falkland Islands – the longest bombing raid in history. His career had begun and ended at the forefront of conflict. Yet, had he been born just three or four years later, he would most likely have become nothing more combative than a Home Counties solicitor with a penchant for golf.

Beetham's military career began one damp October morning in the unlikely setting of the stands at Lord's cricket ground. Turning up promptly at 9 a.m. as instructed, the eighteen-year-old Beetham sat with hundreds of other young hopefuls on the hard wooden benches for six hours, staring at the empty pitch, becoming increasingly hungry and thirsty. Finally, he was issued with bedding and marched away. His war had begun.

Michael Beetham's ancestry has been traced back by some genealogists to the fifth century, as Scandinavian and Norman nobility. The origins of the Beetham family who settled in Britain are in the pretty village of Beetham in Cumbria. No fewer than eleven generations of the family resided at Beetham Hall, which today can be found in part ruin to the south of the village. Exactly how long the family resided at Beetham Hall is unclear but it is known that Beetham Hall was built between the early and mid-fourteenth century, and the family's significance in the local area is still marked in the local church by their battered effigies and tombs, which sadly were all vandalised during the Civil Wars in the mid-seventeenth century.

The family history trail then goes cold but it is presumed that the Beethams remained in the north of England. The trail is picked up again in 1794 when a George Beetham was born in Leeds; this was Michael Beetham's great-great-grandfather and provides the first evidence of a military connection to the family. George joined the 2nd Life Guards in 1812 and served with the regiment during the Peninsular War and then at the Battle of Waterloo in 1815, where he was wounded by a sabre cut to the head during the famous cavalry charge against the French Grand Battery.

The nineteenth century witnessed a succession of four George Beethams. Michael's father, George Clarence Beetham, born in July 1891, was brought up in Yorkshire before the First World War. In November 1915 he enlisted into the York and Lancaster Regiment. Then in January 1917 George crossed the Channel to face the horrors of trench warfare on the Western Front and distinguished himself during the Battle of Cambrai in November, for which he was awarded the Military Cross for his leadership and bravery. Having survived the long and enduring hardship of the trenches, George returned home at the end of the war and married Eva Vivian Adam, the daughter of a Scottish banker.

The couple had a daughter in 1920 and Michael James Beetham was born on 17 May 1923. The family lived on the outskirts of London and at the age of twelve Michael was accepted into the prestigious St Marylebone Grammar School. The academic standards of the school were high but even at this young age Michael had the self-discipline to apply himself and the enthusiasm to compete successfully at athletics, cricket and rugby. By 1939, now aged sixteen, Michael was playing in the first fifteen and was old enough to appreciate the developing crisis in Europe. On 2 September, the day before Britain declared war on Germany, the boys of St Marylebone's were evacuated to Redruth in Cornwall. Michael was billeted with a friendly local family, the Martins, in the attractive coastal village of Portreath.

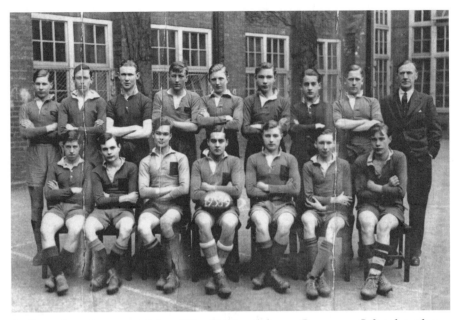

1. Seated centre as captain of the St Marylebone Grammar School rugby third fifteen, March 1939 (St Marylebone Grammar School)

After the Battle of France, as the last British Army stragglers were plucked from the beaches of Dunkirk, it became clear that a German invasion of Britain would be attempted. The formation of a nearby unit of the Local Defence Volunteers gave the senior students and masters the chance to do their bit for King and Country. Because Michael and his fellow senior boys were under the age of seventeen, they were not officially members of the LDV but they were allowed to volunteer to attend the local unit every week under the supervision of the school's masters. The boys learned drill, how to act as lookouts and how to make 'Molotov cocktails'. It was an exciting time for Michael and, like the other boys, he genuinely felt they would be capable of deterring any German invasion along their allocated part of the coastline in Cornwall. They spent their weekly stints with one of the school masters positioned high on the cliff tops overlooking the harbour. The school staff were an inspiration to the boys, making them believe they really could make a difference should the Germans invade. Had Michael and his schoolmates actually looked down from those Cornish cliffs on advancing German storm troopers, there is no doubt the boys would have hurled their homemade bombs with determination, but one hates to contemplate the inevitable outcome.

Michael's first taste of war itself came in the middle of one of his matriculation exams as German bombers were attacking Falmouth. As the air-raid siren wailed over Redruth, Michael and his school chums were ordered to the shelter. Once inside, the exam's invigilator struggled to prevent the boys discussing the unfinished exam paper.

With his exams successfully completed, Michael left Cornwall to return home for the summer holidays. By then his father, having been recalled to the army as a major, was stationed as second-in-command to an infantry training battalion at Hilsea Barracks near Portsmouth. It was now the beginning of July 1940 and Michael was seventeen years old. He had intended to return to school to gain some higher qualifications, after which he imagined himself joining the army as an officer, and while at home he was interviewed by a colonel at Hilsea Barracks with a view of joining the York and Lancaster Regiment. However, Michael's ideas were very soon to change because from his magnificent vantage point on the hills overlooking Portsmouth he witnessed the opening phase of the Battle of Britain as it unfolded in the skies over southern England.

Because it was a high-priority target for the Luftwaffe, Portsmouth was protected by heavy anti-aircraft guns, light anti-aircraft guns and balloons; to Michael, it was a magnificent theatre. The port came under attack as early as 11 July. It was about 6 p.m. when Hurricanes from nearby Tangmere were scrambled to intercept Heinkel He111s, escorted by Messerschmitt Bf110s, which were heading for Portsmouth at 18,000 feet. The Hurricanes shot down two of the Heinkels but some of the bombers managed to bomb the town and port, which caused slight damage to the town and to the aircraft factory of the Airspeed Company and there was some damage to a few French chasseurs in the port.

The air battle in the skies over southern England continued throughout the summer of 1940 as battle after battle took place, and each day Michael became more determined to be part of it. The weather was good and the raging battles were spectacular, although he was fully aware that the young men of Fighter Command were fighting for survival. Then he came to a decision. From that moment on there was to be no more school and he was not going to join the army. It was going to be the Royal Air Force and he spoke with his father to inform him of his decision. Naturally, his father had imagined Michael following his footsteps into the York and Lancasters but he could see how determined his son was and after some discussion he agreed.

Major Beetham and his unit were then moved to Leicester as it was considered more sensible for a training battalion to be in the Midlands rather than remaining in Portsmouth under the constant threat of attack. Having made the decision to join the Royal Air Force, Michael then had to decide what he should do next, because at the age of seventeen he was too young to join up. His father knew a chartered accountant at the accounting firm of Corton & Co. in Leicester and so Michael started working there. Mr Corton, who ran the company, saw Michael as a likeable recruit and paid for him to complete a correspondence course, hoping that Michael would pursue his career with the company after the war.

On his eighteenth birthday Michael applied to join the RAF Volunteer Reserve as a trainee pilot. However, the rush of volunteers at that stage of the war meant that he had to wait before his application was processed. In July he was called before the selection board in Birmingham, where he was interviewed, given a medical and set some aptitude tests to determine whether he was suitable for pilot training. Once he returned home it was an anxious time for him as he had to wait to find out whether or not he had been accepted. He continued working at Corton & Co. but it was not long before he received the good news he had hoped for. He was accepted into the RAFVR as a trainee pilot.

On 6 October Michael Beetham went to No 3 Air Crew Reception Centre at St John's Wood in London. A number of ACRCs had been established across the country, and overseas, to receive the many thousands of young men who had volunteered for aircrew duties. Beetham arrived to find that the ACRC was set up at Lord's cricket ground. It was 9 a.m. and the weather was miserable. There were hundreds of other young hopefuls and he sat in one of the stands overlooking the empty cricket pitch. Ironically, it was the same ground where before the war he had spent many happy hours after school watching cricket, as his school was just around the corner and the boys were allowed in free after 4 p.m. to watch the cricket before going home. Now back at Lord's for the first time since leaving school, it was a completely different scene. Apart from the miserable weather, there seemed to be little or no organisation. There were no refreshments provided and he just had to wait for his number to be called for processing. He had hoped that because his surname began with the letter 'B' he would be called early but that did not prove to be the case. Eventually, at 3 p.m. he was called and he was issued with his mattress, blankets and pillows before he was put into a squad of twenty-five recruits.

The recruits were accommodated in houses and flats all around the local area, and Beetham was accommodated in a spacious flat at Viceroy Court overlooking Regent's Park. He was to share a room with six of his squad members but there was no furniture and he noticed that he was the youngest in the group. At 5 p.m. it was time for their first meal and they were marched across to London Zoo; most of the wild animals had been evacuated, but the monkeys had remained – much to the amusement of the new recruits.

For all volunteer aircrew the ACRC was where their training first began. Beetham was attested into the RAFVR and during the first week he was kitted out with his new uniform. The rest of his time was spent in Regent's Park learning how to march and attending various lectures. There were also inoculations, medical and dental examinations, physical-fitness training and, of course, the inevitable kit inspections. Most of his squad members were much older than him: some had been in the services for some years, as ground crew in the RAF or in the army, some had been in the police force and the others were from a variety of backgrounds and locations. The recruits were paid two shillings and sixpence per day and the evenings were often free, which gave them the chance to enjoy London and share a quiet drink or two. Beetham, of course, was no stranger to London and his local knowledge often proved beneficial to the other recruits.

After nearly three weeks at the ACRC he was posted to No 17 Initial Training Wing at Scarborough. ITWs had been set up across the country to teach recruits basic service skills and to prepare them for flying training. Beetham and his colleagues travelled by train from London to Scarborough, where the ITW had been set up at Scarborough College, and Beetham's course was to be the first. The recruits spent much time in the classroom as part of their ground school training and the subjects included meteorology, theory of flight, navigation and aircraft recognition. It was not all time in the classroom and for the recruits there was much time spent outdoors doing yet more drill and more physical exercise. It was a cold winter at Scarborough, but for Beetham his time at ITW was enjoyable. Away from the barracks the locals in the nearby towns and villages proved very friendly and, of course, the local Yorkshire beer was always very good.

At the end of February 1942 Beetham left Scarborough for No 11 Elementary Flying Training School, which was located at a civilian flying school at Perth in Scotland. He was now 1576038 Leading Aircraftman M. J. Beetham and he travelled to Scotland with twenty of his colleagues. As far as his own future as a pilot was concerned, the next phase was crucial. Although there would be a certain amount of flying instruction at EFTS, the aim of the school was to decide whether the pupils had the ability and potential to succeed as pilots and whether it was worth sending them abroad for further training. It was immediately obvious to Beetham that life at Perth was going to be even better than Scarborough. He was accommodated in a large, rather lovely, manor house and the addition of flying pay meant that he was now paid seven shillings and sixpence per day.

After just a few days of ground school, he was ready for his first flight. The aircraft used at EFTS was the excellent De Havilland DH82A Tiger Moth II. Beetham's first flight at EFTS, and indeed his first flight ever, took place on 2 March 1942. It was a cold day and there was snow on the ground. Unsurprisingly, he was apprehensive before the flight as he had never been airborne before and he had no idea of how he would react. However, all the apprehension disappeared and he was soon airborne in Tiger Moth 6779 with his instructor, Sergeant Bruce, at the controls. Beetham felt fine and he found his first touch of the controls exhilarating. It was a very short first flight, lasting just ten minutes, during which there was just enough time to get used to the cockpit layout and to experience life off the ground. Later that day he was airborne again, with the same pilot and in the same aircraft. This was the first of two exercises during which the instructor taught the student how to climb and descend, by using the control column and the aircraft's engine power, and how to turn by using the ailerons and rudder; all basic skills for a pilot but at twenty minutes and forty minutes respectively, there was little time in the air to learn. The second of these exercises was flown with Pilot Officer Kay, who then became Beetham's personal instructor during his stay at Perth.

The pressure on the EFTS to get the student pilots assessed and then out again in the shortest possible time soon became quite evident. On 11 March Beetham flew three times. At the start of the day he had only learned the simple basics but by the end of the day he had also been taught taxiing the aircraft, carrying out medium-rate turns, how to glide and land the aircraft, and spinning; all this in a combined total of ninety-five minutes in the air. There was no time to rest as he was airborne twice a day for the next two days, when he was assessed on all the skills he had been so rapidly taught. The course finished that same day, 13 March. Beetham had been at Perth for just two weeks and had flown his first five hours but he had obviously done well enough to proceed, although others found they had not; they were destined for other aircrew specialisations or for ground duties.

Beetham next went to the Air Crew Despatch Centre at Heaton Park, Manchester, where he joined many other new trainees destined for aircrew training schools around the world. When war broke out the RAF had had a shortfall of more than a thousand pilots, which led to a large demand for pilot-training facilities. More airfields were needed, as were more aircraft and instructors, and the combination of insufficient resources, uncertain weather and the constant threat of attack required that alternative arrangements be made. Provisional plans for RAF pilots to undergo flying training overseas had already been put in place and this led to the Empire Air Training Scheme, later to become the British Commonwealth Air Training Plan, which was a four-nation agreement between the UK, Canada, Australia and New Zealand; there had been similar talks with South Africa, Southern Rhodesia and the United States of America. The first overseas flying-training schools were in operation by early 1940, and all the schools planned in the scheme were in operation by the end of 1941, including the training of RAF cadets in the USA through the Lend-Lease Act.

While Beetham was at Heaton Park rumours of their destination started spreading among the airmen awaiting disposal. One day it was to be Canada and the next day it was South Africa – or so the rumours suggested. Beetham did not have to wait long to find out where he was destined for, but when he did receive the news it came as a bit of a surprise. He was off to America to be trained under the Arnold Scheme, a scheme named after General 'Hap' Arnold who had visited Britain during April 1941 to discuss the training of RAF pilots. Arnold had agreed to provide one-third of the US Army Air Corps training capacity for the training of RAF pilots in the south-eastern states of America. The scheme meant that RAF pilots would learn to fly in aircraft belonging to the US Army Air Corps and by American instructors, and the first RAF cadets started pilot training in America under the Arnold Scheme in June 1941; by the end of the war some 7,500 British cadets had been trained under the scheme.

Three days later, on 24 March, Beetham left Heaton Park. His parents had travelled to Manchester to say goodbye and he met up with them at the Grand Hotel. It was an emotional time as the family knew it would be some time before they would all be together again. He then travelled to Gourock on the Firth of Clyde, where he embarked on the SS *Banfora* and sailed for North America the following day. The *Banfora* was a 6,000-ton Spanish coaster that had been converted to carry fifteen hundred troops and was one of two merchant ships being escorted by two Royal Navy destroyers; the other merchant ship was carrying German prisoners of war who were being taken to Canada. More used to average speeds of around ten knots, *Banfora* had to work hard to keep up with the escort as the convoy made a number of zigzag manoeuvres across the Atlantic to throw off the German U-boats known to be operating in packs. Everyone was fully aware of the U-boat threat but the RAF recruits on *Banfora* convinced themselves that the two Royal Navy ships would protect them rather than the other merchant ship carrying the German prisoners of war.

Although the passengers were allowed up on deck during the hours of daylight, the poor weather meant that the sea was rough and conditions on board *Banfora* were bad. Accommodation was in the hold, which was extremely dark, and there was water on the floor; it was like the Black Hole of Calcutta during the blackout at night. Although there were hammocks available, Beetham did not fancy the idea of sleeping in one and so he made a bed as best he could in the hold. The food was appalling and every day it was stew with potatoes full of black holes. After a couple of days his squad, which consisted of some rather 'street-wise' individuals and army transfers who seemed good at organising special deals from anyone on board, had managed to negotiate apple pie from the ship's galley at a cost of two shillings and sixpence; it was delicious. Word soon got around about the apple pie and it was not long before there was a queue at the galley every day. It was only a matter of time before the captain and crew noticed this and so that was the end of the good food; it was then back to stew and potatoes for the rest of the voyage!

The journey across the Atlantic lasted just over a week. *Banfora* docked at Halifax in Nova Scotia on the east coast of Canada and, having disembarked, Beetham boarded a Canadian troop train destined for Moncton, New Brunswick. After the dreadful conditions on *Banfora*, the train journey was luxurious. The coaches were old sleeping cars and beds could be made, the food was very good and the scenery quite outstanding. On 7 April Beetham arrived in Moncton, where all RAF cadets were processed on arrival, including those destined for Canadian training bases, and he spent the next three weeks at No 31 Personnel Depot, with hundreds of other RAF cadets, waiting to find out when and where he would continue his pilot training.

During 1941–5 some fifteen thousand RAF cadets were trained in America, approximately half of them under the Arnold Scheme and half under the British Flying Training School scheme in America. Those trained under the Arnold Scheme went to an airfield located at one of eleven cities in the south-east. In the state of Georgia there were airfields at Albany, Macon, Americus and Valdosta. In Alabama there were airfields at Montgomery, Dothan, Selma and Tuscaloosa. In Florida there were the airfields of Lakeland and Arcadia, and there was the airfield of Camden in South Carolina.

At the end of April Beetham boarded a train at Moncton and began the long journey south to the state of Georgia. The journey lasted three days and the views were often stunning. One of the stops, which lasted just an hour, was at the town of Chattanooga, where masses of local people had turned out to welcome the RAF 'heroes of the Battle of Britain'. While the would-be pilots on the train were not exactly the 'heroes of the Battle of Britain', the RAF cadets were nonetheless happy to enjoy the accolade and reception they received.

Beetham's next stop was the RAF Reception Centre at Turner Field, near Albany in Georgia. To help reduce the wastage rate in the Arnold Scheme, a four-week acclimatisation and familiarisation period at an American air base had been introduced. This gave British cadets time to become familiar with life in America before commencing their primary training phase; Beetham was one of the early cadets to benefit from this initiative. Turner Field was a large airfield used for a number of purposes such as an Initial Training Wing for the Americans, similar to the ITWs in the UK, and for the advanced pilot training of RAF pilots.

At Turner Field the cadet quarters were good and the food was excellent; fresh fruit and chocolate – items considered to be luxuries back home – could be found in abundance. However, the mix of RAF cadets into the American system was not without its problems as many of the RAF cadets did not take too kindly to the discipline of the training regime; this was not just the case at Turner Field but also throughout the American flying-training system. The RAF cadets were temporarily in the US Army Air Forces, which had recently formed from the US Army Air Corps, and were, therefore, subject to

American discipline and code. The RAF cadets had to ensure their blankets had no wrinkles and their bed space was immaculate for inspection by the senior American cadet officers, and their food, although wonderful, had to be eaten in just fifteen minutes. When a whistle blew they had to stop eating; anyone seen eating after the whistle was reported, even if he still had food in his mouth. There was also a de-merit system at Turner Field, which meant that any minor misdemeanour received punishment, such as being made to walk around the barrack square for one hour. As one of the youngest cadets Beetham could accept this form of 'discipline' to some extent but many of the other cadets had been non-commissioned officers in the British Army or RAF prior to becoming cadets and did not readily accept the American regime.

The warm weather and high humidity meant that the British cadets wore American tropical khaki uniform, which proved to be very good in the climate, rather than air force blue, but they did retain their blue forage caps with the white air-cadet flash to show their status as RAF aircrew. Life in America during 1942 was quite different to what Beetham had experienced back home. There was no rationing, which meant there was always plenty of food, and there was no blackout. The towns and cities were brightly lit and there were plenty of clubs and bars to frequent. There was also the excitement of being overseas for the first time and the young British cadets were received by the locals with warmth and affection, and were encouraged to become part of the local community.

It was soon time for Beetham to move on to primary training. Six civilian flying schools had been contracted to carry out primary training of cadets under the Southeast Air Corps Training Center, later designated Eastern Flying Training Command, and the location for the RAF cadets' training was decided by one of the RAF administration sergeants based at Turner Field. One of the most popular locations was the Lakeland School of Aeronautics near Tampa in Florida, and one of Beetham's course colleagues, Bob Bowring, a former RAF sergeant ground engineer, had managed to negotiate places at Lakeland for himself and his colleagues at the cost of $1 per cadet. Beetham wondered whether the RAF administration sergeant at Turner Field was a future Charlie Clore, the well-known financier and property magnet, of his time!

Beetham commenced primary training at Lakeland on 3 June 1942. He was in Class SE-42-K, which differed from previous classes as it was a mixed British and American class, and all of the RAF members had completed flying grading. There were eighty-two British cadets in the total of two hundred on the course; the remaining students were American aviation cadets. Conditions on base were good and Beetham found the food and accommodation to be of the highest order but, despite being a civilian flying school, discipline at Lakeland was also strict.

The day started at 5.30 a.m. when a bell sounded and the cadets hauled themselves out of bed and into flying overalls. They had not showered or shaved at that point but they had to form up on the parade square into their two flights, one American and one British, and be counted off by one of the American under-officers. The American flag would then be raised to the sound of a trumpet and afterwards the cadets returned to their barracks to wash and shave before going for breakfast. After a few days the British cadets decided they would not all go on parade and a rota system was put in place so that each day three-quarters of the RAF cadets attended the parade, while the remaining quarter spent a bit longer in bed. Their American colleagues, who were all good-quality cadets from the military academy at West Point, were initially appalled by this behaviour and so they informally warned their RAF colleagues that they could expect to be reported under the American 'honour system' if they continued to breach the rules. The RAF cadets discussed this threat but promptly chose to ignore it and decided to continue their daily arrangement for the early morning parade. Two days later, and having seen that the RAF cadets were not deterred by their threat, the American cadets adopted the same practice as the British at the beginning of each day! Beetham has often wondered how these fine young men got on in later years.

The American syllabus for the twelve weeks of primary flying training included sixty-five hours of flying training and 225 hours of ground school, which was far too much time in the classroom considering that the British cadets had already covered some of the ground school previously at ITW. This led to a reduction in the number of ground school hours for the RAF cadets and they were instead taught about the RAF organisation and procedures, aircraft recognition and current affairs. Some of the older cadets found the exams quite difficult and so the RAF cadets helped each other through the numerous examinations in the course but they were incensed to find out that many cadets had already been returned to the UK because of their academic inability or because of some other administrative or disciplinary matter – all this at a time when the RAF was short of pilots.

The aircraft used for primary training was the PT-17 Stearman biplane trainer and Beetham's first flight in the PT-17 was on 5 June with his instructor, Mr E. W. Johnson. Beetham found the Stearman an extremely enjoyable aircraft to fly: it was very stable in flight and was more powerful than the Tiger Moth that he had previously flown. For the next two weeks the routine was much the same, with one flying exercise a day and the inevitable periods of ground school in between. Beetham found Johnson to be a likeable man and a reasonable flying instructor, although he always shouted at Beetham whenever he did something wrong, regardless of the aircraft's position at the time, as he seemed to find this to be the best way to instruct. The Stearman had an open cockpit and Beetham soon got used to being shouted at, even when upside down or in a spin, although he often felt like telling Johnson to 'shut up' himself. After fourteen exercises Beetham was considered ready to go solo and he flew his first solo in the Stearman, which lasted twenty-five minutes, on 24 June.

The syllabus included elimination check rides at various points, the first of which was after ten flying hours, with further checks at twenty hours, forty hours and at sixty hours before the end of the course. Beetham's first check ride was on 27 June with Mr A. M. Holzappel, when he was assessed to see if he had met the standard required in all the flying disciplines and manoeuvres taught so far; this was followed by a solo flight three days later, which also formed part of the assessment. Beetham passed to the required standard and he proceeded to the next phase of his primary training.

He had now successfully completed the first month of his primary training. There had been little time for rest as the instructional tempo was high: twenty-five training flights in twenty-five days. If Beetham felt the instructional tempo of June had been high then July was even more demanding. He flew six times in the first three days and during one solo exercise he was authorised to practice S-turns over a road. A colleague was to carry out the same exercise and, before taking off, the two young cadets arranged to meet over a designated landmark to conduct some unauthorised air combat. The exercise and rendezvous went according to plan and the air combat commenced, but unfortunately they were spotted by an instructor in another aircraft. After they had landed, the two cadets were called into the instructor's office and were told they had violated flying regulations by dangerous flying and were informed they would be subjected to an elimination check ride. The next day Beetham found himself walking out to his Stearman with one of the senior instructors, Mr R. Lanning. His future as a pilot was in the balance and he was keen to make sure that he made no mistakes. He did not. Thirty minutes later Beetham was back on the ground and to his relief he escaped with just a warning.

While at Lakeland, Beetham's only contact with his own family back home was by letter, whenever he found the time to write, and he was only allowed off camp every other weekend. With two of his colleagues, John Rivaz and Bill Ashford, he was lucky enough to enjoy the warm and generous hospitality of the Carty family who lived near Tampa, about forty miles away, and the three young cadets would be picked up by the family and taken to their home on a beautiful lake where they were able to relax and enjoy their first experience of water skiing.

The rest of July passed very quickly as the rate of instruction increased yet again and Beetham flew a minimum of two, but usually three, sorties a day for the next two weeks. The exercises now included steep turns, elementary eights, lazy eights, pylon eights, more spinning, more stalling, forced landings, precision approaches and landings, aerobatics and cross-country navigation exercises. He flew his final check ride on 27 July and Class SE-42-K completed primary training on 4 August. By then Beetham had flown a total of sixty hours, approximately half dual and half solo, and the intensity of the course meant that he had flown eighty-six training sorties at Lakeland in less than two months, the last sixty-one of which were flown during July. He was one of fifty-one RAF cadets who successfully completed the course; one cadet was held over to the next course and thirty were eliminated from pilot training. This high wastage rate was typical for the Arnold Scheme, which by the end of the war was 45 per cent, twice that of the British Flying Training Schools in America. The reasons for this vary, but much depended on the quality of the instruction as well as the quality and motivation of the cadets, although the Arnold cadets certainly found their training regime far too rigid.

Having completed primary training, Beetham and the rest of Class SE-42-K moved to Gunter Field near Montgomery, Alabama, to commence the basic flying phase. Gunter Field was located four miles to the north-east of Montgomery and had been the municipal airport before becoming the first US Army Air Corps basic flying-training school in the south-eastern part of the USA. The aircraft used for basic flying training was the Vultee BT-13 Valiant trainer, which had a maximum speed of 180 mph and a continuous canopy with the instructor and student sitting in tandem. The undercarriage was retractable and the aircraft was fitted with blind-flying instruments so that student pilots could be taught the basics of flying at night or in bad weather.

The first few days at Gunter Field were spent in the classroom before Beetham flew his first exercise in the BT-13 on 9 August with his instructor Pilot Officer R. G. Wilson. Two days later he was airborne again, after which he spent the first of two exercises in the Link Trainer, where he could practise and consolidate what he had been taught in his first two airborne exercises. This became the pattern for the basic phase with Link Trainer exercises, each lasting an hour, embedded into the flying syllabus. After seven airborne exercises, Beetham flew his first solo in the BT-13 on 22 August.

In addition to the normal handling techniques, instrument flying was introduced, and then night flying. On 10 September Beetham was ready for his night solo. He walked out to the aircraft with his

2. Beetham completed his pilot training in America under the Arnold Scheme. He is pictured here (third from right) with some of his colleagues of course SE-42-K and his flying instructor, Mr E. W. Johnson (third from left), during the primary phase of training at Lakeland in Florida, July 1942.

instructor, only to find the aircraft was unserviceable. He then walked to the second aircraft and strapped in quickly in a rush to get off. Once airborne he immediately realised the air-speed indicator was not working and so he declared an emergency with air traffic control and the controller gave him permission to complete a circuit and then land. The duty instructor in the tower was passing Beetham suitable advice, which involved him assessing his speed as best he could, but because it was dark he could only pick up a few references from the ground. Beetham kept his speed up and landed safely, although it took some distance to bring the aircraft to a halt; fortunately, it was a long runway. He then taxied back to the dispersal, only to find that the pitot head cover had not been removed, which meant that the aircraft's air speed could not be measured! In his rush to get airborne both he and his instructor had overlooked one of the basic pre-flight checks during the walk round the aircraft. Beetham removed the pitot head cover so that he could continue with his flight; it passed without further incident, but it had been a quite traumatic experience, considering it had been his first night solo!

The learning curve continued to get steeper. By October the training he was receiving included flying at night, formation flying, instrument flying, cross-country navigation and flying radio beams. His final exercise of the basic phase was flown on 7 October and he was assessed as ready to move onto the final phase of his flying training. He also found out that he was destined for multi-engine bombers rather than single-engine fighters, which was good news for him because his personal preference at that time was for twin-engine ground attack. However, he was also aware that most cadets were destined for the heavy bombers that were now entering service with Bomber Command because that was where the main build-up was most needed; that is exactly what would happen to him.

When Beetham arrived back at Turner Field for his advanced phase he was in familiar surroundings, having only left Turner four months before. This time he would be on the main flying part of the airfield rather than the Reception Centre situated away from the flying activity. He now had completed 140 flying hours and the end of his flying training was in sight. At that stage of the war there were a number of twin-engine trainers being used for advanced flying training, including the Curtiss-Wright AT-9 Fledgling and the Cessna AT-17, which had only recently been introduced at Turner Field.

The AT-9, otherwise known as the 'Jeep', was essentially a wartime trainer. With a crew of two – the instructor and student pilot

– it had been designed to bridge the gap between single-engine training aircraft and front-line twin-engine operational aircraft. It was a low-wing cantilever monoplane design, with a retractable undercarriage, and had a maximum speed of nearly 200 mph and a maximum operating ceiling of nearly 20,000 feet. Its handling characteristics were similar to light and medium bombers in service at the time, which meant that it was considered to be an ideal training aircraft for wartime pilots, particularly because the aircraft was not considered easy to fly. The AT-17 was a military variant of the commercial Cessna T-50 light transport aircraft and had also been designed to bridge the gap between single-engine trainers and twin-engine bombers. It was similar to the AT-9 in terms of speed but it could operate at a slightly higher altitude. The AT-17 was a similar design to the AT-9 in that it was also a low-wing monoplane design with a retractable undercarriage, but its advantages were that it could carry up to five people and it had electrically operated wing trailing-edge flaps. Also, the handling characteristics of the AT-17 were more favourable as far as student pilots were concerned.

After a short ground school introduction Beetham flew his first sortie of the phase on 16 October, in an AT-17 with his instructor, Pilot Officer V. Jaymes. Beetham's first exercise in the AT-9 was on 20 October and he would fly both aircraft during the phase, although the AT-9 was used for more exercises than the AT-17. Apart from mastering the normal handling aspects of both aircraft, the syllabus included formation flying, beam flying, instrument flying and then night flying. Much of the training pattern was similar to the earlier phases of flying training but one significant difference was that the student pilots did not fly either the AT-9 or AT-17 solo, even though they were assessed as capable of doing so. When not flying with an instructor, exercises were flown with another student pilot at a similar stage of training. This was to give each student as much airborne time as possible; it was not a reflection of the difficulty of operating either aircraft solo. These additional hours were logged as passenger hours, but they all added valuable airborne time for the students and by the end of the phase Beetham had accumulated an additional forty hours airborne.

From the middle of November the phase introduced more formation flying, with up to six aircraft, more instrument flying, a number of cross-country exercises, more beam work and instrument let downs to the airfield. More and more complicated procedures were then introduced, which saw the students operating in formations of six aircraft and having to navigate cross-country, during which they were given timing problems to overcome along the way. The students were now being taught how to think and operate as a formation. Exercises typically lasted between one hour thirty minutes and two hours fifteen minutes, with each exercise providing the student pilot with different problems to overcome. Beetham finished the advanced phase on 10 December when he flew his final check ride.

Flying training was now complete and over the past six months he had flown 238 training exercises totalling more than two hundred hours. By now each RAF cadet had been interviewed by the senior RAF staff to decide whether he would graduate with a commission in the rank of pilot officer or whether he would graduate as a sergeant pilot. Most cadets graduated as sergeants but Beetham was to be commissioned. The fact that he had been well educated and because his father was a major in the army may have been factors, but this was the first of many defining moments in his RAF career. Beetham was also offered the chance to stay in America for a further year as a flying instructor before returning to the UK for his operational tour but, while he felt pleased that he had done sufficiently well to be considered good enough to be an instructor, and it would have given him another year of flying experience, Beetham declined the offer. He simply wanted to get on with his operational tour.

When he and the rest of Class SE-42-K graduated from flying training on 13 December 1942, Beetham was presented with American wings, rather than RAF wings, by a general from the USAAF at a large wings parade ceremony. These were the only pilot wings ever presented to him and he would later have to get his own RAF wings from stores at Harrogate on his return to the UK but he always remained extremely proud of his American wings and would have liked to have worn them on the opposite side of his uniform to his RAF wings, in the same way that Americans that had been trained by the RAF were allowed to do; this was not allowed, however. At the wings ceremony one of the RAF reviewing officers was Squadron Leader 'Dinghy' Young, who passed on his words of encouragement to the RAF's newest pilots before he returned to the UK to join 617 Squadron and to take part in the legendary Dams Raid in May 1943; sadly, Young would be among the casualties that night.

With the wings ceremony over, followed by the customary celebrations, it was now time for Beetham to go home. The journey took him and his fellow graduates back through Moncton, where he spent Christmas and the New Year before going on to New York to embark on the passenger liner HMTS *Queen Elizabeth* for the voyage home. His short stay in New York was mainly spent in a bar drinking bourbon and there was little sightseeing done before it was time to board the ship for the journey home. On 6 January 1943 *Queen Elizabeth* set sail for Glasgow with Beetham and more than ten thousand American troops and five thousand RAF personnel on board. There was no escort allocated because *Queen Elizabeth* managed thirty knots at full speed and there was no ship in the Royal Navy that could keep up with her; *Queen Elizabeth* would simply weave her way across the Atlantic at full speed and would out-run any danger that presented itself.

Conditions on board were luxurious compared to those experienced on *Banfora* on the outward journey in March. The food was excellent and the troops were fed extremely well twice a day, although the large number on board meant that meals were served in shifts. Beetham was on the shift that had breakfast at 5.30 a.m. and dinner at 6.30 p.m. Initially it seemed a long time to wait between breakfast and dinner but there was plenty of food to be had and the fact that the clock was moving forward at the rate of one hour per day as the ship sailed eastwards helped reduce the time between meals. However, because of the Americans on board there was no alcohol.

During the voyage home Beetham was able to reflect on his time in America. The flying training had been of a high standard but navigation had been made easy because of the good weather and visibility, and because of the few but significant navigation features in America, such as one railway or one major road. Even at night navigation had been relatively easy because the navigation techniques taught usually had taken him from beacon to beacon, and the towns were well lit because there was no blackout. However, the American 'honour system' had caused difficulties with the British and was evidence of the difference in attitude of training between the US and RAF cadets. Nonetheless, Beetham had had a great time and the American people had been extraordinarily hospitable; something he would never forget. The voyage back to Glasgow lasted just four and a half days and on the final day the Americans had a parade when they were awarded a medal for operations in Europe. This provided the British personnel some amusement as the presentation took place before the troops had even set foot in Europe. However, after nearly nine months away, it felt good to be back and it was now time to prepare for war.

CHAPTER 2

Bomber Pilot

Having left *Queen Elizabeth* at Glasgow, Pilot Officer Michael Beetham went to No 7 Personnel Reception Centre at Harrogate, where personnel returning to the UK after training overseas were processed. He spent the next few days handing in his tropical clothing and visiting the various military tailors on site, where he found his personal uniform allowance was just sufficient to cover the cost of a new RAF blue uniform and the other personal kit he required. Now the proud owner of some RAF wings, one of the WAAF suppliers kindly agreed to sew them onto his battledress for him but he was no longer allowed to wear the American wings that he had worked so hard for.

Due to the surplus of pilots in the training system Beetham had to wait a few weeks until he could carry on with his flying training. He spent February at the military camp at Filey, otherwise known as RAF Hunmanby Moor, and was then posted to No 7 Elementary Flying Training School at Desford, where he joined No 11 Advanced Flying Unit on 12 March. It had been three months since he had last flown and the aim of the course was for him to regain his flying currency in preparation for the next phase of training and also to re-familiarise himself with flying in the UK. He had returned to the UK full of confidence but, having flown in good weather throughout his time in America, where he had hardly experienced any cloud or poor visibility, the weather conditions in the UK came as a bit of a shock and he had to work particularly hard as there was much to learn. His refresher flying was carried out on the Tiger Moth II, an aircraft he had flown during his elementary flying training at Perth a year before.

After three weeks at Desford he went to No 18 (Pilot) AFU at Church Lawford, to the south-west of Rugby, for his advanced flying training on the twin-engine Airspeed Oxford. Affectionately known as the 'Ox-box', the Oxford had been the first twin-engine mono-plane trainer in the RAF. Beetham flew his first training exercise in the Oxford on 13 April with his instructor, Sergeant Richmond. The sortie was a simple aircraft-handling and basic navigation exercise lasting just one hour. He flew again the next day and four times the day after, the third sortie of which was solo. The tempo remained high for the next two weeks as Beetham was introduced to instrument-flying techniques on the Oxford, which were flown dual with an instructor. By the end of the month he had flown twenty-six times and had accumulated twenty-eight hours on type. He was then attached to No 1533 Beam Approach Training Flight, still at Church Lawford, for the beam-approach phase of the course.

Having completed the beam training, the final phase at Church Lawford was the night-flying phase, which was a mix of dual and solo flying. The night-flying phase followed a typical pattern of one exercise flown dual during the evening, followed by a solo exercise later that night. At the end of the phase the students were also intro-duced to night direction finding and precision navigation techniques. Beetham celebrated his twentieth birthday just a few days before the end of his training at Church Lawford. He had done extremely well as a pilot and had now accumulated over three hundred flying hours as he moved towards his final stages of training.

On 1 June Beetham was posted to Cottesmore, near Oakham, to join No 14 Operational Training Unit. Cottesmore was one of Bomber Command's main training bases and preparations were already underway for the construction of new concrete runways in anticipa-tion of the arrival of Bomber Command's new heavy bombers. The OTU was equipped with the Vickers Wellington, as well as some Avro Ansons and Airspeed Oxfords, and by the time Beetham com-menced his course the decision had already been made to operate the new four-engine heavies with just one pilot rather than two because Bomber Command could not train the number of pilots required, and also the new specialisations of flight engineer and bomb aimer had emerged to help reduce the workload of the navigator.

Beetham found life on the OTU quite different to what he had experienced before. Aircrew from the various flying specialisations were now brought together for the first time and it was the task of the OTU instructors to get them to work competently together as a bomber crew. Getting a crew to work well together relied on the right mix of people and it was generally left to individuals to start to form a crew. Some naturally gravitated towards each other, having perhaps already met somewhere previously in the training system, whereas others joined by recommendation. Beetham's crew initially consisted of five members for training on the Wellington. When he had first arrived at Cottesmore he did not know any of the other students but he had got to know a navigator, Frank Swinyard, through living in the officers' mess. Swinyard knew a sergeant bomb aimer, Les Bartlett, and Bartlett knew a young sergeant wireless operator/air gunner, Reg Payne, who happened to know another gunner, Fred Ball. And so the Beetham crew formed.

At just twenty years old Beetham was the youngest member of his crew. The oldest was Frank Swinyard, who had been born in 1916 and had worked as a company secretary before volunteering for the RAF. The second oldest was Les Bartlett, born in 1917, who had started a career in pharmacy before the war and although he was in a reserved occupation had volunteered for the RAF in 1941. Fred Ball was twenty-two years old and before the war had worked in the jewellery business. Reg Payne was the second-youngest member of the crew by a matter of weeks. He was born in March 1923 and had worked as a junior records clerk at the British Legion. When war broke out he was too young to volunteer for active service but as soon as he was seventeen years old he joined the Local Defence Volunteers and six months later, when he was old enough, he volunteered for the RAF.

The five young men seemed to bond well together immediately and each member was ready for the challenges that lay ahead. There was much to learn in a relatively short period of time. The length of the OTU course varied but was typically up to eighty hours' flying for the pilots and about forty hours for the other crew members. Beetham flew his first OTU sortie with his instructor, Flight Lieutenant Donald, on 23 June – a daytime familiarisation sortie that lasted for one hour and fifty minutes. Beetham was airborne again soon after for his solo check ride and then, in Wellington 891 'N', he took off with Frank Swinyard, Reg Payne and Fred Ball on board for the crew's first training flight together; the bomb aimers still had more training to complete before they could join their crew for the flying phase. The crew's first solo lasted for two hours; it had been a long day with the three flights totalling more than five hours.

The OTU syllabus was designed to give the crew the basic hand-ling and operational skills that would stand them in good stead when they moved on to a heavy bomber. This was an extremely busy period as there was so much to learn. In the six days since his first flight in the Wellington, Beetham had flown twelve times, and the crew had now been joined by the bomb aimer, Les Bartlett. Their daytime training varied from local familiarisation sorties to cross-country navigation exercises, often leading to a simulated bombing run against a target; these training sorties, in particular, brought all the crew's skills together. The number of night training sorties was also beginning to increase and these introduced high-level bombing techniques. Away from the course Beetham enjoyed socialising in the officers' mess or going out with his crew to a pub in the local area, but it was a busy period and the course was extremely hard work. Although he was close to his family in Leicester he rarely went home; he could not drive and there was little time off. Furthermore, his priority was very much towards his training and his crew.

In early August the OTU moved to a newly constructed airfield at Market Harborough, and Beetham flew his first sortie from there on 15 August with his instructor Flight Lieutenant Glenn and later that day his crew was cleared to go solo from the new airfield. They then began a concentrated phase of night flying, and because of the move to Market Harborough and their inevitable break in flying continuity it was necessary to increase the tempo of the course. The crew were now getting used to the pattern and intensity of flying operations at night. The last training sorties of the course included a number of exercises known as 'raids', some of which were flown by day, some were flown at night and some were a mix of day and night exercises. The culmination of their intense training was a night-flying exercise on 31 August that lasted five and a half hours; their longest sortie by far. The crew had now finished the OTU. Beetham had flown forty-four training sorties on the Wellington, totalling eighty hours, of which forty-seven were by day and thirty-three were at night.

After some well-earned leave Beetham and his crew arrived at Wigsley, a satellite of Swinderby near Lincoln, to join No 1654 Heavy Conversion Unit. The introduction of the new four-engine heavy bombers had given Bomber Command a problem in terms of how its crews would be trained. The Lancaster, for example, was significantly different to the Wellington flown at the OTU, and Bomber Command's initial solution had been to give each front-line squadron additional aircraft, typically four, to form a conversion flight. This was not ideal because the squadrons were not established for training purposes and the level of instruction proved variable. Conversion flights were then formed for each group within Bomber Command, but again this was problematic, and finally Heavy

Conversion Units were formed with the task of converting crews to a specific aircraft type and to prepare finally each crew for its tour of operations. No 1654 HCU had been the first Lancaster HCU to form and when Beetham arrived in September 1943 the HCU was equipped with both Halifaxes and Lancasters.

At Wigsley the Beetham crew became seven when Sergeant Don Moore, the flight engineer, and Sergeant Ian Higgins, the mid-upper gunner, joined the crew. These two individuals were quite different: Don Moore was in his late twenties, married with a young child and had previously served as an engine fitter in the RAF before he volunteered for service as a flight engineer. By contrast, Ian Higgins, known as Jock, was very much the single man and determined to live life to the full. The Beetham crew was now complete and it was as diverse as any other crew in Bomber Command.

Beetham's first training sortie on the HCU was on 20 September, when he flew as second pilot in a Halifax. This was the first time he had flown a four-engine aircraft and it proved to be his one and only flight in a Halifax. The sortie was a dual familiarisation exercise with his instructor, Pilot Officer Bernard Gumbley, a twenty-eight-year-old New Zealander who had just completed his tour of operations with 49 Squadron and had been awarded the Distinguished Flying Medal. Beetham's next sortie, on 24 September, was to be unforgettable as it was his first flight in a Lancaster. Flying as second pilot to Gumbley once again, Beetham taxied out to the runway, advanced the throttles and then pulled back on the control column.

The Lancaster climbed away and, once airborne, Beetham could settle down. The cockpit was spacious and his position on a raised floor on the left-hand side of the cockpit, with the large canopy, allowed him good all-round visibility. His initial concern was how to cope with all the dials – there seemed to be so many – but it was not long before he was comfortable with the cockpit layout. In terms of handling, everything felt intrinsically right. The sortie of two and a half hours soon passed and it had felt good to be at the controls of a Lancaster at last. Even though he had flown the Halifax just once, and the Wellington prior to that, he felt there was no comparison in the handling performances of the aircraft. The Lancaster handled beautifully and, although it required some physical effort, he found it to be really quite manoeuvrable.

He flew his solo check ride with Gumbley on 2 October and was now ready for his first crew solo. Having crewed into the aircraft it was Don Moore's responsibility as the flight engineer to assist Beetham during engine starting by monitoring each engine in turn. Behind Beetham on the left side of the main cockpit was the navigator, Frank Swinyard. Sitting at the back of the main cockpit, adjacent to the leading edge of the wing, was the wireless operator, Reg Payne, and in the nose of the aircraft was bomb aimer Les Bartlett. In the rear turret was Fred Ball and in the mid-upper turret Jock Higgins. Beetham taxied out to the runway and they were soon airborne. For their first solo the crew were not permitted to venture away from the local area and it was soon time to land. The flight lasted just thirty-five minutes and it passed without incident; it had been a successful and most memorable day.

The following day Beetham flew another short trip of consolidation and he was now considered ready to venture away from the local circuit. He first flew a cross-country exercise at 12,000 feet, culminating in a practice target run and air gunnery, and then flew his first night dual sortie, again with Gumbley. Later that night he flew his first night crew solo. Beetham was no stranger to flying at night and now had ten Lancaster training sorties behind him but flying the Lancaster solo at night for the first time was a very different experience. There were not the usual visual references available and even getting around the aircraft in the dark proved a challenge. The night crew solo only lasted forty minutes but it had been a long day, with three training sorties, two of which had been at night, totalling more than six hours airborne.

The next phase of training involved three daylight training sorties dedicated to combat manoeuvres and fighter affiliation using a Hurricane as the adversary. These were the only dedicated training sorties for Beetham to learn how to evade an attacking fighter and for the crew to learn how to work together when threatened. Considering the high probability of this happening there was little time to learn and if it had not been obvious to them before, then it was certainly obvious to them now: they would have to learn fast or not survive at all. The crew would make up for this gap in their training and their lack of experience by often discussing what they would each do in certain circumstances; each crew member would rehearse this in his own mind time and time again.

The final phase of the HCU course involved two more night exercises. The first was a night cross-country navigation exercise flown at 16,000 feet with eight 25-lb practice bombs on board, which were dropped on a bombing range at the Isle of Man. The second was flown dual as a searchlight and night fighter interception exercise. The Beetham crew flew their last training exercise on 20 October, another cross-country exercise flown at 20,000 feet that culminated in dropping six 25-lb practice bombs on the bombing range.

Their training was now over and the crew were posted to 50 Squadron at Skellingthorpe. It was time to say goodbye to all those who had worked so hard to prepare them for their forthcoming tour of operations, now just days away. Beetham had been taught well by his instructor, Bernard Gumbley, who was only too glad to pass on his knowledge and experience to his young student during the ten sorties they had flown together. Unfortunately, Gumbley would not survive the war. He later returned to operations with 617 Squadron and was flying a specially modified Lancaster with a 22,000-lb 'Grand Slam' bomb on a daylight raid against the Arbergen railway bridge on 21 March 1945 when his aircraft was hit by flak and was seen diving in flames; Bernard Gumbley and his crew were killed.

By the time Beetham left Wigsley he had flown nearly thirty hours on the Lancaster. Crucially though, he had now amassed more than four hundred flying hours in just over eighteen months of pilot training. He had been well trained and Pilot Officer M. J. Beetham was assessed as 'above the average'. As far as his training was concerned, that was it – finished. There was to be no more. The responsibility for his crew from now on would be his, and their lives would be in his young hands.

Beetham arrived at Skellingthorpe on 26 October 1943. It had been a short journey from Wigsley as the airfield of Skellingthorpe was located just three miles to the south-west of Lincoln. Today the site has long been developed as a housing estate but in 1943 it was a relatively new satellite airfield of 5 Group, Bomber Command. The airfield was constructed on grass fields surrounded by gravel pits, woods and a lake. It had three standard wartime concrete runways, intersecting and linked by a perimeter track. The main runway was nearly two thousand yards in length and fifty feet wide and ran from the south-west corner of the airfield to the north-east, giving the crews a spectacular view of Lincoln Cathedral when taking off in a north-easterly direction. The two other runways were shorter, at fourteen hundred yards in length, and aircraft servicing was carried out at hardened dispersals around the airfield.

On arrival at Skellingthorpe the crew were taken to their respective messes and shown their accommodation. It was a cold damp evening but Beetham was given a warm welcome in the officers' mess, where he was met by one of 50 Squadron's flight commanders, Squadron Leader Parkes, who bought him a beer and updated him on what was going on. Parkes explained that the squadron was currently operating alone from the airfield and was commanded by Wing Commander Robert McFarlane, a highly respected squadron commander who had already been awarded a Distinguished Flying Cross and bar; his second DFC had been for his heroic attack on the German battlecruisers *Scharnhorst* and *Gneisenau* in the English Channel and he would soon be awarded the Distinguished Service Order for his outstanding leadership of the squadron. Parkes also explained that the squadron had been heavily involved in Bomber Command's main efforts during the past few months and that the attention was turning more towards Berlin. It was an extremely busy time and it was going to be a long hard winter, but he informed Beetham that he would be given a chance to settle in as much as possible before taking part in operations.

The following morning the crew reported to the squadron and then proceeded around the station for the issue of their electrically heated flying suits, gloves, socks and boots. Everyone seemed very friendly and keen to pass on whatever they knew to the new arrivals. The next day the crew were allocated their Lancaster, JA961 'A-Able'. It felt tremendous to have their own aircraft and it seemed to be in far better condition than the aircraft they had previously flown at the HCU.

The crew now felt ready to take part in operations, although they would have to wait a little longer before they were given their opportunity. Beetham, however, did not have to wait long. The next day it was announced that operations were on that night and he was scheduled to fly his 'second dickey' trip with one of the squadron's experienced crews. This was standard practice as it gave each new pilot the chance to be shown an operational sortie by an experienced captain and his crew, with the 'rookie' pilot sitting on the jump-seat on the flight deck next to, and to the right of, the pilot. For his second dickey trip, Beetham was allocated to Flight Lieutenant Ian Bolton and his crew. However, during the early evening the operation was cancelled because of poor weather over the target area and the crews were stood down. This was something he would have to get used to.

Although disappointed at the operation being cancelled, Beetham did not have to wait too much longer for his second dickey trip and on 3 November he was again allocated to the Bolton crew for a raid against Düsseldorf. Compared to other cities in Germany, Düsseldorf was a relatively short hop: a round-trip of just four hours. Understandably, Beetham was apprehensive as he had no idea what it would be like to fly on operations, but he was extremely excited as well. This was it, at last, and he felt confident because he knew that the Bolton crew was experienced and very efficient.

They got airborne as part of a mixed bomber force of nearly six hundred Lancasters and Halifaxes. Crossing the Dutch coast Beetham got his first sight of enemy searchlights and anti-aircraft fire, although nothing came their way. They carried on towards Düsseldorf; over the Ruhr there was more anti-aircraft flak but it seemed to be concentrated below them and they continued onwards. Approaching the target area it became more traumatic: the search-lights, anti-aircraft fire and the fighter flares all lit up the sky around them but the crew just gritted their teeth and pressed on. Over the target it was awe-inspiring to see the explosions on the ground, and the fires, but he wondered how anyone could carry on fighting a war under such conditions. They turned for home. Beetham felt relieved they had reached the target unscathed and he started to relax during the transit home. It was an even bigger relief when they crossed the English coast and they could now switch on their navigation lights. It was only then that he realised just how many aircraft were around them. Each set of lights that came on was another aircraft and one by one more and more aircraft became visible to him. Everyone was required to keep a sharp look out all the way back to Skellingthorpe, where they were eventually given permission to land.

Once back on the ground there were lots of people around, including the station commander, to find out how things had gone. The crew were then debriefed by the intelligence officer and afterwards they were allowed to go for bacon and eggs before finally going to bed. Beetham was obviously relieved that all had gone well. In the space of just a few hours he had experienced the excitement, trauma, fear, pride and elation of operational flying, and was fully aware that from now on the responsibility for the crew and all the decisions made would be his – there would be no one else to turn to. His crew were all waiting to welcome him back and they wanted to know all about the trip and what it was like to fly on operations. Beetham re-enacted the whole mission but he was also mindful to give them a confident message and to reassure them that everything would be fine.

As for the Bolton crew, they would not complete their tour of operations. On the night of 2/3 December they were shot down during a raid against Berlin. Bolton and four of his crew managed to escape out of the aircraft and were taken prisoners of war, as was a war correspondent from the *Daily Express* who had been flying with the crew that night, but two of his crew members were killed.

The night after the Düsseldorf raid the Beetham crew flew a cross-country navigation exercise lasting four and a half hours, which took them down to Taunton, then up to the Isle of Man and across to Carlisle before returning back to base. Beetham was ready for more operations and each morning he would go down to the squadron at about 10 a.m., only to find that his name was not on the operations list; he was not helped by the weather as a number of operations were being cancelled at the time. He found this most frustrating but the squadron commander, Robert McFarlane, did take him to one side to explain that it was a difficult period for the squadron and he did not want to risk sending a crew on their first operation to Berlin, and so his crew just needed to be patient.

For the next two weeks there were more training sorties, which were a mix of day and night exercises ranging from fighter affiliation to training with specialist equipment and yet more cross-country navigation exercises. It was now early winter and conditions at Skellingthorpe had started to deteriorate. The weather was wet and there was lots of mud about, but away from the squadron the crew could enjoy the hospitality of the local pubs in and around Lincoln. However, each member of the crew was keen to get on with operations and even though they were flying regularly enough there was still a nervous sense of waiting for that first 'op'. The squadron had now been joined by 61 Squadron, which had moved from Syerston to Skellingthorpe; the two squadrons would operate alongside each other for the rest of the war.

On 19 November the crew were called to the flight office, where they were briefed to do a search over the North Sea for the crew of a Lancaster that had ditched on returning from a raid on Ludwigshafen the night before. The weather forecast was not good and the search area was along the enemy coastline. Beetham took off and headed for the search area. He arrived to find the weather conditions to be as bad as predicted; the cloud base was five hundred feet or lower in places and it was pouring with rain. Even though it was daylight it proved to be extremely difficult, if not impossible, for the crew to see anything except the very rough sea. The conditions meant

3. The Beetham crew at the start of their operational tour with 50 Squadron at Skellingthorpe, November 1943. From left: Sgt Fred Ball (air gunner), Sgt Les Bartlett (bomb aimer), F/O Mike Beetham (pilot), P/O Frank Swinyard (navigator), Sgt Reg Payne (wireless operator), Sgt Don Moore (flight engineer) and Sgt Jock Higgins (air gunner) (Les Bartlett)

that Beetham had to work hard to avoid climbing back into cloud or hitting the sea but the crew stayed on task until dusk in the remote hope of spotting a small dinghy or anyone in the water. The search proved fruitless. As their fuel was getting low the crew eventually had to abandon the search and return to Skellingthorpe. It was a quiet transit back as each member felt so low having not been able to locate their missing colleagues.

Because the search area had been so close to enemy territory the crew were told the following day that they were to be credited with their first op of the tour, even though it had not at all been what they had imagined their first op to be. However, if the crew were disappointed that their first op had not been against a major German target, their disappointment did not last long. Three days later, in the morning of 22 November, the crew arrived at the flight office to find they were 'on ops' that night. McFarlane explained to Beetham that the high operational tempo for the squadron now meant that it was their turn to commence full operations. Beetham was naturally excited and told McFarlane they were ready. His crew were allocated JA899 'D-Dog' and just after midday they took the aircraft on the customary night-flying test, or NFT as it was known, which lasted just twenty-five minutes. The main briefing was at 1.30 p.m. and the crew found out their target. It was Berlin! Beetham was a little surprised because his crew had previously been protected from Berlin for their first operation but McFarlane explained to him that the target was likely to be almost only Berlin for a while as Bomber Command now faced its biggest test of the war.

To the crews of Bomber Command, Berlin was understandably the 'Big One' because of what the city represented in Nazi Germany and because it provided the key link between the Western and Eastern Fronts. Berlin was, and still is, a very large city. In 1943 it was not only Germany's largest city but it was the third-largest city in the world with a total area of nearly four hundred square miles. Because of its location deep into the heart of Germany, Berlin had hardly been touched during the early years of the war. There had been a retaliatory raid in August 1940 during the Battle of Britain, but Bomber Command's effort had been small scale. Berlin had then been attacked a number of times during the latter half of 1941 but poor results and high losses brought an end to the campaign. For the next year there had been no further raids on Berlin. The distance meant that bombers would be exposed to ground defences and night fighters during the long transit, and Bomber Command losses at that stage of the war had been steadily increasing. Thus the Air Officer Commanding-in-Chief, Air Chief Marshal Sir Arthur Harris had decided to leave Berlin alone until more aircraft and better equipment were more readily available.

By October 1943 there had been a number of changes that had given Harris the opportunity to launch a major campaign against Berlin. The introduction of the US Eighth Air Force into the overall strategic bombing campaign was already proving significant, as was the introduction of the Pathfinder Force, which had improved bombing techniques and, in turn, had given better bombing results. Significantly, though, the introduction of the four-engine heavy bombers and Bomber Command's expansion in terms of the number of squadrons had meant that more aircraft than ever before were now available. Harris had ordered three attacks against Germany's capital during August and September 1943, which effectively marked the start of the Battle of Berlin, although the main effort did not start until November.

As Beetham sat through the main briefing during the afternoon of 22 November it became increasingly clear that the raid he was about to take part in was to be Bomber Command's biggest effort against Berlin to date. After the main briefing the crew went over their individual areas of responsibility, such as plotting the route to be taken and establishing the aiming points once at the target. Just before 3 p.m. the crew had their meal and then got dressed. As dusk began to fall Beetham made his way out to the aircraft. There was still enough daylight to see Skellingthorpe's ground personnel lining the perimeter track and runway; they had come to wish the crews good luck and to wave them on their way. It was a tremendous sight.

The Lancasters roared down the runway one by one and then it was Beetham's turn. Full of fuel and with its bomb load, it was a long take-off run for the Lancaster but he eventually climbed away. As they crossed the Dutch coast he could see bright flashes of light flak beneath them but the transit to the target area proved uneventful; the cloud cover beneath them acted in their favour as it prevented any searchlights from picking them up. As they approached the target Beetham saw the occasional track marker put down by the Pathfinders and saw the red and green flares gradually descending into the cloud. He made the final turn in towards the target, the bomb doors were opened and at last they released their bombs and turned for home. The flak was moderate but was below them and Beetham flew a steady weave away from the target area to avoid presenting an easy target to any night fighters patrolling the local area. Although their route home took them close to various enemy defences, the cloud cover prevented any searchlights breaking through and there was only occasional light flak along the way. There was a final burst of flak as they approached the Dutch coast but everything then quietened down. Soon it was time to contact Skellingthorpe and then Beetham brought the Lancaster in to land; the sortie had lasted seven hours and fifteen minutes.

Bomber Command's effort against Berlin that night had been 764 aircraft, the largest number of bombers sent to Berlin to date. Fortunately for Beetham the bad weather at many of the Luftwaffe's night-fighter bases had prevented many from getting airborne. The cloud cover over the target area meant that it had been somewhat difficult to assess the success of the raid but bombing had been spread over a large area of Berlin, resulting in considerable damage to the residential areas and several industrial areas. Bomber Command's losses had been relatively small: twenty-six bombers, including one Lancaster from 50 Squadron, had failed to return.

The following morning Beetham found out that his crew would be back on operations that night. It was Berlin again. Harris had decided that his force should return to Berlin immediately, although this time the number of bombers would be halved and, with the exception of the Pathfinders, it would be an all-Lancaster effort. The route chosen was the same as the previous night but this time the weather at the Luftwaffe's night-fighter bases was more favourable and the night fighters were able to hassle the main stream. Conditions over Berlin were again cloudy, which meant the Pathfinders had to use sky-marking techniques. For Beetham the sortie passed without incident until he arrived back over Lincolnshire to find the aircraft's flaps were unserviceable. He was instructed to divert to nearby Wittering, which had a longer runway than Skellingthorpe, for a flapless landing and he landed the aircraft without any problems. It had been another long night; twenty Lancasters had failed to return but the raid had caused further destruction of Berlin in the industrial and residential areas of the city.

By mid-afternoon the following day the Lancaster had been fixed and Beetham made the short flight back to Skellingthorpe. He landed to find there were to be no operations for 5 Group that night as Bomber Command's total effort against Berlin during the previous two nights had exceeded eleven hundred bomber sorties. This gave the crew a well-earned rest, and many of the squadron's personnel made their way into Lincoln for the evening. The following day a further trip to Berlin was planned but the operation was cancelled not long before take-off because of poor weather.

The next day it was to be Berlin again; the third raid against the city in just five nights. The first part of the sortie was quiet but cloud cover disappeared close to the Frankfurt defences. Searchlights were soon illuminating the main force and enemy fighters started to appear. The first signs of Berlin were the searchlights of the outer defences and soon Beetham could see the red glow of Berlin as the bombers in the earlier waves found the target. Conditions were good enough to bomb the target visually and he was soon turning for home. There was more searchlight activity followed by the inevitable flak as they approached Hamburg, and one searchlight battery managed to capture their Lancaster and the flak suddenly became more intense. Beetham immediately dived to port and he then climbed steeply to starboard to escape the beam. The rest of the return transit passed without incident until they were ready to descend back to base. Dense fog had meant that a recovery into Skellingthorpe was impossible and so the crew was initially diverted towards Pocklington and then to Melbourne in Yorkshire. It was not long before Beetham saw the flare path breaking through the fog and he touched down at the first attempt – the first squadron aircraft to do so. Three Lancasters behind them were not so lucky. The first swerved off the runway and became bogged down in soft ground. The second missed the runway completely and hit a vehicle on the ground before ploughing in to another Lancaster; both aircraft caught fire but amazingly both crews escaped, although the vehicle driver was killed. The third Lancaster tried to land several times but flew into a farm house during its final attempt. Both occupants of the farm house were killed, as were all but two of the Lancaster crew. If all this had not been bad enough for the squadron, a fourth Lancaster was missing over Germany.

The fog covering the east of England was still there the following day and it was two days before the weather had cleared enough for the crews to return to Skellingthorpe. The raid against Berlin on the night of 26/27 November had proved costly for the Lancaster force. Twenty-eight aircraft were shot down on the return leg when much of the main force had become scattered, and fourteen more crashed back in England due to the bad weather; these losses represented nearly 10 per cent of the Lancaster force dispatched to Berlin that night. Despite the overall losses to Bomber Command, Beetham's last three operations had been to Berlin and he noticed the confidence spreading through his crew. His next operation was to Leipzig on the night of 3/4 December. When the target was revealed at the briefing there was a sense of relief among the crews as it proved a welcome change from Berlin. He thought this had to be easier than what he had endured so far but his crew were about to learn a salutary lesson as proof that there was no such thing as a straightforward or easy operation and it was not just Berlin that would prove to be tricky.

Like Berlin, Leipzig was deep in the heart of Germany and it was a major target in Bomber Command's effort to destroy key aircraft and ball-bearing factories. The route was familiar, as it was much the same as for Berlin. Having dropped their bombs Beetham's crew turned for home but then came a moment he would never forget. There was a shout from Jock Higgins in the mid-upper turret just as a string of cannon shells from a Junkers Ju88 flew past the port side of the aircraft. There were thuds as the Lancaster was hit in the wing and Beetham's response was instinctive as he quickly put the Lancaster in a hard corkscrew manoeuvre to port. By now his gunners were returning fire and the Ju88 disappeared. It was all over in a matter of seconds. The crew surveyed the damage: the port wing had been hit several times, the flaps were damaged and a fuel tank had been punctured. The fuel from the punctured tank soon disappeared and the crew had to jettison everything they could in order to make it back across the Channel. Without the use of flaps Beetham was again diverted to Wittering and he touched down with little fuel to spare, having been airborne for nearly eight hours.

The crew returned to Skellingthorpe to find they had been granted seven days' leave. Aircrew on operations were typically, but not always, given seven days' leave every six weeks. Beetham went home to visit his parents and spent many hours chatting to them and was able to bring them up to date with what he had been doing. It was a lovely break but it was soon time to return to Skellingthorpe. He returned from leave eager to continue with his tour of operations. He had now flown six operational sorties and was glad to be back among his crew colleagues once more. They were no longer the new crew and were becoming established members of the squadron, having been to Berlin three times.

Bad weather meant that two operations were cancelled before Beetham flew his next operation. The target was Frankfurt, which was a welcome change from the long transits to Berlin and Leipzig. He was allocated the Lancaster ED588 'VN-G George', which became legendary when it completed 125 operational sorties, of which all but the first ten were flown with 50 Squadron from Skellingthorpe. Of more than 7,300 Lancasters built only thirty-four completed one hundred operational sorties and only a handful completed more operations than 'G-George'. When Beetham flew it to Frankfurt on 20 December it was the aircraft's fifty-first operational sortie. The raid was not particularly successful as the target area was covered by cloud and the Germans had successfully used decoy fires on the ground to add confusion, which resulted in bombing being scattered over a large area; there were also losses for 50 Squadron as two Lancasters failed to return. 'G-George' survived that night, but it would not survive the war, failing to return from a raid on Königsberg on the night of 29/30 August 1944.

There were no operations flown by Bomber Command over Christmas and for a short while at least everyone could enjoy a short break. Beetham was on the operations board again on the night of 29/30 December. The briefing was held at 2 p.m. and Beetham's crew were one of fifteen squadron crews, more than a hundred young men, crammed into the Nissen hut briefing room. The squadron commander pulled back the curtain covering the map and revealed the target – Berlin again! Beetham swallowed. It was only the crew's seventh trip but already this was to be their fourth to Berlin.

It was to be another maximum effort for Bomber Command, with more than seven hundred Lancasters and Halifaxes taking part, attacking in five waves, and all to be phased through the target in twenty minutes to saturate the defences. Mosquitoes were to carry out diversionary attacks against Magdeburg and Leipzig and Beetham's wave, the third wave, was briefed to feint towards Leipzig before turning towards Berlin at the last minute. The weather forecaster had briefed the crews to expect heavy cloud over most of Germany with widespread fog and poor visibility, which they hoped would restrict night-fighter activity. For the raid Beetham was allocated LL744 'VN-B', a new aircraft that had recently been delivered to the squadron, and it would be this Lancaster the crew would go on to fly throughout the rest of their tour; to the crew it became affectionately known as 'B-Beetham'.

The crew went out to the aircraft dispersal at 4 p.m. ready for take-off an hour later. The normal crowd of station personnel had gathered to watch the squadron depart and the aircraft were soon airborne. Beetham climbed to 19,000 feet and crossed the Dutch coast, after which he climbed further to the aircraft's maximum height of around 21,000 feet. The route took them to the north of the Ruhr and then south-east past Osnabruck and Hanover towards Leipzig. Twenty miles short of Leipzig he turned towards Berlin as briefed. By now there was much more activity, with searchlights trying to penetrate the cloud and pick up the bombers. Although there was plenty of flak there was nothing too close and fortunately there was no sign of any fighters. He could now feel the turbulence from the slipstream of bombers, which was always a bit disconcerting, and he could see the Wanganui marker flares ahead of him.

Because of the cloud they would have to bomb blind. The markers were well concentrated and he could see a glow of fires through the cloud where the aircraft had already bombed. Beetham held the aircraft straight and level during the final two minutes of the bombing run – it always seemed a very long two minutes – as the bomb doors were opened and then finally the bombs were released on the middle markers. He felt their 4,000-lb 'cookie' go and then the canisters of incendiaries, and it was always a relief when their bomb load had gone and the bomb doors could be closed again. He then turned northwards before finally turning for home.

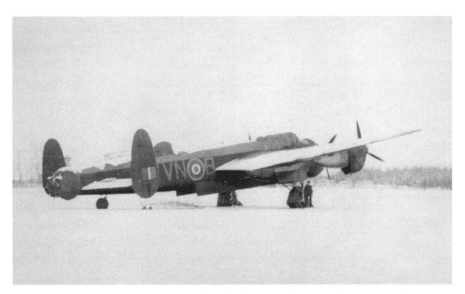

4. Beetham's trusted mount LL744 'VN-B', otherwise known to the crew as 'VN-B-Beetham', pictured at Skellingthorpe during the hard winter of 1943–4. Beetham flew this Lancaster twenty-one times on operations (Les Bartlett).

It was a long transit home but there were no problems. The weather cleared as they got closer to home and they landed safely back at Skellingthorpe at half-past midnight. At the debriefing they reported a quiet and uneventful trip, which was good for Berlin, after which the crew enjoyed their bacon and eggs before going to bed at 2 a.m.

The following morning Beetham went down to the flight at 10 a.m. to see whether ops were on again that night. He was met by his flight commander, who questioned him about the previous night. Beetham confirmed that it had been an uneventful trip and the flight commander then told him to go with him out to the aircraft dispersal. They drove out to the dispersal to find two of the ground crew standing on top of the starboard wing, which had been covered in scaffolding, and Beetham was staggered to see a large hole through the wing's outer fuel tank. He could clearly see where a 30-lb incendiary bomb, dropped from an aircraft above, had gone straight through the outer part of the wing. Fortunately the fuel tank had been empty at the time and had been purged by nitrogen, and so no fire had occurred. Beetham's corporal fitter jokingly asked him what he had done to his new aircraft, and his flight commander asked him whether he had felt anything unusual over the target. Beetham explained that all he had felt over the target area was the normal amount of turbulence but had not noticed anything untoward at the time.

It had been a lucky escape and it would be some days before their aircraft was ready for operations again but Beetham started to think about what might have happened had the incendiary bomb hit the engine or the fuselage and how close the rest of the other aircraft's bomb load must have passed. Would he have been standing there now? Perhaps luck was on their side. He knew only too well how important luck would be, as well as the skill of his own crew, if they were to get through the rest of their tour unscathed.

On New Year's Day Harris ordered another raid against Berlin, which involved Beetham once more. The target was again covered by cloud, which led to scattered bombing, and the route taken meant that the sortie was eight hours and fifteen minutes long – the longest flown by the crew to date. Four nights later it was Stettin, another long night and a sortie of eight hours and forty minutes, which set another record for the crew. The Stettin raid was the last before a period of full moon and so Beetham spent more than a week waiting around for his next operation. The weather at Skellingthorpe had also taken a turn for the worse and there was much snow around but the station's personnel worked hard to keep the airfield open and there were a couple of training flights to keep the crew active.

After a raid on Brunswick, Beetham's next four operations were all to Berlin and they marked a new phase of operations against the capital. Bomber Command studies had concluded that less than 25 per cent of Berlin had been damaged, which was less than the assessment of damage to other major cities at the time. The first of these raids involved 769 aircraft and was the largest force dispatched to Berlin to date.

The second, on the night of 21/22 January, was more interesting as it was a special operation and Beetham's was one of twenty-two Lancasters detailed to carry out an attack against Berlin while the main force of 648 aircraft attacked Magdeburg. The objective was to deceive the German defences and make them think the main target was Berlin and not Magdeburg, and Beetham was tasked to fly ahead of both the Pathfinder force and the main force. As he was flying the only Lancaster from Skellingthorpe involved with the decoy raid, both the station commander and the squadron commander had briefed him prior to take off and had instructed him not to take any risks. All this extra attention and concern made it feel as if he was on a one-way mission and no one expected him to come back. Besides, what did they mean by telling him not to take any risks? As far as Beetham was concerned all operations over Germany were risky and he saw no reason why this should be any different!

Beetham was first airborne from Skellingthorpe and it felt great to be ahead of everyone else. The transit outbound went well and at the designated point he turned for Berlin. Once in the target area he could see that Berlin was covered in cloud and he could see the glow of searchlights against the cloud but, being out in front, there were no Pathfinder markers for them to aim at and so the crew bombed the target as best they could before heading north towards Sweden and then for home. The flak was very light and was falling well below. Over Sweden it was a clear night and he could see the lights of the towns since there was no blackout there. The rest of the transit home proved to be quiet and, although one of the Lancasters failed to return from the diversionary raid on Berlin, the spoof tactic generally worked well as the German controllers were very slow to identify Magdeburg as the main target. However, for a variety of reasons, the bombing at Magdeburg did not prove to be accurate and there were heavy losses; fifty-seven aircraft of the main force failed to return.

The fourth in this latest series of raids against Berlin also proved memorable. Beetham was in the fifth wave and by the time he reached Berlin the enemy night fighters were active in the area. Having dropped their bombs, he turned for home and he then noticed a Junkers Ju88 ahead of them, attacking another Lancaster. Beetham immediately told the bomb aimer, Les Bartlett, to man the front turret and to start firing at the Ju88. They both then watched the Ju88 make a slow turn to port and commence a spiral descent towards the ground. Once back at Skellingthorpe the crew filled out a combat report and claimed the Ju88 as damaged. It was not possible to determine anything more because they had lost visual contact with the Ju88 as it spiralled towards the ground.

At the end of January the crew were given a few days' leave. It had been a busy month with nearly sixty hours of operational flying. Beetham was promoted to the rank of flight lieutenant and had now flown fifteen operational sorties, nine of which had been against Berlin. One of the ground crew had taught him how to drive, using the perimeter track of the airfield as a road, and so he bought

5. Beetham pictured in January 1944 during his operational tour with 50 Squadron

a car; a 1931 Morris Minor, which cost him £30. Having then got his provisional driving licence, and with an aircrew entitlement of two hundred miles' worth of petrol a month, he was now on the road – but he had learned to fly a Lancaster before he could drive a car!

When the crew returned from leave the next ten days were spent conducting training flights rather than operations as Bomber Command was carrying out a number of minor operations rather than any major efforts. One training flight proved unforgettable for Beetham and ended in tragedy for two of his crew. On 12 February the crew took off in Lancaster W4119 'VN-Q' for a fighter affiliation sortie. On board were Beetham and his crew, and Pilot Officer D. A. Jennings and two of his air gunners; the idea was that the two pilots would share the sortie, as would the four air gunners on board. Beetham flew the take-off and first thirty minutes of the sortie before he handed over control and command of the aircraft to Jennings.

Soon afterwards there was a shout of 'port outer on fire' from one of the crew members. Beetham was down in the nose compartment and immediately noticed flames coming from the engine. Having decided there was nothing more that could be done, Jennings then gave the order to abandon the aircraft. Beetham was handed his parachute by Don Moore and he then jumped out through the front escape hatch in the floor of the bombing compartment. He was immensely relieved that his parachute opened and he could now survey the scene around him. He could see a few other parachutes and so he knew that some of his crew had also managed to escape. There was a cloud layer below and he could see the Lancaster descending in flames with a trail of dark smoke behind. Other than that, he had no idea where he was. He had been in the nose compartment at the time and they had been conducting their training above cloud, and so he had lost his sense of positioning over the ground. Having descended through the cloud, he was relieved to see that he would come down in a field rather than the sea and he could now see a number of parachutes in the sky around him. He was surprised how quickly the ground seemed to rush up to him but he landed safely. He then saw two other parachutes on the ground nearby, but he had no idea who they were. A farmer was approaching him with a shot gun as he thought the German invasion had started but Beetham was quick to shout out 'RAF, RAF'. Somewhat relieved, the farmer invited him into the farmhouse and the next to come in was Frank Swinyard. At that point the farmer brought out a bottle of whisky but it did not last long!

Reg Payne had been the last member of the crew to vacate the aircraft successfully through the rear door before the Lancaster crashed at Revesby in Lincolnshire. Sadly, Beetham's rear gunner, Fred Ball, and his flight engineer, Don Moore, who for some reason had decided to go to the rear of the aircraft rather than follow Beetham to the front escape hatch, had not managed to get out; nor had the two gunners from Jennings's crew, who were also at the rear of the aircraft. It was a tragic blow. Fred Ball and Don Moore had survived fourteen operational sorties only to lose their lives during a training sortie over Lincolnshire just a matter of miles away from their home base.

Beetham and three of the crew attended Fred Ball's funeral in Birmingham and Frank Swinyard attended Don Moore's funeral in London. There was the inevitable inquiry to determine the cause of the crash and the loss of life, and a few days later the crew were joined by Flight Lieutenant Ted Adamson, the squadron's engineer leader, and Pilot Officer Johnny Blott, the squadron's gunnery leader, who had already been awarded the DFC. These were good and very experienced replacements as both had already completed their tour of operations and Beetham felt it quite a compliment that they had volunteered to join his crew for the remainder of his operational tour.

There were just two more operations during the rest of February: to Leipzig, which passed without incident, and to Augsburg when Beetham had to return to Skellingthorpe on three engines following the loss of oil pressure on the starboard outer engine during the return transit. The next major effort ordered by Harris was to Stuttgart on the night of 1/2 March. At over eight hours it was another long night for the crew, although poor weather over Germany prevented German night fighters from getting airborne and it proved to be the quietest trip for the crew to date.

The next week saw operations planned and then cancelled due to poor weather. After that the crew were one of just forty-four Lancasters that took part in a raid against an aircraft assembly plant at Marignane near Marseille in the south of France. This provided the crew with a different challenge as it was the first time they were to drop bombs on French soil and it required precision bombing from 10,000 feet, which was well below their normal bombing height of above 20,000 feet. The route took them over Le Havre and then down across the Alps, and Beetham could then see the coastline of southern France and the Mediterranean before turning in towards Marseille. Their target was three hangars at the airport and, having released their bombs, Beetham turned for home. He looked down at the devastation beneath them with fires raging across the area and smoke billowing into the night sky. There was then the long and tedious transit home and the crew landed safely back at base after just under nine hours airborne: another record for the crew.

Following the Marignane raid the crew were again given a few days' leave. Beetham returned from leave to find that he had been awarded the DFC in recognition of his gallantry during operations. His citation read:

> On the night of 3/4 December 1943, the aircraft of which he was captain was attacked by a Ju88 after leaving the target. The port centre petrol tank was holed and much fuel was lost, but due to his skilful handling he managed to reach this country and land safely. Then, on the night of 25/26 February 1944, he was captain of an aircraft detailed to attack Augsburg. Shortly after leaving the target, the starboard outer engine failed. Once again, Flight Lieutenant Beetham proved

his skill and brought the aircraft safely back to base on three engines. He has always shown a high standard of efficiency and has proved himself an excellent captain of aircraft. For his consistent devotion to duty, his gallantry in the air, and the offensive spirit which he has shown in battle, he is awarded the Distinguished Flying Cross.

There was also a DFC for Beetham's navigator, Frank Swinyard, and a Distinguished Flying Medal, the equivalent award for non-commissioned officers, for his bomb aimer, Les Bartlett.

On 24 March it was Berlin again, their tenth trip to the city. The weather forecast predicted clear skies over the target area but fog was forecast by 3 a.m. in Lincolnshire. At 7 p.m. Beetham took off from Skellingthorpe. The transit across Denmark and the Baltic Sea did not cause any problems but many aircraft strayed off track and into the defences of Kiel and Lübeck. Once over Rostock there were more searchlights and flak but the strong tailwind took them quickly to Berlin. Fortunately, over the target area a thin layer of stratus cloud had formed, which made it difficult for the searchlights to pick them up and so there were no problems during the target run.

Once off the target Beetham could see some night-fighter activity but nothing too close. They managed to avoid the defences of Leipzig, Brunswick, Osnabruck and Hanover and then they were crossing the Dutch coast and on their way home. However, the fog had arrived in Lincolnshire earlier than predicted and Beetham was eventually diverted to Foulsham in Norfolk, where he landed with the aid of FIDO (Fog Investigation Dispersal Operation or sometimes referred to as Fog Intense Dispersal Operation or Fog Intense Dispersal Of), which was developed during the war for dispersing fog from an airfield by using ignited petrol fed from large pipes along each side of the runway.

FIDO systems were used at many airfields during the war but, although he knew about it, Beetham had never seen it before and had not been trained for it, and so he did not really know what to expect. He was given a heading to steer towards the airfield and as he got closer he could see a bright orange glow ahead of him. As he descended and entered the fog all forward visibility disappeared. Beetham was now concentrating on listening to the controller who was talking him down and flying on instruments with precision accuracy. He was fully aware just how thick the fog had become as he made his final approach to land and it was a hairy moment as he continued to descend lower and lower – through 600 feet, 500 feet, and then 400 feet – without knowing where he was or being in sight of the ground. Then, as he descended through 300 feet, he visually picked up the runway lights straight ahead of him and exactly where the controller had told him they would be. FIDO had done its job and had lifted the fog high enough for a safe landing to be made. Once on the ground Beetham was extremely mindful to keep the aircraft straight on the runway because he could see the ignited fuel either side of him and in no way wanted to veer off the side of the runway!

This proved to be Beetham's last trip to Berlin and also the last major effort against the city by Bomber Command, bringing an end to the Battle of Berlin after sixteen major raids and over nine thousand sorties flown during the winter of 1943–4. It was the longest and most sustained bombing offensive of the Second World War, during which nearly thirty thousand tons of bombs had been dropped. Although there would be some minor operations by small numbers of Mosquitoes against the city during the remaining period of the war, there was nothing of any strategic importance. The Battle of Berlin had cost Bomber Command more than five hundred aircraft and Skellingthorpe had suffered 168 killed during operations against Berlin alone.

Beetham flew two more operations during March, the second of which was the disastrous raid against Nuremberg on the night of 30/31 March. It was a night close to a full moon and Beetham had expected the raid to be cancelled. As one of the more experienced captains he knew where the searchlights and flak batteries were located and during the transit he realised they were being continuously blown towards the Ruhr by the wind, which was stronger than forecast. Although Swinyard's calculations were suggesting they should turn to port, Beetham kept turning starboard, away from the known defences, and because the visibility was good enough for him to see the defences on his left and other aircraft being shot down. The main force became so scattered that 20 per cent of the bombers did not pass within thirty miles of one turning point and the German night fighters also scored considerable success, resulting in many bombers being shot down before reaching the target.

On reaching the target Beetham found the area covered by cloud and the defences were not causing any great problems. They bombed as best they could and on the way home managed to avoid any night fighters and other local defences, although the wind continued to be a challenge. They eventually returned to Skellingthorpe unscathed but others were not so lucky and the Nuremberg raid proved to be a bad night for Bomber Command. Of the 795 aircraft that took part, ninety-five failed to return, including three from 50 Squadron, and ten more were written off back at base; Bomber Command casualties that night were 535 killed and a further 180 wounded or taken as prisoners of war.

The disaster of the Nuremberg raid effectively brought to an end, for the time being at least, the massed attacks against major German cities; it would be some time before these tactics were employed again. The winter nights were now drawing to a close and Harris realised that his bombing offensive deep into the heart of Germany would have to stop. Furthermore, plans for the forthcoming Allied invasion of Europe meant that Bomber Command's attention was now needed elsewhere. Harris switched his emphasis to targets in occupied Europe, and Beetham's next operation was against an aircraft assembly plant at Toulouse on the evening of 5 April as part of a small Lancaster force of 144 aircraft from 5 Group with one Mosquito to mark the target, flown by the legendary Wing Commander Leonard Cheshire, then commanding 617 Squadron; this was the first time the tactic of using a single Mosquito to carry out low-level target marking was used. The raid was significant for 5 Group as its commander, Air Vice-Marshal Ralph Cochrane, had been informed by Harris that 5 Group was now an independent force, which meant that whenever required the group could use its own aircraft for marking rather than having to rely on the Pathfinder force.

Beetham flew six more operations during April, two of which were against railway marshalling yards near Paris: at Juvisy and La Chappelle respectively. Bomber Command crews were always very careful when bombing targets in occupied France as a directive had told the crews to identify the target positively before releasing their bombs to minimise the risk of civilian casualties. This meant bombing at a lower height, which offered the benefit of enjoying spectacular views over Paris, although they were fortunate never to encounter any night fighters in the area.

A pattern was now developing in the way Bomber Command conducted its operations. There would be a maximum effort every two nights, with only a minor operation on the night in between. For example, Bomber Command flew a total of 1,116 operational sorties on the night of 22/23 April, including Beetham's involvement in a 5 Group effort against Brunswick; two nights later there was another maximum effort by Bomber Command, totalling 1,160 sorties, and another on the night of 26/27 April to Schweinfurt, which Beetham flew on.

His next sortie was a 5 Group effort to an explosive factory at St Medard-en-Jalles near Bordeaux, but fires caused by the earlier bombers meant they were unable to identify the target accurately and so the crew did not bomb. Because of the importance of the factory, however, the bombers – including the Beetham crew – returned the following night to complete the task.

The Beetham crew had now completed twenty-nine of their required thirty operations and their next, which they hoped would be their last, was to an aircraft factory at Toulouse on the night of 1/2 May. The contrast between this operation, a more specialised raid against a target in France, and their first operation against Berlin demonstrates just how Bomber Command's offensive during the

6. The Beetham crew at the end of their tour of operations, May 1944. Standing from left to right: Sgt Jock Higgins (air gunner), P/O Johnny Blott DFC (air gunner), F/L Mike Beetham DFC (pilot), F/O Frank Swinyard DFC (navigator), P/O Les Bartlett DFM (bomb aimer). Sitting from left to right: F/L Ted Adamson (flight engineer) and Sgt Reg Payne (wireless operator) (Les Bartlett)

winter had changed. Now, fewer than half the bombs dropped were against targets in Germany and the balance would continue to swing further during May, when three-quarters of Bomber Command's sorties were flown against targets in France and other occupied territories. Also, when they had flown their first raid against Berlin in November it was part of a force of 764 aircraft taking part in the only major operation that night and involved all the major groups within Bomber Command, with twenty-six aircraft lost. Now, although Bomber Command was flying a similar number of sorties overall, the groups were operating separately against six different targets and the overall losses would be considerably lower.

There had been times during the past six months when the crew felt their final operation would never come, but the end was now in sight, although there was no time to be complacent; too many crews had failed to return from their last operation. Once again the crew flew their trusted mount LL744 'VN-B Beetham', the twenty-first time they had flown the aircraft in their last twenty-four operations. The crew had always been vigilant throughout the tour, but on this occasion Beetham sensed they were more so and there was a certain amount of extra tension among them all. As things turned out he need not have worried. The aircraft did not let them down and the operation passed without incident. When Beetham touched down safely at Skellingthorpe there was obvious relief all round. Then, at the debriefing, the squadron commander had a smile on his face and offered his congratulations and confirmed, much to the relief of the crew, that their tour of operations was over.

CHAPTER 3

Bomber Command to Africa

It was now May 1944 and so much had happened in such a short period of time. Beetham had joined 50 Squadron as a young twenty-year-old flying officer just six months earlier and had done his tour through the hard winter of 1943–4, which had been a difficult time for Bomber Command, with losses as heavy as at any other time. Berlin had been a major target in that period and the Beetham crew had completed ten out of the sixteen raids on the 'Big City' flown by Bomber Command during the Battle of Berlin. He had completed his tour of operations before his twenty-first birthday and was now a flight lieutenant with a DFC. To survive the whole tour had required considerable skill and luck too. The crew had had several narrow escapes, and had seen many of their comrades shot down. Being such a young man and dedicated to the task, Beetham had not worried unduly in spite of having several worrying moments. It was of course a relief to complete the tour but at the same time he was sorry that it had all come to an end and that he would be leaving the squadron, his many friends and the tremendous spirit that existed.

There was time for just one more sortie before leaving 50 Squadron, a familiarisation flight for a replacement crew about to start their tour of operations. That night the squadron was once again on operations but not the Beetham crew. It was probably just as well as it was the ill-fated raid on a military camp near the French village of Mailly-le-Camp when forty-two Lancasters failed to return and among the losses were five aircraft from 50 Squadron; twenty-five of the squadron's aircrew were killed. Before leaving Skellingthorpe the crew visited their trusted mount, LL744 'VN-B', one last time. If there was such a thing as a lucky aircraft then 'VN-B' was certainly it for the Beetham crew. They had flown it twenty-one times on operations and each time it had proved reliable and got them back safely, despite losing an engine on one occasion and suffering damage on two others. Unfortunately, though, the aircraft did not prove as lucky for its next crew as 'VN-B' would not survive the month; the aircraft failed to return following a raid on Brunswick on the night of 22/23 May and six of the crew were killed.

Having completed their tour of operations, the five original crew members went their own separate ways, and all five would survive the war. Les Bartlett then returned to his pre-war profession of pharmacy and retired in the village of Hamble near Southampton. Reg Payne worked in the engineering industry before retiring in Kettering, where he has since worked tirelessly as the president of his local branch of the Royal Air Force Association. Jock Higgins joined the Palestine Police Force and then moved to Canada. A keen golfer, Jock died on the golf course in 1993. Frank Swinyard became a certified accountant after the war and then joined the Merchant Seamen's War Memorial Society as the company secretary and accountant. He devoted the rest of his life to making the venture a success and died in 1991.

After some leave Beetham travelled down to Lulsgate Bottom in Somerset to join No 61 Course at No 3 Flying Instructors School. His next posting was to No 5 Lancaster Finishing School at Syerston in Nottinghamshire, which had been introduced to bridge the gap between the HCU and the front-line squadron, but first he had to be trained as an instructor. He commenced the course at Lulsgate Bottom on his twenty-first birthday and two days later flew his first exercise in the Airspeed Oxford. Although Beetham was an experienced pilot and captain he found instructing to be a different skill altogether. He spent the next three weeks being taught how to pass on his knowledge and experience to students and how to become a good instructor. He then went to the LFS as a newly qualified instructor, where – although he had three hundred hours on the Lancaster – he spent the first week learning how to teach evasive manoeuvres and how to teach flying on three, and even two, engines before he was qualified to teach student pilots all aspects of the Lancaster course.

For the rest of the year Beetham taught many crews how to fly and operate the Lancaster before they went on to their tour of operations. One of his student pilots was Flying Officer Norman Hoad, who was later shot down and taken prisoner of war but remained in the post-war RAF and later retired as an air vice-marshal. Hoad also became an established artist and a founder member of the Guild of Aviation Artists and a vice-chairman of the Armed Forces Art Society.

By the end of 1944 the balance had well and truly swung in the Allies' favour following the successful D-Day landings and the subsequent breakout from Normandy towards Germany. However, crews still needed to be trained as it would be several more months before the war in Europe would come to an end. Beetham remained at Syerston until March 1945 but it was only a matter of time before he would be needed back on operations, although it was also evident that the war in Europe was approaching its end. He was then posted to 57 Squadron at East Kirkby as the squadron's checking pilot with the task of checking each pilot every ten operational sorties to make sure they were still competent at flying corkscrews and other defensive manoeuvres, and they could still handle the aircraft safely on three engines. While this luxury could not be afforded during Beetham's operational tour with 50 Squadron, there were now plenty of pilots and these sorties became known as the 'ten-sortie' and 'twenty-sortie' check rides.

There was a welcome break from the routine check rides on 8 May, the day the war ended in Europe, when Beetham flew on Operation Exodus. This was the repatriation of British and Commonwealth prisoners of war from mainland Europe, and throughout May more than three thousand round trips took place, returning 74,000 prisoners of war. The Lancaster could carry up to twenty-five passengers and Beetham flew from East Kirkby to Juvincourt in France.

The weather was good and after landing he shut down in the queue of Lancasters on the perimeter track. A truck eventually arrived two hours later, and twenty-four former prisoners of war got out. They were all British Army and had been captured at Dunkirk five years before. They had only recently been informed of their imminent return to Britain and appeared somewhat bedraggled and bemused. Many had never flown in an aircraft before but they were soon briefed on the safety aspects of flying and told not to touch anything. They boarded the aircraft and sat or stood in any available space they could find. There was a lieutenant colonel among the group whom Beetham allowed on to the flight deck, but otherwise there were some passengers in the bomb aimer's compartment in the nose of the aircraft, some sat on the main spar and alongside the wireless operator and others were crammed into the fuselage as best they could.

They were soon airborne and on their way back to Dunsfold in Surrey, which acted as a reception centre for all returning prisoners of war. It was a beautiful day and so Beetham crossed the English coast over the white cliffs of Dover as a way of welcoming them all home. After landing he shut down on the perimeter track opposite the main hangars and his passengers got off the aircraft to be met by a group of young women of the Women's Auxiliary Air Force. Seeing that his passengers were now in good hands he bid the repatriated soldiers farewell and returned to East Kirkby, where he found a party in full swing. It had been a most memorable and extremely rewarding way of spending VE-Day.

While Europe was celebrating the end of the war, Beetham was preparing to deploy to the Far East, where the war against Japan was still ongoing. At the Second Quebec Conference of September 1944, held between the British, Canadian and American governments, Britain's prime minister, Winston Churchill, had agreed to send a large part of Bomber Command, known as Tiger Force, to the Pacific once Germany had been defeated in Europe. As 57 Squadron was one of the nominated squadrons to deploy to Okinawa, Beetham prepared to go to war once more. By the end of June he had been promoted to the rank of squadron leader and appointed as a flight commander. Then, after America dropped two atomic bombs on Hiroshima and Nagasaki, followed by Japan's surrender on 15 August, all plans to deploy to the Far East were put on hold and later disbanded altogether.

Towards the end of August the squadron was due to take delivery of the new Avro Lincoln B2, a larger version of the Lancaster and designed to operate at higher altitude. The squadron had been designated the first trials squadron before the aircraft was to be deployed to the Far East. News had come through from Bomber Command that the squadron's first Lincoln was ready for collection from Waddington and so Beetham flew from East Kirkby to Waddington in a Lancaster to pick the new aircraft up. Having first reported to the air traffic control tower, he picked up and read some pilot's notes to familiarise himself with the new aircraft, and then promptly flew it to East Kirkby.

The arrival of the new aircraft meant there was much interest on the station and a few days later he was able to put the Lincoln through a hard routine of climbs and descents, steep turns and stalls, and assessed its performance on three engines. He then flew a further sortie to assess the aircraft in the circuit and during landing. His overall assessment of the aircraft was that it had some improvements to the Lancaster but he did not find the Lincoln as good to handle and felt it to be a rather cumbersome beast.

The following month he took part in Operation Dodge, the repatriation of the British Army from Italy and the Mediterranean, when he flew to Bari in Italy, a flight of seven hours, before returning three days later with twenty army personnel on board. He then flew to Berlin for a visit, via Tibenham in Norfolk for customs clearance; compared to the long night transits during the winter of 1943–4 it seemed a relatively short trip of just two and a half hours. Flying in daylight at low level, he could see the extensive damage to the towns and cities of the Ruhr and western Germany before he landed at RAF Gatow.

During the following two days Beetham was able to observe for himself what life was like in Berlin in the immediate aftermath of the war. He and his colleagues were escorted by a wing commander from Gatow, and Beetham found it fascinating to tour the city. He thought it was a complete shambles and at times it was impossible to walk along the footpaths unhampered; only the roads had been cleared. There was enormous damage and very few buildings were unscathed. An obvious place to visit was the Reichstag, which had been constructed during the nineteenth century to house the parliament of the German Empire. When they got there they found it guarded by a Russian soldier and so they had to work out how to get past the guard. One of them had an idea. He had a NAAFI pass and he duly waved it in front of the guard, saying in a loud voice, 'Marshal Zhukov, Marshal Zhukov'. It worked and the guard let them pass, although there was not much to see due to the extensive damage caused by the Allied bombing. Later on they were walking around another part of Berlin when they came across some planks blocking the walkway. They moved the planks, only to reveal a dead body, and so they hastily replaced the planks and moved on. That evening they visited a nightclub with their escort. There was a small band playing, and many young waitresses but Beetham and his escort were not allowed to fraternise with the local German population; even so, with plenty of drink available, it proved to be a good evening.

The visit to Berlin proved to be a sombre reflection on the events of the war, but Beetham had no regrets about the part he had played during the Battle of Berlin. At no time did he feel at all threatened by the people of Berlin and he found most to be rather bedraggled, although everyone was understandably glad and relieved that the war was over.

Now that he was no longer required to deploy to the Far East, Beetham had to make a decision about what to do in the longer term. He was still only twenty-two years old and was keen to stay in the post-war RAF, but he could see that the end of the war would mean squadrons being disbanded and large numbers of wartime personnel demobbed. While this would undoubtedly suit some, particularly those who had families or previous occupations, there was nothing he would rather do than stay in the RAF. What he did not know was the scale of the planned reduction in the armed forces, which were expected to fall from about five million personnel at the end of the war to just over one million by the end of 1946 and then to just over 700,000 by the beginning of 1949. The reduction in RAF manpower was expected to reduce to less than 400,000 by early 1948 and to 250,000 by 1950.

Government policy meant the priorities were on the development of Bomber Command and Fighter Command and to a lesser extent Coastal Command. Even though there would be the inevitable reduction in the number of expensive overseas bases, a number of transport elements would still be required. It was planned that the RAF's front-line strength would eventually be in the region of 165 squadrons, totalling about fifteen hundred aircraft, with most squadrons being retained in the UK, although sixty squadrons would be based overseas in Germany, the Middle East and Far East.

Not only was Beetham keen to stay in the post-war RAF, but he was also keen to secure a permanent commission rather than a short-service commission. His opportunity came in September when he received a written offer of a permanent commission, followed by a telephone call from the group personnel officer, who proposed a posting for Beetham to the staff at the Officer Advanced Training School, which was about to move from Cranwell to nearby Digby.

The OATS course was three and a half weeks long and focused on junior command for officers destined for flight and squadron commander appointments. Beetham had previously done the course as a student towards the end of the war and had found that the practical skills on the course were well taught and the comforts of Cranwell quite remarkable. But, even though he had enjoyed his time as a student, he was not at all keen on the idea of joining the staff because he wanted to remain flying, even if that meant losing his rank of squadron leader. He made his point clearly and quite forcefully to the personnel officer but, for now, he did not get his way. He was instructed to proceed to Cranwell for an interview with the newly appointed commandant of the RAF College, Air Commodore Richard Atcherley. The commandant listened to what

Beetham had to say but he appeared rather cross and he made it clear to Beetham how a posting to the RAF College would be beneficial to his career.

During the journey back to East Kirkby Beetham wondered whether he had done the right thing but he did not have to wait long before he knew the outcome. A few days later he received a telephone call from his personnel officer. Beetham accepted the fact that he may have to lose his acting rank but insisted he wanted to remain flying and asked if he could be found a posting to a squadron as a flight lieutenant. The personnel officer called back later to tell him that he was to be posted to 35 Squadron at Graveley as a flight commander instead of Cranwell, and the 'bad news' was that the squadron was about to move to the Middle East. Beetham was delighted. As a flight commander he would retain his rank of acting squadron leader and he found it quite extraordinary that anyone could think that a posting overseas could be bad news. In fact, he thoroughly looked forward to it.

There were not many permanent commissions on offer at the time and there is no doubt that Beetham was very lucky, not only to be retained in the post-war RAF and granted a permanent commission but also to obtain a further flying tour in rank. As far as he was concerned, he had learned a valuable lesson when dealing with personnel officers during his career. From that moment on he would always ask for what he wanted and would then stick to it. While this tactic would clearly not work for everyone in the RAF, it seemed to work well for him!

Beetham arrived at Graveley in November 1945 to join 35 Squadron. Graveley was situated to the south of Huntingdon in Cambridgeshire and, because it had been one of Bomber Command's units designated for the Far East as part of Tiger Force, the squadron operated the Lancaster Mark I (FE) – the 'FE' simply standing for 'Far East', meaning that the aircraft had been converted for tropical use. A second Lancaster squadron, 115 Squadron, was also at Graveley, and the Bomber Command squadrons operated alongside each other. Beetham quickly settled in as he was familiar with the aircraft and the squadron's tactics, and soon learned that the squadron was to deploy to Shalufa in Egypt, close to Port Suez. He was issued with his tropical kit and got up to date with all the required inoculations. In January he went on embarkation leave before his deployment but was recalled to Graveley just a few weeks later to find out that the deployment to Egypt had been cancelled and the squadron had been selected to represent Bomber Command in a number of forthcoming flypasts instead.

The next few weeks were spent carrying out formation flying. Throughout March and April the squadron gradually increased the size of its formations from three aircraft, to six aircraft, then nine and finally twelve. By the end of April the squadron was fully competent at twelve-aircraft formation flying and precision timing in preparation for the flypasts that were soon to follow. The squadron formation was led by the squadron commander, Wing Commander Alan Craig, a former Pathfinder pilot who had been decorated with the DSO and DFC, and at twenty-four years old was one of the youngest wing commanders in the post-war RAF. Beetham got on extremely well with his squadron commander from the start and the two men formed a friendship that would last for many years.

The first formation flypast was on 4 May, when the squadron provided a twelve-aircraft flypast over Holland to mark the anniversary of the nation's liberation. Throughout May the squadron did little other than carry out more practice formation flying in preparation for the next event. On 8 June the squadron flew over London for the Victory Day flypast and Beetham had on board a *Daily Telegraph* reporter, Mr Townsend, to capture the event from the air.

7. 35 Squadron was selected to represent Bomber Command in a number of flypasts and half of its formation of twelve Lancasters is seen approaching London for the Victory Day flypast on 8 June 1946. Beetham is flying the third aircraft 'TL-A'.

The squadron had also learned that it was soon to depart on Operation Lancaster to represent Bomber Command at the Army Air Forces Day Celebrations at Long Beach Field, California, and to take part in a goodwill tour of America. The invitation had come from General Carl Spaatz of the US Army Air Force, who had commanded the US Eighth Air Force when it had first moved to England in 1942, to mark the close association with Bomber Command and to repay some of the hospitality given by Bomber Command to American personnel during the Second World War. It was to be the first visit to the USA by a foreign squadron since General Italo Balbo had taken a flight of Italian aircraft to the World's Fair at Chicago in 1933. For Beetham this was great news and more than compensated for the fact that he was not going to the Middle East. Life was just getting better and better.

The news was also well received by the squadron's personnel as most had never been to America before. The plan was for the squadron to take sixteen Lancasters and crews to America, with five members of the squadron's ground crew travelling with each aircraft throughout the tour. Twelve Lancasters would be used for the formation flypasts during the tour with four aircraft nominated as reserves. Beetham had been allocated Lancaster SW315 'TL-A' for the tour, an aircraft he had flown almost continuously during the previous three months of training and for the two flypasts over Holland and London.

The total size of the detachment was to be 230 officers and men. In addition to those travelling in the Lancasters, there was an advance party of thirty officers and men led by the station commander, Group Captain Richard Collard, and a ground party of more than eighty engineers and support personnel. It was a good team to represent Bomber Command. The vast majority of aircrew had operational experience with Bomber Command and many had distinguished themselves on operations; among the detachment there was one holder of the DSO, twenty-three had been awarded the DFC and eleven held the DFM. Also accompanying the squadron was the BBC news correspondent and former wartime reporter, Charles Gardner. It had been Gardner's detailed broadcast in July 1940 when he witnessed an aerial engagement between RAF fighters and German aircraft attacking a British convoy in the Channel that catapulted him to fame as a wartime broadcaster and, somewhat controversially at the time, brought the reality of war home to radio listeners during the early days of the Battle of Britain.

On 8 July Beetham eased back on the controls of 'TL-A' for the start of the goodwill tour of America. He was the fourth to get airborne from Graveley and the first leg was a short transit down to St Mawgan in Cornwall, where the sixteen crews spent the night, and the following morning the formation headed out over the Atlantic towards the Azores. The advance party had gone on ahead in an Avro York, which would accompany the Lancasters throughout the tour. The leg to the Azores passed without incident and he touched down at Lagens Airfield nearly seven hours later.

The crews had the following day off. The weather forecast across the Atlantic was not good but the crews took off as planned on the night of 11 July for the transit to Gander in Newfoundland, Canada. Crossing the Atlantic by air in 1946 was a challenge and not many had done it at the time. The weather was very cloudy and Beetham soon learned that fog was forming at Gander, so he was somewhat relieved after an hour and a half to hear that the Lancasters had been recalled to the Azores. Beetham touched down back at Lagens three hours after he had taken off, two hours of which had been spent in cloud.

The crews had a few hours' rest before trying again the following day. This time they took off in daylight and the weather across the Atlantic was much improved and they reached Gander in just under nine hours, the last two of which had been at night.

The squadron then had a few days to prepare for their move south, and this gave the engineers the chance to check the aircraft over one more time and to rectify any minor defects. On 17 July the squadron took off from Gander for Mitchell Field on Long Island, New York. The flight took just over six hours and Beetham joined up in formation with the other Lancasters over Boston. The weather was clear over Long Island and Craig led the main formation of twelve aircraft over Mitchell Field, followed by the remaining four Lancasters. One by one they peeled off to make their final approach and land. One of the squadron's main priorities throughout the tour was to always be on time and Craig was the first to touch down, at exactly 4 p.m., the specified time of arrival.

Mitchell Field was the headquarters of Air Defense Command, responsible for the air defence of the USA, and the crews were met on arrival by the Chief of Air Defense Command, Lieutenant General George E. Stratemeyer, and the base commander, Colonel L. R. Parker. Also welcoming the squadron to America was the British representative to the United Nations Military Committee, Air Chief Marshal Sir Guy Garrod, plus many other local dignitaries.

The sixteen Lancasters lined up in front of operations and the RAF personnel formed up in ranks as the American Air Force band played the national anthems. That evening the squadron enjoyed the very best of American hospitality at a welcoming reception, cocktail party and a dinner at the officers' club.

The arrival of 35 Squadron made the newspapers the following morning, but there was little time to relax. Twelve Lancasters took part in a flypast over Manhattan that afternoon, flying in from the battery and passing directly over the Empire State Building at the specified time of 1.20 p.m. The Lancasters then flew over Thirty-Fourth Street and disappeared in the hazy sky over the Bronx and then Queens before returning to Mitchell Field. The flypast was a great success and there were more plaudits from the local media and the population of Manhattan. The hospitality in New York was unforgettable. That night the RAF personnel were all invited to the trotting races at the Westbury track and the senior officers were dinner guests of the Roosevelt Raceway officials. The following day they were taken to Jones Beach before being entertained for dinner at Mitchell Field; one of the Lancasters was made available for the public to view during the day and to meet some of the crew, and the next day they were all invited to watch a baseball game at the Yankee Stadium.

It was a great start to the tour but it was soon time to move on. After saying their farewells on the morning of 21 July the squadron set off westwards for Scott Field near St Louis, Illinois. The transit took nearly six hours, across Pennsylvania, Ohio and Indiana, which gave Beetham time to take in the marvellous view of the landscape beneath. Once over St Louis the squadron circled the area in formation for all to see before they landed to be met by the base commander, Colonel Neal Creighton. For the next four days the hospitality proved to be, once again, unforgettable. There was a full entertainment programme, which had partly been arranged by the St Louis Chapter of the American Red Cross, including visits to the Vouziers mansion at Florissant, a tour of the Anheuser-Busch brewery, a sight-seeing tour of St Louis, a night at the Municipal Opera, an evening at Forest Park Highlands and a visit to the midget auto races.

The squadron then left Scott Field for Lowry Field at Denver, Colorado. It was another transit westwards, this time across the states of Missouri and Kansas, and five hours later Beetham joined up in close formation as the squadron arrived over Denver before landing at Lowry Field, where they were met by the commanding general, Brigadier General Thomas Lowe, and the acting British consul, Cyril Ward. That evening there was a reception for the officers at Denver University, hosted by Chancellor and Mrs Caleb F. Gates, and two days later the gates of Lowry Field were opened to the local residents to see for themselves the Lancasters close up and to speak to the crews.

The final leg of the journey, to Long Beach Field near Los Angeles in California, provided Beetham with a marvellous view over the Rockies and Grand Canyon. On arrival at Long Beach Field the squadron was met by the base commander, Colonel K. C. McGregor, and the British consul general, J. E. M. Carvell. Also present was the Commander-in-Chief Bomber Command, Air Marshal Sir Norman Bottomley, who had flown out to California to join the detachment, and among the other notable guests greeting the squadron were a number of British actors living in Los Angeles, including Nigel Bruce, Richard Greene and Peter Lawford. The entertainments programme over the next few days was full and there were opportunities to visit the National Broadcasting Company studios of Hollywood, the Rose Bowl sports arena in the Pasadena Valley, the Hollywood Bowl amphitheatre, the Long Beach Pike with its rollercoaster and other rides and to see sites such as Long Beach Harbour, the Cahuenga Boulevard – one of California's eight-lane super highways – and the beach at Santa Monica. There really was something for everyone, and one of the highlights for Beetham was visiting the Hollywood film set where he met the award-winning film and stage actress Ginger Rogers.

The main event of the tour was the Army Air Forces Day, which was held on 1 August to celebrate the thirty-ninth anniversary of the service. Four airfields were made open to the public: Long Beach Field, March Field, San Bernardino and Victorville. The theme of the anniversary was 'Air Power is Peace Power' and the day started with an Army Air Force cavalcade of nine B-29 Superfortress heavy bombers, nine C-47 troop carriers, twelve P-51 Mustang fighters, twelve A-26 Invader bombers and nine B-25 bombers. Later in the day it was the turn of 35 Squadron to provide a flypast. The twelve Lancasters took off from Long Beach at intervals of thirty seconds before joining up and flying in formation over the Long Beach area and then on to Los Angeles, Hollywood and Beverley Hills. Beetham had a reporter, Bernard Greene, on board to capture the event. The flight lasted an hour and a half, and the Lancasters proved to be an extremely popular attraction for the local population. That night there was a formal dinner at the Hollywood-Roosevelt Hotel to mark the anniversary.

The week spent at Long Beach was truly memorable for Beetham and was undoubtedly the highlight of the goodwill tour. Two days later it was time to start the long journey home. First stop was Kelly Field at San Antonio, Texas, and during the next few days he was able to enjoy visits to a ranch and a rodeo, and to catch up on some shopping in San Antonio. The next leg was to Andrews Field in Washington DC, a transit lasting seven and a half hours, and the following evening the squadron was hosted by the British ambassador and Air Chief Marshal Sir Guy Garrod at a garden party on the lawn of the British embassy. The following day the squadron flew a formation flypast over Atlantic City, Philadelphia, Baltimore and Washington. Beetham had two Washington reporters on board to capture the occasion and the highlight was a flypast over the White House, which was the final flypast of the American tour.

The squadron next flew to Westover Field, Holyoke in Massachusetts, where there was another reception followed by local visits. During the stay the officers were flown to Boston and given a tour of the city before they were entertained at a tea party by the British consul general, Bernard Ponsonby Sullivan. There was then an open day at Westover to provide the locals with the opportunity to meet the RAF crews and to view the Lancasters before the squadron flew on to Mitchell Field, New York. Again, this provided Beetham with the opportunity to see many local sites, and while they were at Mitchell Field the ground crew carried out the final servicing of the Lancasters in preparation for the transit back to the UK.

The return to the UK took the squadron back through Gander and the Azores. It had been six weeks since Beetham had first crossed the Atlantic at the start of the tour and he had had a fantastic time. The transit to St Mawgan passed without incident and then, on 29 August, the squadron completed the last leg back to Graveley. The route took them along the south coast of England and the squadron formed up and conducted a flypast over London before landing back at Graveley, where they were met by Sir Norman Bottomley and many other distinguished guests.

The speeches that followed were full of praise for both the squadron and the Lancaster. The tour had gone extremely well and once again demonstrated the technical reliability of the Lancaster. Beetham had flown SW913 'TL-A' throughout the tour, totalling more than ninety hours of flying time, without any problems what-soever. Following yet another reception to welcome the squadron home, the crews were given two weeks of leave. It was the end of a truly unforgettable trip and a most wonderful experience. Further-more, it had given Beetham a further insight into America and its people, and the knowledge he had gained would certainly help him throughout the rest of his career.

Beetham returned from leave and went straight into rehearsing for the Battle of Britain flypast, which took place on 14 September. His return to Graveley was brief; just three days later both 35 Squadron and 115 Squadron moved to their new home at Stradishall, about ten miles to the south-west of Bury St Edmunds in Suffolk. The flypast over London was the last of the squadron's ceremonial commitments and it then reverted to normal Bomber Command duties once more. Beetham's first task at Stradishall was to take some overseas visitors, including a colonel from Russia and a professor from China, on local flights to demonstrate the capability of the Lancaster's H2S radar. It was nearly time for him to move on as his tour as a flight commander with 35 Squadron was coming towards an end.

In February 1947 Beetham was posted to High Wycombe as a personnel officer at HQ Bomber Command. Now he had to revert to the substantive rank of flight lieutenant, which was not unusual at the time because the RAF was still reducing its numbers and many officers found they had to accept a reduction in rank, and ground tours, if they wanted to remain in the post-war RAF. This reversion in rank was hardly a temporary arrangement as it would be five years before Beetham became a squadron leader again. His appointment as P2a meant that he was now responsible for the postings and career management of Bomber Command's aircrew at the rank of flight lieutenant and below, and he was one of about a hundred staff officers working in the headquarters for the new C-in-C, Air Marshal Sir Hugh Saunders.

Having not been in a staff tour before, Beetham was in unfamiliar territory but he got on very well with his immediate superior, Squadron Leader Nigel McFarlane, whom he had known during the war, and he found the post to be a fascinating insight into personnel issues. Bomber Command was not in good shape: twenty-two of its squadrons were now commanded by ex-prisoners of war, many of whom had returned to peacetime Britain determined to renew their

operational careers and, while the RAF was trying to be as fair to
them as possible, many of the squadrons were not well led.

With the memories of the goodwill tour to America still fresh
in Beetham's mind, the opportunity to return to North America
soon came his way. He responded to a summons to the C-in-C's
office wondering what he might have done wrong, but he need
not have worried. He was warmly greeted by Saunders and the
conversation soon turned to the goodwill tour of America the
year before. Saunders then informed Beetham that he was due to
go on a visit to North America and Canada the following month
and he wanted Beetham to accompany him as his aide-de-camp.
Saunders explained that it would not be appropriate for his own
ADC to go, because she was a female officer, and Beetham offered
the additional benefit of being able to act as the second pilot for the
trip. Beetham was delighted. It had been just twelve months since
he had taken part in the goodwill tour and he was excited at the
thought of returning to North America again so soon.

Before the trip he had first to find out about the duties of an ADC
and then go to Hemswell in Lincolnshire to re-familiarise himself
with the Lincoln so that he could be the second pilot for the transit
across the Atlantic. It had been two years since he had last flown
the Lincoln, and it had been six months since he had flown at all,
but after just four trips with 97 Squadron, including one solo with a
crew, Beetham was certified qualified to act as second pilot for the
transit to North America.

Then at Heathrow Airport on 24 August he climbed into Lincoln
'OF-K', a specially prepared aircraft from 97 Squadron, and sat
alongside the aircraft captain, Squadron Leader Bretherton, for the
start of the journey to Washington DC. Saunders then climbed on
board and they were soon on their way for the first leg, a long transit
across the Atlantic to Gander, which was completed in eleven and
a half hours. After a day of rest the crew completed the trip to
Bolling Field, Washington DC, in just over seven hours, where
they were met by the base commander and commanding general
of Headquarters Command, Major General Burton Hovey, who
had worked closely with the RAF when he commanding the 303rd
Fighter Wing of the US Ninth Air Force while based in southern
England during 1944 and again when he assumed command of
Berlin Air Command after the war.

Throughout the visit to the USA, Saunders and Beetham were
escorted by Hovey and his protocol officer, Major Fernandez.

Beetham found Hovey to be a most delightful senior officer and he got on extremely well with Fernandez, who seemed to take care of all the arrangements, which meant there was often little for Beetham to do, and the Americans also provided a Douglas DC-3 Dakota for the duration of the tour. Two days after arriving in Washington they flew to Baltimore and back, followed the next day by a visit to Cleveland, Ohio. After a brief stay in Cleveland they flew on to Fort Worth, Texas and then to Los Angeles, arriving on 1 September. It was a busy itinerary and there was little time to relax given the packed meeting and social programme. Beetham spent the next three days in California, during which there were visits to Muroc Dry Lake, a desert salt pan in the Mojave Desert – now the central part of Edwards Air Force Base – Mather Field and then on to the small city of Arcata. At Arcata he took the opportunity to fly in a Boeing B-17 Flying Fortress, which had been the main heavy bomber of the US Eighth Air Force during the war.

Saunders and Beetham flew north to Seattle in the state of Washington and then two days later on to Colorado Springs, which was soon to become the site of the new US Air Force Academy. It was at Colorado Springs that they joined up again with Bretherton and the Lincoln. Now with Saunders and Hovey on board, they flew to Selfridge Field in Detroit, Michigan, a long flight of more than five hours and the last leg of the American tour. After a short stop at Selfridge Field they flew on to Ottawa in Canada. They then spent two days in Canada, during which they visited the Canadian bases at Trenton in Ontario and Malton near Toronto. They were flown around in a twin-engine C-45 Expiditur flown by Air Vice-Marshal David Carnegie, the air adviser to the UK High Commissioner in Ottawa. Hovey then accompanied them for the last time as they flew to Mitchell Field, New York in the Dakota for the final few days of the tour. Then, on 14 September, Saunders and Beetham left Mitchell Field in the Lincoln for the return journey to Gander and then to Northolt.

Beetham arrived back in the UK on 16 September. It had been another excellent trip full of yet more wonderful memories. The past three weeks had provided him with a valuable insight into the daily life of a very senior officer and had given him the opportunity to get to know his C-in-C personally. After drafting a handful of thank-you letters for Saunders, Beetham handed back the ADC responsibilities and returned to his daily task of managing aircrew postings. Although it was a ground tour, he found the headquarters staff friendly and very helpful and he thoroughly enjoyed his time at High Wycombe.

He found the tour to be educational and a very good experience, particularly when it came to dealing with the Air Ministry and the highly dynamic manning environment. In extreme cases he would get a call from the Air Ministry on a Friday and he would be expected to find someone for a specific location by the following Monday. This was never easy, and one of his main achievements in post was to help persuade the Air Ministry to change its policy on extremely short-notice postings, which meant that from then on individuals were given a minimum notice of two weeks prior to any posting.

Having completed his ground tour, Beetham now looked forward to returning to flying. Up to that point he had spent all his time with Bomber Command and, although still twenty-five years old, he now felt ready for a change. He had made good contacts in the Air Ministry, where cross-command appointments were managed, and he was able to negotiate his next posting during the final weeks of his tour at High Wycombe. One option that had been on offer was an exchange posting to America but, although this sounded very appealing, he had trained in America and had recently completed two high-profile visits to the USA, so Beetham turned the opportunity down. Instead he opted for a posting to 82 Squadron in Africa as it would give him the chance to do something completely different and would provide him with the opportunity to visit a part of the world he had always found most fascinating.

It had been well over two years since Beetham had left 35 Squadron, so he was required to complete a refresher course before joining 82 Squadron. He spent two weeks flying the Wellington Mk X with No 1 (Pilot) Refresher Flying Unit at Finningley in South Yorkshire, which he completed on his twenty-sixth birthday, and then joined the squadron in Kenya at the end of May 1949.

Equipped with Lancasters, 82 Squadron had been seconded to the Colonial Office to undertake an aerial survey of British Africa. Existing maps were hopelessly out of date and modern mapping was considered to be an important contribution to the British territories after the Second World War, so the Directorate of Colonial Surveys was established by the Colonial Office as a central survey and mapping organisation for British colonies and protectorates.

Until 1920 Kenya had been known as the British East African Protectorate, but then took its name from the country's highest peak, Mount Kenya. The south-east part of the country lies on the Indian Ocean and from the coast the low plains rise to central highlands that are bisected by the Great Rift Valley. Kenya has many neighbours and from the south, working clockwise, is bordered by Tanzania, Uganda, Sudan, Ethiopia and Somalia; its tropical climate ranges from hot and humid on the coast to more temperate inland.

When Beetham arrived in Kenya, 82 Squadron was commanded by Wing Commander David Torrens. At any one time the squadron was operating two or three small detachments of aircraft from its main base at RAF Eastleigh, in the eastern suburb of the capital city of Nairobi, which was the RAF's main operating base in East Africa. Beetham spent his first three months operating from Eastleigh but, because the aerial survey could only be done in daylight and in good weather conditions, he then moved around Africa for the rest of the year. The general pattern was to spend about seven months of the year in East Africa, operating from Eastleigh, and five months in West Africa using Takoradi in Ghana as the squadron's main operating base. Using these bases as a hub, the detachment would fly to a small operating strip in that area of Africa and then operate from that remote location until the task in the area was complete. Each squadron detachment was typically two aircraft and three crews with thirty supporting ground personnel and Beetham was appointed as one of the detachment commanders.

The technique used for the aerial survey was to use the aircraft's Gee-H navigation aid, which had been developed during the war to enhance the Lancaster's blind-bombing capability, and a beacon on the ground, which had been surveyed and set up in a known position by the Royal Engineers. On board the Lancaster was a visual indicator that enabled Beetham to fly circles at a suitable height of about 15,000 feet above the ground. Starting from a range of two hundred miles from the beacon, he would fly decreasing circles, getting progressively closer to the ground beacon, while the survey camera on board photographed the ground beneath them; the circles became tighter and tighter until they became too tight for the operation of the camera, which typically happened at about eighty miles from the beacon. Flying had to be very precise and sorties lasted up to ten hours, which proved to be tiring for the crews. At the end of each week the films would be collected by a Dakota and flown back to Eastleigh to be developed and assessed by the Royal Engineers. The planned scale of photography was 1:30,000, which was selected as a compromise to suit topographic mapping and the various specialist departments who required the information to assess, for example, the geology and agriculture of the region.

Air navigation in Africa often provided the crew with great challenges, particularly when navigating cross-country between detachments in bad weather and in the vicinity of mountains. The transit from Eastleigh to Takoradi took more than twelve hours and when carrying ground crew in the rear fuselage it was not possible to climb above 12,000 feet, because of the lack of oxygen for the passengers, so a wide margin of safety was applied to the minimum altitude during transits. While navigation during the aerial surveys proved relatively simple – through using the aircraft's Gee-H when within range of the beacon – it proved far more challenging at the end of the sortie when recovering back to base. This was especially the case when operating in West Africa, where the maps provided were somewhat rudimentary and in extreme cases the positioning of lakes on the map could be anything up to a hundred miles in error.

An example of a detachment was between April and September 1950 when Beetham's detachment operated from Zwartkop in the Transvaal, South Africa, to conduct a survey of the British protectorates of Bechuanaland, Basutoland and Swaziland. From Zwartkop the detachment moved on to Ndola, Rhodesia, where it remained until September, when it flew to Takoradi and then back to Eastleigh at the end of March 1951.

The following month Beetham was sent on a short-notice high-priority detachment to RAF Habbaniya in Iraq, about fifty miles to the west of Baghdad. A crisis was developing with Iran, following the decision of the newly elected prime minister, Dr Mohammed Mossadegh, to nationalise Iran's oil reserves and this resulted in a British embargo of Iranian oil. As there were no up-to-date maps of the region Beetham led the detachment to Iraq via Aden. RAF Habbaniya was situated on the west bank of the Euphrates, near Lake Habbaniya, and had every facility that he could have asked for. The weather was perfect for the task, which meant that the detachment photographed the whole of Iraq in just six weeks, during which Beetham personally flew 153 hours, of which ninety-five were flown in one month alone.

Life as a detachment commander in Africa provided Beetham with exactly the challenge that he was after. Operating from a remote location for a period of five or six weeks, often up to fifteen hundred miles from his main operating base, with two or three aircraft and crews plus thirty or forty ground crew, and being responsible for the welfare and discipline of the detachment, proved to be a good test of his personal leadership and was his best tour in the development of his man management skills. He never experienced any problems with the discipline of his men and everyone seemed to enjoy the detachments. His occasionally unorthodox style of leadership seemed to work well: his simple threat to return anyone causing a problem back to the main operating base was enough to prevent any problems from emerging in the first place. During the past two years he had lived in various local hotels and houses, hired whatever local transport he could in order to get the job done and had sampled all the local delicacies that he cared to. He had also flown nearly twelve hundred hours during his tour, and one of the Lancasters flown was PA474, better known today as the 'City of Lincoln' of the Battle of Britain Memorial Flight; it would not be the last time he flew this particular aircraft.

Overall, Beetham could have asked for no more from his tour with 82 Squadron, but he was keen to return back to the rank of squadron leader as soon as possible and had taken the opportunity during his time in Africa to sit both the promotion exam and the qualifying exam for Staff College.

First and foremost he wanted to return to the rank he had previously held but he was also aware that if he was going to get anywhere in the RAF he had to complete the required staff training. He knew that Staff College was a prerequisite to commanding a squadron and this was something he was becoming increasingly keen to do. He had set his mind on passing the two exams as soon as he could and he sat both exams alone during one detachment to Takoradi with just an invigilator to keep him company. He was also fortunate that the squadron's work in Africa was considered important and suitably high profile, and in terms of his own personal career progression there was plenty for his flight commander, Squadron Leader Andrew Humphrey, to assess him on, given that he was a detachment commander with more responsibility than a flight lieutenant might normally have on any other squadron.

Beetham returned to the UK in July 1951. As the Canberra jet bomber was soon to enter service with the RAF he saw this as his next opportunity, particularly when he found out that he was to be promoted back to the rank of squadron leader, as he very much wanted to be part of the transition of Bomber Command into the jet age. Following a brief holding post at HQ 1 Group at Bawtry, he managed to secure a posting to the Canberra force as the chief ground school instructor at 231 Operational Conversion Unit at Bassingbourn in Cambridgeshire, with the task of setting up the ground school facility.

The intention was that the OCU would run three main courses: a long course of conversion to type and weaponry, a short course of conversion to type only and a photo-reconnaissance course. Because the trainer variant, the Canberra T4, was not due to enter service for another two years, the Meteor jet trainer was used for dual-control training. This meant that before Beetham could start flying the Canberra, he had to first complete a jet conversion course on the Meteor 7 at No 205 Advanced Flying School at Middleton St George in County Durham.

Although he had already amassed more than 2,500 flying hours, mainly on the Lancaster, there was a stark difference between flying a four-engine heavy bomber with a crew and flying a twin-engine Meteor jet on his own. His first flight in a jet aircraft was on 14 November, and he flew twice more that day, also dual, before he flew his first jet solo just two days later. By the end of the month he had completed the course, which included general handling, asymmetric flying, high-altitude and high-speed flight, instrument flying, formation flying and aerobatics. Not only were there vast differences in speed and manoeuvrability to get used to, he also had quickly to learn the art of fuel management when flying a jet aircraft. It was an extremely intense course, with the flying phase lasting just two weeks, during which he flew twenty-six sorties, up to four times a day, totalling twenty hours.

Soon after returning to Bassingbourn, Beetham was delighted and honoured to find out from the station commander that he had been awarded a King's Commendation in the New Year's Honours List for his work with 82 Squadron in Africa. He spent the first three months of 1952 flying several more training sorties in the Meteor and then, on 4 April, he flew his first conversion flight in the Canberra B2.

During the next three weeks he flew the Canberra five more times, but the build-up of the Canberra force proved to be much slower than had initially been expected. The original plan was for Bomber Command to have twenty-four squadrons, with each squadron equipped with ten B2s, in wings of four squadrons at six bases. However, by the time Beetham first flew the Canberra only three squadrons, all at Binbrook, had started to take delivery of the aircraft. Just days later, he was informed that he had been selected for Staff College and so instead of continuing to the Canberra force he now suddenly found himself on his way to Staff College at Andover. It was the end of April 1952.

CHAPTER 4

A Career Unfolds

For any officer with the aspiration to reach air rank, attending Staff College has always been an essential part of their career development. That is not to say air rank is guaranteed for those who have attended Staff College, far from it, but Beetham was very much aware that he needed to attend Staff College if he was to go on and command a squadron and to realise his full potential within the service. He felt fortunate that his opportunity came along during what seemed otherwise to be a slight lull in the build-up of the jet bomber force in Bomber Command.

The Staff College at Andover had been established in 1922 as the RAF's first staff college with the task of training its officers in the administrative, staff and policy aspects of the Royal Air Force. The college generally provided a year-long course for promising squadron leaders as preparation for their staff duties in key appointments at the Air Ministry or at command or group level. Its first commandant was Air Commodore Robert 'Henry' Brooke-Popham, and among the twenty students attending No 1 Course in March 1922 was Squadron Leader Charles Portal, who went on to become Chief of the Air Staff during the Second World War, and Squadron Leader Keith Park, who commanded Fighter Command's 11 Group during the Battle of Britain. At the end of the Second World War it was decided there was a need for two RAF Staff Colleges and a second college was established at Bracknell in Berkshire. Each college developed its own characteristics, but its fundamental attitudes were still rooted in the pre-war Andover tradition.

When Beetham was selected to attend Staff College in 1952 there was no specific reason why he should attend Andover rather than Bracknell. Although he might have been initially disappointed not to be going to Bracknell, and wondered why he had been one of the few selected to go to Andover, it was just a matter of timing and he soon realised there were several advantages of attending Andover. He knew that his background was very narrow and he now needed to break out of purely thinking in terms of Bomber Command and to learn more about the rest of the RAF; after all, the RAF was operating in many different roles all over the world and his personal knowledge was extremely parochial. Staff College would provide him with his first opportunity to think more widely.

Beetham arrived at Andover on 28 April to join No 10 Course. The course was welcomed by the commandant, Air Commodore Walter Cheshire, who had only taken over his appointment the month before, having previously been the Air Officer Commanding RAF Gibraltar. Beetham soon settled into his new surroundings. While lectures formed a considerable portion of the teaching at Staff College, the bulk of the instruction was given in syndicates, taking into account the varying experience of the students, and there were many exercises to be completed. The course content was as expected for the development of a future senior officer. Staff duties focused on written and oral communications, and there were several presentations on the organisation of the RAF and its personnel. There were also lectures on the importance of mobility for the RAF, which included supply and movements and the maintenance of equipment, and there were lectures on all aspects of warfare, including naval and land warfare, which included the history of warfare and smaller conflicts.

The warfare lectures brought into discussion the political and economic environments, including the introduction of international law, and there were briefings on the North Atlantic Treaty Organis-ation. This was a part of the course that Beetham found most fascinating. The world had changed significantly in the seven years since the end of hostilities in Europe. Although Britain, America, France and the Soviet Union had been allies against the Axis powers during the Second World War, disagreements over many issues, particularly the shape of post-war Europe, had existed both during and after hostilities. NATO had come into existence in 1949 when its member states agreed to mutual defence in response to an attack by any external nation or organisation. For its first few years NATO was little more than a political association but the conflict between North and South Korea, which had started in 1950 and was still ongoing during Beetham's time at Staff College, galvanised the member states and led to the formation of a more integrated military structure under the direction of the USA. The Cold War that followed would dominate the years ahead and shape politics, coalitions, propaganda, technology and, of course, the development of military equipment and weapons – both conventional and, very soon, nuclear.

While the course content was generally the same at Andover and Bracknell, there were some notable differences between the two courses. Andover had fewer students than Bracknell, typically about sixty at Andover compared to 120 at Bracknell, and about half of the Andover students were from overseas. Although the British Army and Royal Navy had their own Staff Colleges at Camberley and Greenwich respectively, there were a handful of army and navy students on the course in addition to the overseas students, which gave No 10 Course a fine mix of nationality and services, as well as a balance of knowledge and expertise. Another difference was because of the variance in language skills of the overseas students at Andover, which meant the Andover course was often conducted at a slower pace and in a more relaxed style than at Bracknell. This gave the RAF students at Andover the general perception that their course was less intense, and often less formal when compared to their Bracknell colleagues. Furthermore, the number of overseas students meant that the course content differed slightly to that at Bracknell when it came to the more classified lectures because the overseas students were not privy to any classified material relating to national security. There were also a number of visits during the course to industry and other service units, which included army and navy establishments. These visits were often combined with Bracknell, but if the classification of the visit, or part of the visit, meant the overseas students were not able to attend, then the policy at Andover was that their RAF students would not attend either.

The pilot students were fortunate to be able to maintain their flying currency, and therefore their flying pay, during their time at Staff College and Andover received a monthly allocation of flying hours. Beetham was able to maintain flying currency on one of the many Percival Proctors, a four-seat monoplane aircraft that had been used during the war as a radio trainer and for general communications purposes. Flying provided him with a welcome break from the classroom and he flew the Proctor typically two or three times a month, and also managed to get back to Bassingbourn during a break in the course in August, where he flew four trips in the Canberra and four in the Meteor. By the time he finished Staff College Beetham had flown thirty-four times during the course!

Staff College proved to be an excellent course and Beetham enjoyed it very much. In particular he liked the exposure to all aspects of the RAF and learning about its strategic role within the modern world, which to him was extremely exciting. When he finished Staff College in April 1953 he had yet to reach his thirtieth birthday, but sadly his father had recently died of a heart attack at the age of sixty-two; it was devastating news. His parents had moved back to the family home in Wembley after the war and, following his father's death his mother, who did not enjoy the best of health herself, decided to move to Johannesburg in South Africa, where she hoped the higher altitude would improve her health and she would also be close to her daughter Joan who had settled in Johannesburg after getting married.

It was inevitable that Beetham's career meant that there would be periods when he was unable to see his mother or sister, but he had been able to see Joan during his tour in Africa and he would continue to get opportunities to visit South Africa during the rest of his career. His mother, however, would not remain in South Africa long. Within a few years she developed a heart problem and returned to the UK; she spent her last years living in Ewell in Surrey before she died at the age of ninety.

Away from work Beetham's interests were still focused around reading about military history and playing sport, specifically his long-term enjoyment of tennis and his more recent discovery of the game of golf, which his flight sergeant flight engineer had taught him during his time in Africa. Beetham enjoyed service life in every respect and he was happy to pursue a career in the service rather than take up a new career elsewhere, flying or otherwise. Although he had now successfully completed Staff College, nothing had particularly changed in terms of his own personal ambition. While he may not have had any great personal ambition at that time to reach the top, there is no doubt that he was on his way to greater things. He now had Staff College behind him, at a comparatively young age, and it was a matter of whether he would be given the right opportunities to show that he could operate at a higher rank.

His next appointment was at the Air Ministry in London. The majority of senior officers in the RAF can expect to spend some of their career in Whitehall, and Beetham's career was to be no different. In 1953 the government's Main Building in Whitehall was shared between the Air Ministry and the Board of Trade. Beetham was posted to the Operational Requirements staff as OR1a, where he worked for the director of operational requirements, initially Air Commodore Digger Kyle and then Air Commodore H. J. Fitzpatrick. Beetham took over from Squadron Leader Alan Craig, his former squadron commander at Graveley, who had also taken a reduction in rank at the end of his tour as OC 35 Squadron.

Soon after arriving in London, Beetham went to No 10 Advanced Flying Training School at Pershore in Worcestershire for a refresher course on the Oxford, which meant he would be able to maintain his flying currency while at the Air Ministry; during his tour he would generally fly at least once a month in an Anson from nearby Hendon.

When he was at the Air Ministry he chose to live with his aunt in Epsom and travelled into the centre of London each day. As OR1a he was responsible for bomber and reconnaissance development, working directly for Wing Commander Peter Cundall and Group Captain Nebbie Wheeler. He shared an office with OR1b, initially Squadron Leader Duncan McIver and then Squadron Leader Pat Kennedy, who had the responsibility within OR for the development of fighter aircraft. As OR1a, Beetham held a key appointment that was right at the heart of the RAF's future bomber and reconnaissance capabilities, and it gave him the chance to contribute to a number of major programmes such as the development of the photo-reconnaissance variants of the Canberra, the PR7 and PR9, and bringing into service the RAF's three new V-bombers – the Valiant, Vulcan and Victor.

The Canberra had already started to give Bomber Command a significant increase in capability and during its first years in service was continually breaking height and speed records. By the time Beetham arrived at the Air Ministry the first photo-reconnaissance variant, the PR3, had just entered service and was capable of operating at medium-high altitude, giving Bomber Command the ability to conduct pre- and post-raid reconnaissance using a forward-facing camera. The PR7 then took the capability a step further in terms of height and range, and the first of the PR7s entered service during the first year of Beetham's tour. By the end of 1954 there were four squadrons of PR7s at Wyton, and during the following year a PR7 set the London to New York record of seven hours and twenty-nine minutes, at an average speed of 461 mph. With a prevailing wind, the same aircraft returned to London in six hours and sixteen minutes at an average speed of 550 mph.

Much of Beetham's work with the Canberra was involved with the development of the more capable PR9, a further enhancement of the PR7, but the PR9 was still some way off from entering service; it would become the UK's equivalent to the American U-2 spy plane. Equipped with more powerful engines and an increased wing area, the PR9 was designed to have an operational ceiling in excess of 60,000 feet, which would put the aircraft above the surface-to-air missile threat at the time. The initial design work was done at English Electric, but Napiers were also subcontracted to modify a PR7 as the test aircraft, which made its first flight as a reconfigured design in July 1955. The nose area had been completely redesigned, giving the PR9 a very different cockpit layout and canopy design to the other Canberra variants, with the navigator sitting in the nose of the aircraft and the pilot in a fighter-style cockpit.

As the first squadron was not due to take delivery of the PR9 until January 1960, Beetham would not see the variant enter service during his tour but his contribution to its development helped ensure that the PR9 pilot would become the envy of the Canberra force; the aircraft's excellent performance was undisputed and the pilot had the luxury of a good cockpit layout and the benefit of an autopilot. However, with the focus now turning to the development of Bomber Command's main strike capability, an increasing amount of Beetham's time was spent on helping to develop the capability of the new V-bombers, which would soon enter operational service with the RAF.

The American use of an aircraft to deliver the first atomic bombs on Japan during the last days of the Second World War had taken air warfare to another level and in 1947 the Air Ministry had issued the first specification for a new jet-powered aircraft capable of carrying a 10,000-pound weapon load over a range of 3,350 nautical miles at a minimum speed of 500 knots with a delivery height of not less than 50,000 feet. Six aircraft companies were invited to submit tenders: Avro, Armstrong Whitworth, Bristol, English Electric, Handley Page and Short Brothers. As the designs were expected to be radical, an Advanced Bomber Group consisting of eighteen structural engineers and aerodynamics experts was set up at the Royal Aircraft Establishment at Farnborough.

The Avro and Handley Page designs, the Avro 698 and HP80 respectively, both offered significant advantages over the other submissions, but the group did not want to commit to just one design, in case a major design flaw later emerged, and so to reduce the overall risk to the programme the group decided to continue with both designs. In addition, Vickers had been working on a more conventional design, the Type 660, as a long-range high-performance bomber and the design was considered low risk as it was based on proven aerodynamics, rather than theory, and so Vickers was instructed to proceed with development as an interim solution, pending further development of the Avro and Handley Page creations. The Vickers design subsequently became the Valiant, which would be the first of the V-bombers to enter service with the RAF, and the Avro and Handley Page designs became the Vulcan and Victor respectively.

In the meantime the future of Britain's defence strategy had been discussed by the Chiefs of Staff in 1952. NATO was still in its early years and it was evident that Britain's relationship with other countries – in particular the USA – was not sufficiently strong that the support of other nations could be relied on at a time of conflict. It was also clear to Britain that the USA was continuing with full-scale production of thermonuclear weapons and that Russia was doing the same, although it was not known how long it would be before these weapons would be ready for operational use.

To the Chiefs of Staff it was clear that Britain needed its own nuclear capability if it was to avoid being sidelined in any future conflict or, worse still, unable to react if threatened by another major power. Britain certainly had the ability to produce nuclear weapons and, after taking all considerations into account, the government decided to proceed with development and production. Later that year, Britain's first atomic device was tested on the Monte Bello Islands, an uninhabited group of islands off the north-west coast of Australia, and Britain became the world's third nuclear-capable power behind the USA and Russia. Work was then put in place to develop a new 10,000-pound air-launched weapon, code named Blue Danube, which would require an aircraft to deliver it on a target potentially thousands of miles away.

The fact that the RAF was trying to bring three different V-bombers into service in the same period of time was not without its problems and there was a time when it looked as if one design might have to be rejected. Many scientists seemed to be against the Vulcan but Beetham believed that he and his colleagues in OR knew better. Although he felt slightly uncomfortable about developing a bomber without defensive armament, experts had pointed out that without defensive armament the bomber would perform better, more like a fighter, and its electronic counter-measures would provide any protection needed.

These were exciting times for Beetham, and over the coming months he gained a valuable insight into the capabilities of all three V-bombers. His responsibilities took him to Vickers at Weybridge, where he was able to observe and have an input into the design of the cockpit layout of the Valiant. The Valiant prototype had first flown in May 1951, just over two years after the contract had been issued, and Beetham was fortunate to get the opportunity to fly the aircraft during its test and development flights.

The design of the aircraft was quite conventional, with simple aerodynamics, and the four Rolls-Royce Avon jet engines were mounted in pairs in each wing root rather than in wing-mounted pods. The wings were swept at forty-five degrees for the first third of the wing, which then reduced to twenty-four degrees at the wing tips; this was because the ratio between the wing thickness and chord (the width of the wing from leading to trailing edge) could be reduced closer to the tips. The wing loading was low by more recent standards and the tail surfaces were also swept back, with the horizontal tail plane mounted relatively well up the vertical fin to keep it clear of the jet exhaust. The aircraft's Mach number was limited to around 0.82 Mach, with the aircraft typically cruising around 0.76 Mach at heights up to about 50,000 feet.

Beetham flew the Valiant a total of seven times during his tour at the Air Ministry, including four times with his former colleague and fellow flight commander on 35 Squadron, Shorty Harris, who had left the RAF for a career as a test pilot with Vickers. The Valiant B1 entered service soon after with 138 Squadron at Gaydon and by the time production came to an end in 1957 a total of 107 aircraft had been built. Of the three prototypes built, one had been completed to B2 standard, which was designed to operate at low level, but, although the Air Ministry had ordered seventeen aircraft, the B2 programme was later cancelled.

Not only did Beetham fly the Valiant during his tour at the Air Ministry but he was also able to gain valuable knowledge and experience of the two other V-bombers through his many visits to Handley Page at Radlett in Hertfordshire and to Avro at Warton in Lancashire. He made his first flight in the Vulcan in April 1955 and he then first flew the Victor in August. As with the Valiant, all his flights in the V-bombers were flown in the co-pilot's seat during the development programme and he was able to gain much early knowledge of these aircraft, both of how they performed aerodynamically and of their operational capability. Not only did

1   Beetham (second left) pictured at Graveley in 1946 while serving with 35 Squadron. On the left is the station commander, Group Captain Richard Collard, and second right is OC 35 Squadron, Wing Commander Alan Craig. Furthest right is Squadron Leader Shorty Harris.

2   Pictured (centre) at Long Beach Field, Los Angeles, with the British actress Merle Oberon during the American tour of 1946

3 Pictured (centre) with the American actress and legend Ginger Rogers during a visit to the Hollywood studios, July 1946

4 Being interviewed by Richard Hosking of the Federal Broadcasting Service in Salisbury, Southern Rhodesia, after Beetham's record-breaking flight of 16 April 1959

5   Beetham (second right) and his crew at Cape Town after his record-breaking flight from Marham, 9 July 1959

6   Beetham (second left) during his tour as the station commander at Khormaksar in Aden meeting Air Vice-Marshal Johnnie Johnson (third right), the AOC Air Forces Middle East, after a flight in a Belfast during 1965

7 Relaxing with Lucinda and Alexander in Aden during 1965

8 Promoted to air commodore while still the station commander at Khormaksar, Beetham opening the corporals' mess on 10 October 1966

9 Imperial Defence College 1967. Beetham is fifth from the left in the second row from the back.

10 Beetham (left) arriving at Wildenrath on 19 January 1976 to assume command of RAF Germany and the Second Allied Tactical Air Force. In the centre is the deputy commander, Air Vice-Marshal Bill Bailey, and on the right is the station commander, Group Captain Leech.

11 A formal ceremony was held at the Joint Headquarters at Rheindahlen on 20 January 1976 to mark the joint arrival of Beetham as commander of the Second Allied Tactical Air Force and C-in-C RAF Germany and General Sir Frank King, the newly appointed commander NORTHAG and C-in-C British Army of the Rhine.

12 Flying in a Wessex helicopter from Gutersloh, Beetham is pictured (second left) visiting the Harrier force deployed in the field in Germany, 1 July 1976.

13 Enjoying a light-hearted moment with the Chief of the Defence Staff, Sir Andrew Humphrey (centre), following his arrival in Germany on 5 January 1977. On the left is Sir Frank King, the C-in-C BAOR and commander NORTHAG. Humphrey was a personal friend but died suddenly less than three weeks later and his death triggered a change in senior appointments that would see Beetham appointed as the next Chief of the Air Staff.

14 Welcoming the prime minister, James Callaghan, to Germany in April 1977

15 Pictured with Sir Frank King. The two men enjoyed an excellent working relationship and the rapport between the two commanders in Germany was there for all to see.

16 Beetham was given a good send-off from RAF Germany. His wife, Patricia, is handed a farewell bouquet and his son, Alexander, is standing on the right. On the left is his PSO, Wing Commander Ian Macfadyen, and his wife Sally.

17 Departing Wildenrath and RAF Germany on 22 July 1977

18 Beetham's first visit to a flying station as the new Chief of the Air Staff was to RAF Valley, where he flew the new Hawk T1 jet trainer for the first time on 10 August 1977.

19 The commemorative dinner for the sixtieth anniversary of the RAF at the Mansion House in London, 31 March 1978. Beetham is seated fifth from right, next to the Lord Mayor, Air Commodore the Right Honourable Sir Peter Vanneck (centre); the principal guest, the Duke of Edinburgh, is seated fifth from left. Among this most distinguished line-up are seven marshals of the Royal Air Force, including Sir Arthur Harris (seated third from right).

20 Visit to Lossiemouth on 31 August 1978, during which Beetham (third left) flew in a Jaguar of 226 Operational Conversion Unit with Squadron Leader Chris Pinder (second left). Second right is Beetham's PSO, Mike Stear, and far right is Flight Lieutenant Dave Holme. Standing next to Beetham (third right) is Group Captain Dennis Caldwell, the station commander of RAF Lossiemouth, and far left is Wing Commander Bruce Latton, OC 226 OCU

21 Chatting with pilots of the Republic of Korea Air Force during his visit to South Korea in October 1978 (ROKAF)

22 The Beethams with the Maharajah of Jaipur during their visit to India, January 1980 (IAF)

23 Beetham poses with his wife at the Taj Mahal during their visit to India, January 1980 (IAF)

24 The Beethams greeting Sir Arthur Harris at a Bomber Command reunion dinner held at Grosvenor House on 19 April 1980. The dinner was held in Harris's honour just days after his eighty-eighth birthday and was attended by more than twelve hundred members and guests.

25 Welcoming the Queen Mother and Prince Andrew to RAF Leeming to mark the sixtieth anniversary of the Central Flying School Association, 4 July 1980

26 At the opening of the Tri-National Tornado Training Establishment at RAF Cottesmore, 29 January 1981. Also pictured are the Chief of the West German Air Force, Generalleutnant Friedrich Obleser (left), the Chief of the Italian Air Force, Generale Lamberto Bartolucci (second right), and the Commander-in-Chief of the German Navy, Vizeadmiral Gűnter Fromm (right).

27 Meeting personnel at Ascension Island in the immediate aftermath of the Falklands conflict, 28 June 1982. In the background (arms folded) is Beetham's PSO, Group Captain David Cousins.

28 Having been taught how to play golf by one of his SNCOs in Africa in 1950, Beetham liked to find time to get on the golf course whenever possible. He is seen here teeing off during a match between the RAF and the aerospace industry at the Moor Park Golf Club in June 1982.

29 Beetham (seated front row, third from right) was among more than sixty guests invited by the prime minister, Margaret Thatcher, to a formal dinner at 10 Downing Street on 11 October 1982 to celebrate the success of the Falklands Conflict

30 Pictured left leaving the Ministry of Defence for the last time as Chief of the Air Staff, 15 October 1982. Next to Beetham is Air Chief Marshal Sir Douglas Lowe and on the right is Air Vice-Marshal Paddy Hine.

31 Sixty-four years after completing their tour of operations with 50 Squadron, four of the former crew members met up again in June 2008 at the memorial situated on the former site of RAF Skellingthorpe in Lincoln. Left to right: Ted Adamson, Les Bartlett, Beetham and Reg Payne (author)

32 With England cricket captain, Andrew Strauss, at Lords during a break in a one-day international match with Australia, 6 September 2009

he fly in the V-bombers, he also managed to fly the Canberra and Meteor many times and during his ground tour at the Air Ministry he flew ten different types.

Beetham also became involved in the early stages of the ill-fated TSR2 (Tactical Strike and Reconnaissance, Mach 2) programme, for which he wrote the draft specification. The introduction of Soviet radar-guided surface-to-air missiles meant that aircraft flying at subsonic speed, even at high-level, could no longer be considered safe, as the shooting down of America's U-2 spy plane, piloted by Francis Gary Powers, by a SA-2 over the Soviet Union in 1960 would later prove. The Canberra, for example, had no defensive armament and it relied on operating at high level and at relatively high speed to avoid being shot down; the combination of its speed and altitude made interception by fighters incredibly difficult. However, this new threat posed by the latest SAMs meant the RAF now required a new supersonic all-weather aircraft that could deliver a weapon on target over long distances at a speed of up to Mach 2.

The specification for the TSR2 required the aircraft to deliver tactical nuclear or conventional weapons at low level and in all weathers. The aircraft would also be required to carry out photo-reconnaissance at both medium and low level in daytime or at night. Furthermore, the aircraft needed to be able to operate from prepared air strips with a short take-off capacity. For the purpose of the requirement, low level was considered to be below 1,000 feet, the expected operating range was to be 1,000 nautical miles and the aircraft needed to be able to operate from a runway of no more than 1,000 yards.

The Air Ministry's requirement would eventually be issued in March 1957, after Beetham had left his post, as General Operational Requirement 339, and would prove to be an immense challenge for industry given the technology at the time. There then followed some years of industrial, political and inter-service debate before the TSR2 first flew in 1964. Built by the British Aircraft Corporation, the TSR2 had many technically advanced features that made it the best-performing aircraft of its day. Yet the programme would controversially be cancelled by Harold Wilson's Labour government the following year in favour of the American General Dynamics F-111 swing-wing bomber as a cheaper option.

The decision proved divisive and critics were further outraged when a number of unfinished TSR2 airframes were hastily scrapped. Somewhat ironically, though, the F-111 programme would also later be cancelled; Beetham believed it was a great mistake to abandon the TSR2 as it was a remarkable aircraft. The decision to scrap it, and then the F-111, would mean that the RAF had to wait a long time for an aircraft as capable to enter service. In the end the RAF would get the Tornado, after many intervening traumas and great expense, but Beetham felt the TSR2 would have been a very-high-performance aircraft, with longer range than the Tornado, and its avionics could have been updated over time.

At the end of 1955 Beetham's replacement, Squadron Leader Dougie Lowe, was posted to the Air Ministry early, which gave Beetham the chance to share his responsibilities with Lowe for the last six months of his tour. Plans were now being put in place to replace the Canberra bomber squadrons with the new V-bombers and so Beetham started manoeuvring his own position to secure a posting to the V-force, preferably on promotion so that he could command a squadron. He also now had an additional factor in his life to consider as he had met Patricia Lane during his early days at the Air Ministry and the couple had decided to get married at the end of his tour in London.

When Beetham finished his tour at the Air Ministry in May 1956 he was set to return to flying but was instead chosen by the task force commander for the forthcoming Operation Buffalo, Air Commodore Ginger Weir, to be his personal staff officer. Operation Buffalo was to be the first major nuclear trial in Australia, involving the first air drop of a British atomic weapon. This came as mixed news to Beetham. It would clearly delay his return to flying and would mean postponing his wedding but he fully recognised the importance of the trial and that it would give him a rare opportunity to gain a valuable insight into the development of the nation's nuclear capability. The wedding was postponed until after the trial and, in the meantime, the plan was for Patricia to return to her home in New Zealand and once the trial was complete Beetham would fly from Australia to New Zealand, where the couple could get married before they returned to the UK.

Operation Buffalo represented the culmination of work which had started in 1947 when the prime minister, Clement Attlee, had first announced that Britain should develop an atomic bomb. The very special relationship between the UK and Australia meant that nuclear tests could take place overseas because, unlike the vast countries of the USA and Russia, there was nowhere suitable to conduct such tests at home. There were obvious problems with nuclear testing, such as preparing a suitable range, establishing radiological safety standards for the Australian population and accurately forecasting meteorological conditions, and improving safe firing conditions. In February 1956 a conference had been held at HQ Bomber Command to discuss the programme for Operation Buffalo and Operation Grapple. Buffalo was part of Britain's main atomic bomb development programme and was the name given for the trials held at Maralinga in South Australia between July and November 1956; Grapple was the name given to the megaton weapon trials that would take place later at Christmas Island in the Pacific Ocean during 1957–8.

Situated nearly five hundred miles to the north-west of Adelaide, Maralinga was identified as the site for the testing range for Buffalo after much searching, which had started as early as 1952. To the west of the Woomera Range, and measuring some sixteen miles east–west and twelve miles north–south, the Maralinga area was considered sufficiently large for Buffalo. The land was reasonably flat and the southern edge was considered far enough north of the transcontinental railway. The plan was for the main party to arrive in early August and the first drop was due to take place on 11 October by a specially modified Valiant of 49 Squadron. Also taking part would be Canberra B6s of 76 Squadron, which were to be used for cloud sampling; this was a new role given to the squadron the year before and the squadron would operate a detachment of aircraft and personnel in Australia to support the various trials.

The range had to first be prepared and there was much construction work to be done to ensure the task force had sufficient accommodation and technical buildings. Altogether there would be some 1,350 personnel at Maralinga: 500 would be RAF and RAAF personnel supporting the trial; 350 scientists; an Indoctrinee Force of 250 volunteer servicemen who would experience the effects of a nuclear explosion and examine the effects on the ground on weapons and equipment; and a further 250 Australian servicemen with the responsibility of running and maintaining the range area. Time was short and the extremely high temperatures, combined with shortages of water and the challenges of providing acceptable hygiene conditions, meant the Australian construction engineers were pushed to the limits.

To assist Weir during the detachment was the commander of the Air Task Group, Group Captain Paddy Menaul, but the man with the overall responsibility for the trials was Sir William Penney, a British physicist who was responsible for the development of British nuclear technology and specifically the atomic bomb after the Second World War. His area of speciality was the physics of hydrodynamic waves and during the war he had been at Los Alamos in the USA as part of the British delegation for the Manhattan Project, where he worked on the blast effects of the atomic bomb and its optimum height for detonation. After the war Penney had been chosen to head Britain's High-Explosive Research Project and with the work centred at Fort Halstead he led the final arrangements to test the first bomb in the Monte Bello Islands in 1952. Then in 1954 he was appointed to the board of the newly formed United Kingdom Atomic Energy Authority, with responsibility for nuclear development.

Beetham joined Weir during the final planning stages at the Air Ministry and then accompanied him to Australia in a Canberra B6 of 76 Squadron. Leaving Weston Zoyland on 4 July, the journey to RAAF Edinburgh near Adelaide took one week, with overnight stops at Idris (Libya), Habbaniya (Iraq), Karachi (Pakistan), Negombo (Ceylon), Changi (Singapore, for two nights) and Darwin (north Australia). The final leg from Darwin to Edinburgh took over three hours, most of which was over unpopulated desert area, and the clear weather meant that Beetham could see the vastness of Australia broken up only by the marvellous view of Alice Springs.

On 15 July Beetham flew with Weir on to Maralinga in a Devon of the RAAF. At that stage the main accommodation village, which was being constructed in the south-west corner of the range, was not complete, and the task force was operating from 43 Mile Camp located in the centre of the range area. He then spent the next few weeks going back and forth between Maralinga and the rear base at Edinburgh, where conditions were considerably better. The main body of scientific staff now started to arrive and the village was completed at the end of the month. By mid-August Penney had arrived in Australia and the final preparations were underway.

Understandably, there was much media interest in the nuclear trial, both in the UK and in Australia. Back in the UK the government had to balance the information given out with the national security aspects of such a trial. The British public were certainly very much aware of the nation's development of a nuclear capability but previous trials appeared to have provided the British public with too little information and too late. In Australia there was a genuine worry about the reaction to the trial by the Australian people and in the few months leading up to the trial an opinion poll estimated that more than half of Australians were against the tests. It was then a matter for the British scientists to reassure the Australian scientists and government, who in turn would reassure the Australian public that any nuclear fallout would be blown well out to sea. All public statements were made by Australian ministers, rather than by British scientists or a spokesman, although Penney did hold a press conference in Sydney the day after he arrived in Australia, when he produced a masterful performance in providing sufficient information to understand the tests being carried out and to dispel some erroneous notions.

The plan for Buffalo was for four bursts. Two bursts would be part of the weapon-development programme and would be on towers, one would be an air burst and one would be a ground burst; the order of firing was tower burst, ground burst, second tower burst and finally the air burst. Except for the air burst, firings were planned to take place at 7 a.m. local time. Meteorological conditions would obviously play a major part in the final decision to go ahead with each firing, and weather forecasts would be made three times a day. Once D-1 had been declared, there were to be three more forecasts between midnight and the planned firing time, with two balloon ascents in the final two hours. Finally, at 6.55 a.m., just five minutes before the planned firing time, the final decision would be made whether to fire or not. For the air burst, practice flights were to commence on 12 September.

Round One – called One Tree – was originally planned to take place on 29 August but had to be repeatedly postponed because of the weather. Everyone found this period most frustrating and the press were prone to criticise the detachment for alleged inefficiency. As far as safety was concerned, Weir was satisfied that everything that could be done had been done. Everyone had gone to immense trouble within the limits of their knowledge at the time, careful briefings had been given and no one was to be exposed to any undue risk.

To relieve the boredom of waiting for the weather to improve, Beetham flew with Weir in a Hastings on a day trip to the town of Alice Springs in the geographic middle of Australia near the southern border of the Northern Territory. With both Western and Aboriginal influences, Alice Springs has many historic buildings and Beetham found that it was like stepping back in time to a different era, but he and his colleagues were extremely well hosted by the locals during the day, and it had felt good to get away.

The weather conditions finally improved and on 19 September Beetham flew from Edinburgh to Maralinga, a journey he had made many times before but this time he would not return to Edinburgh for ten days. Round One – a tower-mounted test of the new plutonium warhead Red Beard, with an expected yield of sixteen kilotons – eventually took place on 27 September. At the time of the explosion Beetham was less than three miles away from the blast and as close as any observer was allowed. He had been briefed to turn his back to the direction of the blast and not to look at the flash. The explosion was extremely loud and like no other explosion he had ever heard. He could feel the blast wave and, having then turned to look, he saw the big mushroom cloud ascending slowly into the bright blue sky.

The following day the first of the indoctrinees and observers, wearing protective clothing and respirators, entered the target area to survey the effect of the blast. In a Whirlwind helicopter, Beetham was among the first to observe the area. The flight lasted an hour and a Geiger counter on board gave updates on the levels of radioactivity experienced as the helicopter flew closer and closer to the point of detonation. For those on the ground exposure in the target area was limited to a maximum of two hours, after which each man had to pass through a decontamination centre.

Round Two – called Marcoo – was a ground firing of a Blue Danube bomb with a low-yield uranium core, estimated to be below two kilotons, and took place on 4 October. Again, Beetham was with Weir at Maralinga to witness the test. The bomb made a crater 160 feet across and 40 feet deep, and the main cloud soared higher than expected. A Canberra of 76 Squadron was involved in the cloud sampling and fallout was recorded as thinly spread over a large area out to about thirty miles.

Penney then decided to change the firing order for the last two tests and so the air drop by the Valiant became Round Three – called Kite – which was the RAF's operational test of the Blue Danube bomb. The expected yield was forty kilotons when detonated at a planned height of twelve hundred feet above the ground, but there was a risk that the fusing might fail, in which case the bomb would detonate on hitting the ground. Because of the risk, however slight, a low-yield version was to be dropped instead and it would detonate at five hundred feet above the ground, giving an expected yield of about three kilotons.

On 8 October Beetham and Weir once again left Edinburgh for Maralinga, ready to witness one of the most important events in the post-war history of the RAF. At 2 p.m. on 11 October, Valiant WZ366 took off from Maralinga airfield. Captained by Squadron Leader E. J. G. Flavell, and with Menaul on board as an observer, the aircraft climbed to 38,000 feet. Having established communications with the ground, the aircraft descended to 30,000 feet and entered the range. The Valiant completed a number of fly-through manoeuvres before the weapon was released at 3.27 p.m., after which the Valiant turned steeply away.

Telemetry showed that the weapon detonated at the planned height and it was described in Penney's report as causing a brilliant flash and fireball with a terrific dust cloud and stem. After observing the mushroom cloud the aircraft landed back at Maralinga. A second Valiant, WZ367 flown by Flight Lieutenant N. Bates, was also airborne in the area to monitor the drop with specialist testing equipment fitted in its bomb bay. The test was considered a great success. The atmosphere was very dry and an inversion meant that the cloud stopped at 14,000 feet. A limited amount of fallout was recorded at Maralinga village, although this was not considered dangerous in any way. Otherwise, fallout was recorded as minimal. News of the successful drop soon found its way back to the UK in a simple signal to the Chief of the Air Staff, Sir Dermot Boyle, reporting that the device had successfully exploded. A few days later Weir signalled HQ Bomber Command praising the professionalism of all those service personnel involved in the trial.

The final burst, Round Four – called Breakaway – which was a slightly different variant of Red Beard with an estimated yield of less than sixteen kilotons, took place during the early hours of 22 October. The cloud rose to about 35,000 feet and fallout was recorded as far away as 190 miles. Later that day, Beetham was again able to observe the crater from a Whirlwind helicopter before he left Maralinga for the last time.

Beetham had been in Australia for more than three months. He has remembered all four explosions ever since – the blinding flash and large mushroom cloud. Witnessing the nuclear tests would have a major influence on all his later strategic thinking, particularly regarding NATO's policy on retaliatory response and the employment of nuclear weapons. It certainly convinced him that it would never be practicable to impose limits on any nuclear conflict.

Apart from witnessing an important part of Britain's nuclear development programme, Beetham had also managed to find the time to sample the delights of the country and to visit many of

Australia's major cities; Weir had certainly been keen to travel around as much as possible and wherever Weir went Beetham went too.

With the trial over, the original plan had been for Beetham to fly on to New Zealand, get married and then return to Australia for his transit back to the UK, leaving his wife to make the long journey back to the UK alone because she was not entitled to service transportation home. However, the worsening situation in Suez as a result of Egypt's decision to nationalise the Suez Canal had meant that all of the air transport was taken off the Buffalo programme to support the developing crisis in Suez. For those stuck in Australia there was a certain amount of re-planning required to transit the personnel and equipment back to the UK by sea, which meant that things turned out in Beetham's favour. Weir kindly agreed to a Canberra training flight to take him to New Zealand and from there he could eventually return to the UK by sea rather than having to first return to Australia.

On 2 November, with Beetham on board, the Canberra flew from Edinburgh to Christchurch in New Zealand and the following day Beetham married Patricia, with the Canberra crew included as their guests. After a few days on their own the Beethams spent the next ten days in Christchurch before setting sail for the UK on the SS *Rangitata*. The long voyage gave the couple some valuable time together after their long period of separation. It was the perfect way to return home.

CHAPTER 5

A Valiant Record Breaker

The Beethams arrived back in the UK five weeks later, having experienced a wonderful honeymoon across the Pacific via Pitcairn Island, and a most leisurely voyage home through the Panama Canal and across the Atlantic Ocean courtesy of the New Zealand Shipping Company. Once back in the UK, Beetham learned another valuable lesson about government financing when a civil servant from the finance department telephoned him and asked if he had any additional expenses for the journey home. Although his wife was not entitled to claim the journey at public expense it was explained to him that his journey back from New Zealand was £50 less than it would have been from Australia and so he was entitled to make a claim up to the value of the difference, provided that he could provide any receipts up to the entitled amount. This had never occurred to Beetham at the time he was travelling home and he had certainly not kept any bills or receipts, and so he missed out on £50; such was the vagueness of government allowances and entitlements.

Once back in the UK, Beetham initially had no idea where his next posting would be. After a few phone calls and enquiries he found out that he was to be posted to the newly formed V-force, although initially it was unclear whether he would be posted to the Valiant or the Vulcan. His preference was the Valiant, although it was some time before he found out that he had been granted his choice. There was a long training programme ahead, although he had done much of it previously, but this was the entry route into the V-force for everyone, regardless of background and experience.

The Beethams moved into a flat in Mablethorpe and in February 1957 Beetham was posted to the RAF Flying College at Manby in Lincolnshire to complete an all-weather jet refresher course on the Meteor. He attended No 113 Course and flew thirty-six hours, completing the course on 11 April with an 'above average' assessment. It felt good to be back in a cockpit of a high-performance aircraft once again.

Having completed his refresher course, Beetham joined No 115 Long Bomber Course at 231 OCU at Bassingbourn. His wife moved with him, as she always would; she quickly adapted to the nomadic lifestyle of being married to an officer in the RAF. Beetham was no stranger to the Canberra but nearly six years had passed since he had previously been at Bassingbourn and since then the OCU had gained the Canberra T4 trainer variant, which had significantly improved the instruction for pilots. It had been adapted from the B2 with side-by-side ejection seats for the two pilots, which made it a rather cramped cockpit environment. The left side of the cockpit, where the student pilot sat, was essentially a B2 and duplicate flying controls had been added to the right-hand side of the cockpit for the instructor pilot; the instrumentation layout was reasonably standard. Beetham's first five instructional sorties were flown in the T4, after which he flew a mix of exercises in the T4 and B2. The course lasted sixty flying hours and he completed it on 19 July, again with an 'above average' assessment.

The final phase of his training prior to joining the V-force was at 232 OCU at Gaydon, to the south of Warwick, where he attended No 26 Medium Bomber Course. The OCU had a number of Canberra T4s for the pre-Valiant training phase and for practising various runway approaches, and Beetham's first four months of the course were spent on the T4, during which he flew a mix of general handling exercises, circuits and landings, and several ILS (Instrument Landing System) approaches; ILS was a ground-based instrument approach system that gave precision guidance to the pilot to enable a safe landing in bad weather. Beetham was also introduced to the Valiant simulator and flew nine familiarisation and general handling sorties, which included several practice emergencies.

Having completed the Canberra phase, Beetham's first instructional sortie in the Valiant was on 16 December. Although he had previously flown the aircraft during his tour at the Air Ministry, this was his first formal instruction. Compared to the Canberra, the Valiant was in a different class. The Valiant was a much larger aircraft and its four powerful Rolls-Royce Avon engines gave the aircraft a maximum speed of 0.84 Mach at heights in excess of 30,000 feet and an operational ceiling of around 50,000 feet. It could carry a single nuclear weapon of ten thousand pounds or a weapon load of twenty-one thousand pounds but, like the other

V-bombers, had no defensive armament. The maximum take-off weight of the Valiant was over twice that of the Canberra, and its large external fuel tanks, fitted under each wing, extended the operational range to about 4,500 miles.

For Beetham, his previous experience of operating in a large crew in the Lancaster meant that he quickly adapted to the crew aspects of the Valiant. It had a crew of five in a pressurised cockpit: two pilots, two navigators (one plotter and one bombing) and an air electronics officer. Only the two pilots had ejection seats, which meant the other three crew members had to abandon the aircraft through the crew door on the port side of the fuselage. This was not considered ideal and the Air Ministry had initially looked at ideas for an escape compartment for the crew and also at fitting ejection seats for each crew member, but in the end the only practical and affordable solution was the one put in place.

The remainder of the course was flown in the Valiant. After three dual instructional sorties, with Beetham flying as the second pilot, he was cleared to go solo. Thereafter, the course was a mix of dual and crew exercises, by day or by night, with the crew exercises typically lasting four or five hours. Promotion to the rank of wing commander came on 1 January 1958 and by the end of the course, which he completed in mid-January, he had been told that he was to command 214 Squadron at Marham.

Situated about ten miles to the east of Downham Market in Norfolk, the RAF station at Marham is synonymous with generations of RAF bombers. In 1958 it was home to three Valiant squadrons: 148, 214 and 207 Squadrons. Beetham took over command of 214 Squadron from Wing Commander Len Trent, a New Zealander who had been awarded the Victoria Cross for leading a heroic raid by Venturas of 487 Squadron against a power station at Amsterdam in May 1943. Beetham moved into the commanding officer's married quarters at Marham. Then, in March, his wife gave birth to their first child, Lucinda.

The role of 214 Squadron was high-level strategic nuclear bombing, which included maintaining QRA (Quick Reaction Alert). Valiants now equipped nine RAF squadrons but the continuously improving capability of the Soviet Union's SAMs meant Bomber Command had to rethink its V-bomber tactics. Three of the Valiant squadrons – the two other Marham squadrons and 49 Squadron at Wittering – were assigned to develop low-level conventional bombing tactics and their aircraft's anti-flash white paint scheme was replaced by the more familiar green and grey camouflage for low-level operations. Of the other Valiant squadrons, 543 Squadron at Wyton remained in the strategic photo-reconnaissance role and 214 Squadron, Beetham's squadron, was one of two Valiant squadrons assigned to the new role of air tankers; the other was 90 Squadron at Honington.

214 Squadron was chosen to be the trials and development unit while also maintaining its bombing capability. This, initially, did not come as good news for Beetham. As far as he was concerned, this was not what he had joined the V-force to do and he certainly did not want to be seen to be carrying out a non-operational task. There was also little guidance given to him from the air staff in terms of what the future role of an air-to-air refuelling tanker should be. He assumed the objective was to extend the range of the V-force because at that stage there had not been any suggestion of exploring the concept of refuelling fighters; that would come later, but the rest he would have to work out for himself. However, he soon realised the importance of the task he had been set and it would prove to be one of those defining moments in his career as he would have the chance to help develop a vital new capability for the RAF. Very few people in Bomber Command, and indeed the RAF, knew much about air-to-air refuelling at the time, and Beetham would now be in a key position to take the RAF forward in its strategic thinking, as well as its tactical development, to enhance its long-range capability through the employment of air-to-air refuelling.

The concept of in-flight refuelling was not new – its origins date back to the very early days of the RAF when the idea of transferring fuel between aircraft in order to increase time in the air had first been explored. More recently, in 1953, a Hose Drum Unit had been fitted to a Canberra by Flight Refuelling Limited as a trial to see what potential the aircraft had as a tanker. Yet it was to be the Valiant that would become the RAF's first dedicated air-to-air refuelling aircraft.

The refuelling trials were expected to last two years. Trial No 306 was to test the capability of aircraft tanker and receiver equipment and Trial No 306A was to develop rendezvous procedures and techniques. Beetham had not been given a specific trials directive; much would be left to the expertise and professionalism of his squadron, and so he sat down with his key personnel to discuss how the squadron was going to achieve its task.

The initial training for both air and ground crews was carried out by Flight Refuelling Limited at Tarrant Rushton, near Blandford

8. Valiants of 214 Squadron carrying out in-flight refuelling during trials in 1958

Forum in Dorset, while a Flight Refuelling School was set up at Marham for all subsequent training. Part of the squadron immediately began conversion to the Valiant B(K)1, which was modified from the B1 standard by fitting a Mark 16 HDU mounted on the bomb-mounting hard points in the rear of the aircraft's bomb bay and a 4,500-lb fuel tank in the front of the bomb bay. This meant the aircraft bomb doors had to be opened while carrying out in-flight refuelling and this modification gave the Valiant the capability of transferring 45,000 lb of fuel at a rate of 4,000 lb per minute. By fitting an in-flight refuelling probe to the front of the navigation and bombing system scanner bay and connecting it internally to the aircraft's fuel system, it was possible to extend the range of the Valiant. External floodlights allowed for refuelling at night and the task of controlling the in-flight refuelling was given to the radar bombing navigator who operated the HDU control panel.

Flight refuelling trials began almost immediately. Beetham flew two sorties in March with one of his flight commanders, Squadron Leader John Garstin, and his crew, during which he practised dry contacts, where there was no transfer of fuel, with other aircraft from the squadron. In April Beetham flew two more trial sorties with Squadron Leader Coventry and his crew and one trial sortie with the Vickers test pilot, Brian Trubshaw. As with the earlier flights the previous month, all of these trials were to practise establishing contact in the air but without transferring any fuel as the squadron had to wait for clearance from Boscombe Down before any transfer of fuel could take place. In between the air refuelling trials, the squadron's crews had to maintain their bombing currency and proficiencies, and during Beetham's early months as OC 214 Squadron his airborne time was split equally between bombing and air refuelling trials.

The RAF was not the only air force developing its air-to-air refuelling capability and during June Beetham had the opportunity to fly from the nearby American base at Sculthorpe in a Boeing KB-50J of the 420th Air Refuelling Squadron. The KB-50J was an air tanking modification of the B-50 Superfortress, which itself was a development of the B-29 Superfortress, and had just arrived at Sculthorpe a matter of weeks before. During the training sortie he was able to gain a valuable insight into American operating procedures and he observed air-to-air refuelling with a Douglas B-66 Destroyer. The American tankers were fitted with a boom that was 'flown' onto the receiving aircraft by the boom operator. This was a different technique to the British probe-and-drogue system being developed by 214 Squadron, where the pilot of the receiving aircraft would manoeuvre his aircraft until he made contact with the drogue; gradual and gentle forward motion of the receiving aircraft would push the hose back into the tanker aircraft until fuel flowed, at which point the receiving aircraft would maintain a constant position with the tanker.

Beetham's experience of observing the American technique during the sortie nearly ended in disaster during one of the refuelling demonstrations when a connection burst and fuel started spilling out inside the tanker's fuselage. The captain immediately declared an emergency. Fortunately the crew managed to get the situation under control and the aircraft landed safely back at Sculthorpe but it had been an uncomfortable moment.

The balance between bombing and refuelling changed markedly in July, when the squadron's effort became focused on the development of its air-to-air refuelling capability, and for the next two months all of Beetham's flying was involved with the trials. At the 1958 Farnborough Air Show during early September he led two Valiants in line astern and 'plugged in' to demonstrate the new air-to-air refuelling capability, a demonstration he repeated later that month during a Battle of Britain flypast over London, when the route took them overhead other Battle of Britain functions taking place at Cottesmore, Upwood, Honington and Marham.

During October the squadron continued to develop and improve rendezvous procedures, which meant the Valiant tankers could join up with their receiving aircraft wherever and whenever they were most needed; these RVs could take place over land or sea, by day or by night. By now it had also become evident that the Valiant's role as a tanker would not only extend the range of the V-bombers but it could also be used to increase the range and endurance of fighters.

By early 1959 the Valiants were successfully transferring fuel to each other, initially by day and then by night. The culmination of this trial period was on 23 February, when Beetham flew a long-range trial sortie from Marham around the UK lasting over twelve hours, during which he successfully took on a full load of fuel during one refuelling bracket. Having proved the in-flight refuelling capability of the Valiant, it was then a matter of determining how far the RAF's long-range operational capability could be extended. This led to a number of long-range demonstration flights during 1959, and Beetham was at the forefront of proving the RAF's new capability. He had built up a number of contacts in Africa during his time with 82 Squadron, and the first of these long-range refuelling flights was on 16 March, when he flew from Marham to Embakasi Airfield at Nairobi in Kenya. The flight of 4,350 miles lasted just over eight and a half hours, during which he refuelled over Malta. After three nights in Nairobi he returned to Marham in just under ten hours, again carrying out refuelling over Malta.

The long flight to Nairobi had gone well and the following month, on 16 April, Beetham took off from Marham in XD861 at 2.30 a.m. (GMT) for a second long-range refuelling exercise. This time his destination was Salisbury in Southern Rhodesia and he was to be supported by two Valiants pre-positioned at Idris in Libya. Signals had been sent the day before to Salisbury and Idris stating the amount of fuel required, and final confirmatory signals were sent following a detailed meteorology brief just three hours prior to take-off. Beetham set course for the Mediterranean where, high above the North African coast near Tripoli, he joined up with a second Valiant flown by Squadron Leader John Garstin. The two aircraft then flew eastwards to overhead Misurata before turning south, where refuelling commenced. The refuelling lasted fifteen minutes, after which Garstin turned back to Idris, leaving Beetham to continue his journey to Salisbury. Beetham later passed over a timing point at Salisbury at 12.42 p.m. (GMT), having covered the 5,320 miles in ten hours and twelve minutes, at an average speed of 520 mph, which set an unofficial record time from the UK to Salisbury.

The record-breaking flight attracted much media interest at Salisbury. Beetham reported to the press that the flight had gone smoothly, explaining that the purpose of the long-range flights, which would continue to increase in range, was to perfect air-to-air refuelling operating procedures, especially rendezvous techniques and signals communications. This underlined what he had said just twenty-four hours earlier when the Air Ministry had invited the press to hear about the work being done by the RAF on air-to-air refuelling. Beetham also stressed the two most important things on such flights were accurate navigation and signals communications. What emerged too was the amount of versatility and teamwork required and how his squadron had achieved an efficient synthesis of the various factors involved: the aircraft, in both the giving and receiving of fuel, the crew techniques required and the equipment developed by FRL.

The return transit took place four days later and the two Valiants carried out a successful rendezvous over Lake Victoria; the development of rendezvous procedures was an important part of the trial and would be crucial to the development of long-range tactics and procedures. The two Valiants then conducted one refuelling bracket over the lake, transferring 35,000 lb of fuel before a second bracket was carried out over Idris, during which another 30,000 lb of fuel was transferred. The return transit, against a headwind, was timed at eleven hours exactly, which set another unofficial record time.

On 10 June Sir Alan Cobham visited 214 Squadron at Marham and the visit provided a wonderful opportunity for the squadron to meet one of the true pioneers of air-to-air refuelling. Cobham had formed FRL in 1934 specifically to develop air-to-air refuelling equipment and techniques that could be employed commercially. FRL had later developed the probe-and-drogue method of in-flight refuelling, which had been the technique used by 214 Squadron during the trials. Beetham had got to know Cobham well during his time as OC 214 Squadron and he spent some of his time working closely with FRL at Tarrant Rushton.

Cobham's visit to the squadron came at a time when the squadron was making significant progress with the trials and just before Beetham was to fly two more long-range demonstration flights, each one further extending the operational range of the Valiant. The first of these was on 17 June, when Beetham flew from Marham to Waterkloof Air Station in Pretoria, South Africa, in eleven hours and fifteen minutes. Having refuelled overhead Kano in Nigeria, he was joined for the final stage of the flight by four Sabre jet fighters of the South African Air Force, which intercepted the Valiant between Pietersburg and Beit Bridge. The formation flew over Haartebeespoort Dam and then overhead Jan Smuts Airport at 12.55 p.m. before landing at Waterkloof Air Station at 1.05 p.m.

Again there was much local media interest on arrival. The air correspondent for the *Rand Daily Mail* captured the event in some detail, explaining how he had personally witnessed the arrival from the air traffic control tower at Waterkloof. The time between the UK and overhead Johannesburg was eleven hours and three minutes, which set another unofficial record. The official record for London to Johannesburg was held by a Comet airliner, which had set a time of thirteen hours and one minute in 1957, including a refuelling stop of fifty-three minutes at Khartoum, although in 1953 a Canberra bomber, Aries IV, had flown between Britain and Cape Town in twelve hours and twenty-one minutes, including two refuelling stops.

While in South Africa Beetham was delighted to have the opportunity to join up briefly with his sister, Joan, and her family before making the return journey to Marham on 22 June. The flight was completed in eleven hours and forty-nine minutes, another unofficial record. Then, on 9 July, Beetham flew Valiant XD858 from Marham to Cape Town in eleven hours and fifty minutes. The route took them overhead London's Heathrow Airport before heading for Cape Town; Valiants were pre-positioned for two refuelling brackets at El Adem in Libya and at Kano in Nigeria, which enabled him to set another unofficial record: the 6,060 miles from London to Cape Town were timed at eleven hours and twenty-eight minutes.

At Cape Town there was an estimated crowd of three thousand people who had travelled to the airport to witness the event. The Valiant swept over the D. F. Malan Airport at 2.56 p.m., then made a wide circle and disappeared into the distance before coming in to land at just after 3 p.m. Beetham was met on arrival by the air adviser to the High Commission, Group Captain F. J. Rump. Again there was much local media interest and Beetham and his crew attended a press conference soon after landing. The historic flight made the front page of the *Cape Argus* newspaper that evening, under the headline 'Valiant Breaks London–Cape Record by 54 Minutes', and the following day the story made the front page of the *Cape Times* under the simple headline of 'Record Breaking UK Bomber'.

Beetham received two signals of congratulations from the UK. The first was from the senior air staff officer at Bomber Command, which read: 'C-in-C sends you and crew congratulations on successful conclusion of your splendid flight. Please inform all concerned.' The second signal was from the station commander at Marham: 'Another remarkable milestone in the history of the Royal Air Force and 214 Squadron. My warmest congratulations to you and your crew and to all your officers and men who have made possible this historic flight.'

Beetham's flight to Cape Town had emphasised to the people of South Africa just how important long-range aviation had become. The world suddenly seemed much smaller and the *Cape Argus*

9. Beetham taxiing in at Cape Town after his record-breaking flight from Marham on 9 July 1959. This was the first non-stop flight from the UK and was timed from overhead London at eleven hours and twenty-eight minutes, breaking the previous record by fifty-four minutes.

followed the main headline story with a shorter article titled 'Small New World'. The first air journey between Brooklands in Surrey and Cape Town had been made in 1920 by Pierre van Ryneveld and Quintin Brand, who had completed the journey in forty-five days, and then in 1935 Amy Johnson completed the journey in four days six hours and thirty-five minutes. After the Second World War the journey time was reduced to less than twenty-four hours, but now the time had been dramatically reduced to less than twelve hours and a number of journalists picked up on the impact this would have on South Africa. To the South African people this historic flight had demonstrated just how much the world had shrunk in a short time and highlighted the importance of maintaining good relations around the world.

The return journey from Cape Town to London was flown on 14 July and was timed at twelve hours and twenty minutes; this shattered the previous record time by fifty-six minutes. These were the first non-stop flights between the UK and Cape Town but remained unofficial records because they were not timed from take-off at London to landing at Cape Town outbound and because Beetham did not land at London inbound. Nonetheless, his two flights not only broke the speed records in each direction, they also provided a most convincing demonstration of the potential of air-to-air refuelling for the RAF.

Initially there had been little British media interest in these long-range flights, which was mainly due to the fact that Bomber Command had not wanted to draw attention to them should anything go wrong. Throughout the period of the long-range flights Beetham had always enjoyed the full support of his new AOC-in-C, Air Marshal Kenneth Cross, and he had always personally briefed the AOC of his intentions and the reasons behind the importance of proving this new capability. Needless to say, having successfully set the unofficial speed record between London and Cape Town, Bomber Command was quick to attract the media's interest, and a photograph of two Valiants conducting air-to-air refuelling, including the mention of Beetham's historic non-stop flight to Cape Town, was used to front a Royal Air Force recruiting advertisement in the *Daily Telegraph* during October 1959.

For his personal vision and pioneering work in these long-range air-to-air refuelling trials, Beetham was awarded the Air Force Cross in the New Year's Honours List on 1 January 1960. He received many personal letters of congratulations, most notably

from Air Chief Marshal Sir Harry Broadhurst, who sent his heartiest congratulations, Air Marshal Sir Walter Cheshire, who commented on his excellent pioneering work that had been worthily
recognised, Air Marshal Sir Kenneth Cross, who sent his heartiest
congratulations and felt the award was well earned, and also from
Mr A. W. Goodliffe, the chief engineer at FRL.

Each of these long-range flights had further extended the
operational capability of the Valiant and had shown the potential
offered by air-to-air refuelling. It was inevitable that the capability
would be further demonstrated in the months ahead and records
were being broken on a regular basis. In May a Valiant of 214
Squadron, flown by Squadron Leader John Garstin, flew non-stop
from Marham to Changi in Singapore; the 8,110 miles was flown
in fifteen hours and thirty-five minutes. Garstin then went on to
fly the longest endurance flight, which was flown around the UK:
7,400 miles were covered in eighteen hours and five minutes. It had
always been planned that the Vulcan would become involved in the
long-range trials, and the following year a Vulcan of 101 Squadron,
flown by Squadron Leader Mike Beavis, supported by nine Valiants
of 214 Squadron, which carried out refuelling brackets overhead
Cyprus, Karachi and Singapore, flew non-stop from RAF Scampton
to RAAF Richmond in Australia; the record-breaking flight of 11,500
miles took twenty hours and three minutes.

May 1960 saw the completion of the major objectives of the air-to-
air refuelling trials, and the following month it was time for Beetham
to hand over command of the squadron to Wing Commander Peter
Hill. While it might not have been the kind of tour Beetham had
initially expected, it had been a most enjoyable, challenging and
rewarding tour, and much had been achieved. Under his leadership
the squadron had demonstrated the huge potential of air-to-air
refuelling and what it had to offer the Royal Air Force. Although
he could never have imagined then just how successful he would
eventually turn out to be in his vocation, Beetham was astute enough
to realise that his career was now gathering momentum. Having
completed his flying tour as a squadron commander, Beetham
now needed a wing commander staff tour in a suitably high-profile
appointment, and the following month he was posted to be wing
commander operations at HQ 3 Group at Mildenhall, near Bury St
Edmunds in Suffolk.

CHAPTER 6

The Height of Readiness
and a Close-Run Thing in Cuba

In 1960 Bomber Command had two operational groups: 1 Group, with its headquarters at Bawtry Hall near Doncaster, which controlled the Vulcan bases in Yorkshire and Lincolnshire, and 3 Group at Milden-hall, which controlled the Victor and Valiant bases in Leicestershire, Rutland, Cambridgeshire, Northamptonshire and East Anglia.

Within 3 Group there were six Victor squadrons (at Cottesmore, Honington and Wittering) and three Valiant squadrons at Marham, equipped with US nuclear weapons under a 'dual-key' arrangement and assigned to the operational control of the Supreme Allied Commander Europe. In addition to the V-bomber squadrons, one Valiant squadron at Finningley operated electronic counter-measures and there were two Valiant tanker squadrons at Honington and Marham. 3 Group was also responsible for Bomber Command's reconnaissance element, which comprised two squadrons at Wyton – one with Canberras and the other with Valiants. OCUs supported the squadrons, with crews destined for the Valiant being trained at Gaydon while crews for the Victor were trained at Cottesmore.

The air officer commanding 3 Group was Air Vice-Marshal Michael Dwyer, who had taken up his appointment in May 1959, and Beetham knew him well from his days as OC 214 Squadron. As there was no group captain appointment at HQ 3 Group, Beetham and the wing commander training, Bill Mugford, both worked directly for the senior air staff officer in the headquarters. When Beetham first arrived the SASO was Air Commodore Bill Coles but in December it changed to the legendary Second World War fighter ace Air Commodore Johnnie Johnson.

By the time Beetham arrived at Mildenhall, 3 Group had acquired an even greater offensive capability as the RAF had entered the ballistic missile age in 1959. Until then Britain's nuclear weapons capability was based on free-fall bombs delivered by V-bombers, but it had become increasingly apparent that if Britain wanted to remain a major post-war power and, more importantly, have an independent deterrent, then the procurement of a ballistic missile was essential. As the V-bombers were entering service during the mid- to late 1950s, the air staff had issued operational requirements for new weapons that would improve Bomber Command's strategic nuclear capability.

OR1139 issued in 1955 had called for a ballistic missile with a megaton warhead (OR1142) and a range of 1,500–2,000 nautical miles. OR1149, which followed in 1956, called for a flying bomb with a range of 1,000 nautical miles and OR1159, issued in 1958, called for an extended range (600 nautical miles) version of the air-launched nuclear stand-off weapon Blue Steel. It never became accepted doctrine to replace bombers with missiles, but there were advantages and disadvantages to both systems, and the V-force and ballistic missiles would share the responsibilities for the nation's nuclear deterrent.

The British government had decided that the Blue Streak intermediate-range ballistic missile would become the main British nuclear deterrent but while Blue Streak was being developed an agreement was reached with the US government for the supply of sixty Douglas SM-75 Thor IRBMs, which had an operational range of between 1,500 and 1,725 nautical miles. The sixty missiles were operated by twenty squadrons, divided equally between 1 and 3 Groups, and spread across Norfolk, Suffolk, Cambridgeshire, Lincolnshire, Leicestershire, Rutland, Northamptonshire and the East Riding of Yorkshire.

As wing commander operations, Beetham was responsible to the AOC for the alert states of the V-bombers under his command. The degree of preparedness for operations was governed by a series of 'alert conditions' and 'readiness states' ordered by Bomber Command's Operations Centre at Headquarters Bomber Command at High Wycombe. Beetham was also responsible for maintaining a close liaison with the squadrons and bases, and for working closely with HQ Bomber Command staff regarding the targeting plans for the squadrons. It was the height of the Cold War and he found himself working at an extremely high level of classification, particularly when dealing with politically sensitive target plans in Eastern Europe.

Bomber Command dispersal exercises had only begun a matter of eighteen months before Beetham arrived in post, and squadrons were still adapting to the challenge of being dispersed to pre-planned bases, from where they would be scrambled in the shortest possible time. It was vital to establish good, and more importantly secure, communications with the dispersed aircraft and crews. Some of the facilities at the dispersed bases were very basic and so concrete aircraft hard standings, known as operational readiness platforms, were laid; these ORPs led straight onto the runway. Further improvements included the construction of permanent crew accommodation close to the aircraft, and temporary command posts with efficient lines of communications. A total of twenty-six dispersed sites were constructed, from Lossiemouth in the north of Scotland to St Mawgan in Cornwall, and the nuclear weapons for the V-bombers came from 92 Maintenance Unit at Faldingworth near Lincoln.

While he was at Mildenhall Beetham managed to maintain his flying currency, often taking the opportunity to fly in one of the Ansons based at the airfield, and he generally managed to fly at least once a month throughout his tour. He also took the opportunity to fly with the Valiant squadrons whenever possible, usually flying as the first pilot in the left-hand seat rather than as the co-pilot, such was his keenness to maintain his knowledge and proficiency.

Because he worked directly for SASO, he enjoyed a close working relationship with Johnnie Johnson. The two men got on very well together, not only in the headquarters but also socially on the golf course. From Johnson's perspective, Beetham was an excellent staff officer who could be relied upon to make up for his own lack of desire for staff work. Johnson would invariably sign off work that Beetham had done and prepared for Johnson's signature, without even checking it, rather than make changes and produce more work; such was his confidence in Beetham. During the spring and summer months the two men spent many a late afternoon or early evening at the Royal Worlington Golf Club, reputed to be among the best nine-hole golf courses in the world; he could hardly argue whenever Johnson suggested they play a quick nine holes of golf but it would usually be Beetham who would have to return to the office later that evening to complete the necessary staff work for the day.

Throughout their tour at Mildenhall the Beethams lived in married quarters; in fact they would live in various married quarters for the next twenty years. Their son, Alexander, was born at Mildenhall in August 1961 and the following month Beetham learned that he was to be promoted to the rank of group captain and posted to HQ Bomber Command at High Wycombe. The news came as a complete surprise to Beetham as he had only been at Mildenhall for sixteen months. He had fully expected to complete his tour at 3 Group before he would be considered ready for promotion. There is no doubt that his accelerated promotion was due to his success as OC 214 Squadron during the air-to-air refuelling trials and for his part in developing the RAF's long-range operational capability. But it was not only that – he had also proved to be an excellent staff officer at 3 Group.

Having packed up and moved from Mildenhall at very short notice, the Beethams arrived at High Wycombe in early October. They moved into their married quarters in Bradenham Beeches, just a short distance from the headquarters and on top of a hill adjacent to extensive woodland. It was a delightful place to live.

Beetham took up his new appointment as group captain training and, because there was no air commodore appointment in the chain of command, he worked directly for the SASO, Air Vice-Marshal Paddy Menaul, and ultimately for the AOC-in-C, Air Marshal Sir Kenneth Cross. Beetham knew both officers very well, having worked closely with Menaul in Australia during Operation Buffalo, and Cross had always provided him with valuable support during the long-range air-to-air refuelling trials while he commanded 214 Squadron. Beetham had found Cross to be a rather forbidding figure to his squadron crews, but personally he had always got on well with him.

As group captain training, Beetham was primarily responsible for the training of the V-force, and the standards maintained within it, and to improve the efficiency of bombing accuracy. He was also responsible for organising the annual bombing competition between Bomber Command and the US Eighth Air Force, a competition that was taken extremely seriously between the two nations with much professional pride and bragging rights at stake. The following summer, and completely unexpectedly, Beetham became group captain operations when Alan Frank was promoted and posted and Sir Kenneth Cross decided to move Beetham into the group captain operations appointment so that Frank's nominated successor, Hugh Everitt, could replace Beetham as group captain training.

This change of appointment came as excellent news for Beetham and a stroke of fortune as far as he was concerned; certainly the group captain operations post was seen to be the key group captain appointment within the headquarters. Beetham had enjoyed his nine months as group captain training but he was much more driven by operational matters rather than training, and so he was looking forward to getting involved in the higher-level operational decisions of Bomber Command. As group captain operations he had two key responsibilities. First, he was responsible for maintaining the readiness states of the V-force, and for periodically exercising those readiness states, and secondly he was responsible for Bomber Command's targeting plans.

Beetham took over as group captain operations at a time when Bomber Command was developing a state of increased readiness and preparation. It had approximately 140 main bombers on seventeen squadrons and operational conversion units spread across six main bases. In addition to the main bases, the dispersal airfields had been developed during the late 1950s to enable the V-bombers to disperse and operate at fifteen minutes' readiness. However, the more recent threat of ballistic missile attack meant that a higher readiness state was required and it would soon be necessary to launch the bombers within the warning period expected from the new Ballistic Missile Early Warning System, due to be ready at Fylingdales in 1963, which was expected to be around eight minutes but could be as little as three minutes, depending on the type of missile attack.

The degree of preparedness of the V-bombers was defined as an 'alert condition' and the normal state of the command in peacetime was designated Alert Condition 4. During any period of political tension that was not considered serious enough to warrant a higher alert condition, the command would be placed on Alert Condition 3; this was a precautionary alert condition and could be issued to all or part of the force at any one time, and the alert condition would detail any specific actions to be taken.

The next condition was Alert Condition 2, which was intended to generate aircraft ready for hostilities. This required Bomber Command to prepare the maximum number of aircraft to combat serviceability with crews at fifteen minutes' readiness. Operations rooms and other vital services were fully manned on a twenty-four-hour basis and Bomber Command was required to generate 75 per cent of its aircraft within twenty-four hours. Using the figure of 140 main bombers, this meant that at any one time Bomber Command would have at least 105 strategic bombers available to go to war within twenty-four hours of the declaration of Alert Condition 2. The highest alert condition was Alert Condition 1, which would disperse aircraft to their nominated dispersal airfields, where they would be prepared ready for an operational take-off.

The alert conditions were qualified by a series of readiness states, which prescribed the take-off readiness of the aircraft and crews and were related to the tactical warning that could be expected of an impending enemy attack. Readiness states were applied to the elements within Bomber Command that had already been generated to combat-ready status and could be varied regardless of the alert condition then in force. The first was Readiness State One-Five, otherwise known as fifteen minutes' readiness; this required all combat aircraft to be prepared to take-off within fifteen minutes. The next, and higher, state was Readiness State Zero-Five, otherwise known as five minutes' readiness; for the crews this meant being at cockpit readiness and ready to start engines. The highest state was Readiness State Zero-Two, two minutes' readiness, which required crews to start engines and taxi to the take-off point and wait for further instructions; the intention was that aircraft would then be scrambled for their operational mission.

The system of alert conditions did not mean that one condition would have to be followed by another and during exercises, or if necessary for real, Beetham could recommend to SASO, and therefore to the AOC-in-C, an escalation of Bomber Command assets from Alert Condition 4 to Alert Condition 2, therefore by-passing Alert Condition 3.

There was a lot of work required at the high-alert states, such as the preparation of nuclear weapons, and there was also a time limit regarding how long Bomber Command could maintain its higher alert conditions and readiness states. For example, thirty days was the maximum period Alert Conditions 2 and 1 could be maintained and four hours was considered the maximum time a bomber crew could hold Readiness State Zero-Five, while Readiness State Zero-Two could only be maintained for a matter of minutes. Procedures for the Thor missile squadrons differed, but essentially between forty-five and fifty missiles were permanently maintained at 'T-15', otherwise known as fifteen minutes to launch.

The second of Beetham's two key responsibilities was the targeting plans. The first targeting plan was an integrated plan with the USA and was based on both nations working together in a major conflict; the second targeting plan was a national plan based on there being no participation by any other nation. Both plans were vitally important. The integrated targeting plan with the USA, co-ordinated with Strategic Air Command and called the Single Integrated Operational Plan, took Beetham on regular journeys across the Atlantic with Wing Commander Jack Furner, the specialist targeting wing commander at HQ Bomber Command, and during these visits they would meet with their Strategic Air Command colleagues at Omaha.

In terms of military capability the USA was very much the lead nation, but the two commands enjoyed a strong political and professional working relationship together as the integration of potential targets in Eastern Europe was vital. The second plan was quite independent and could have been implemented nationally. It had different target assignments and routes, and created much additional work for Bomber Command's planners and crews because each V-force crew had to be totally familiar with both targeting plans and prepared to deliver an attack against their nominated target from either plan at very short notice.

Bomber Command had now been given sufficient resources and had arranged for at least one aircraft from each squadron to be permanently on quick reaction alert because, in the opinion of Sir Kenneth Cross, it was military common sense to maintain a permanent alert concept in the face of a growing Soviet threat and to compete with the greatly shortening warning time in the years ahead. It was also necessary for Bomber Command to test the vital aspects of its Alert and Readiness Plan.

As recently as eighteen months earlier, alert exercises had fallen into two classes. One was the 'no-notice' exercise, such as Exercise Mick, which would generally be conducted within the Command's own resources and stopped short of dispersal of the V-force. The other was the Exercise Mayflight type, which included all aspects of the Command's dispersal plan up to and including the scramble of V-bombers, but these exercises were not 'no-notice' as they had to be planned in advance.

Both types of exercise had their limitations but Bomber Command needed to assess its ability to disperse without prior warning, including recalling its people from leave, and so these exercises were combined under the codename Mickey Finn, an annual exercise first held in December 1961, which required the V-force to disperse and be made ready for an operational mission without any prior warning. There were also navigation and bombing competitions for the crews, held in the UK and in America to improve crew standards;

these standards were also regularly checked by group and command standardisation teams visiting the squadrons.

Beetham fully supported the overriding need for operational readiness to demonstrate the reality of the main bomber force in its strategic nuclear deterrent role. This was the peak of the Cold War and he soon found himself working at an enhanced level of security classification on a daily basis. The arsenal of nuclear weapons for the V-force included the Blue Danube kiloton-range weapon for all three V-bombers, Red Beard for the Valiant in its low-level tactical role and Yellow Sun for the Vulcans and Victors. Furthermore, the Vulcan B2 squadrons were to be equipped to carry more advanced nuclear weapons: the stand-off bomb Blue Steel and the WE177B lay-down bomb. Given the standard of V-bombers and their capability, the megatonnage in their bomb bays, and the fact that its crews had now come to grips with the practicalities of waging strategic nuclear war, Bomber Command felt confident that it was now in a position to meet any future task.

The years of preparation very nearly became reality during the Cuban Missile Crisis of October 1962 just three months after Beetham had become group captain operations. Along with the Berlin Blockade, the Cuban Missile Crisis was one of the major confrontations of the Cold War and is generally accepted as the moment in post-Second World War history when the world came closest to nuclear war.

There were some notable factors leading up to the crisis. During 1961 the Americans had deployed medium-range ballistic missiles in Turkey that provided a significant threat to cities and to industrial and military targets in the Soviet Union. There were also fears of Soviet military intervention in Cuba, situated in the northern Caribbean and less than a hundred miles south of Florida. On 1 May 1961 its leader, Fidel Castro, declared Cuba a socialist republic after a force of fifteen hundred American-trained Cuban exiles landed at the Bay of Pigs with the aim of instigating an uprising amongst the Cuban people and to depose Castro. The invasion was quickly stopped by Cuba's military forces and the American president, John F. Kennedy, was forced to negotiate the release of the survivors. However, the incident meant that Castro continued to feel threatened by a possible American invasion and so he built up his military forces, with the backing of the Soviet Union.

America feared that any alliance between Cuba and the Soviet Union would result in the expansion of communism in Latin

America. Furthermore, the relationship contradicted America's Monroe Doctrine of 1823 (named after the American president James Monroe), which states that any effort by a European government to colonise land or interfere with states in the Americas would be viewed by the USA as acts of aggression that would require US intervention. The doctrine was issued at a time when many Latin American countries were becoming independent from Spain, and the USA feared that a European power would take over the former Spanish colonies.

In early 1962 the USA imposed an economic embargo against Cuba and then, in September, a joint US Congressional resolution authorised the use of military force against Cuba should American interests become threatened. There had already been a major American military exercise in the Caribbean earlier that year that focused on the invasion of an island to overthrow a political leader, and the Cuban government saw this resolution as further evidence that the USA was planning to invade. As a consequence, Castro and Soviet Premier Nikita Khrushchev agreed to place strategic nuclear missiles in Cuba.

The stage was now set for a full confrontation between the USA and the Soviet Union, which would have a dramatic impact on the rest of the world, and the situation came to a head during October 1962. From a UK perspective, British intelligence officers were first informed by their US counterparts on 19 October of the location of launch sites on Cuba for Soviet R-12 (NATO designation SS-4 Sandal) medium-range ballistic missiles and R-14 (SS-5 Skean) intermediate-range ballistic missiles. Two days later the British ambassador to Washington DC, Sir David Ormsby-Gore, was personally briefed on the developing situation by President Kennedy and later that day Kennedy sent a personal message to the British prime minister, Harold Macmillan.

On 22 October Kennedy informed the world that missile bases were being built in Cuba, and he appealed to Castro and Khrushchev to remove all the missiles and bases. He also stated that American policy regarded any nuclear missile launched from Cuba against any nation in the Western hemisphere to be an attack on the USA, and this would result in a full retaliatory response by the USA against the Soviet Union. Kennedy's appeal produced no response and so he ordered a naval blockade of Cuba to prevent Russian ships from bringing additional missiles to the island. In response, Khrushchev authorised his senior officers in Cuba to launch their tactical nuclear weapons if Cuba was invaded by American forces.

The situation remained deadlocked for a week as the two leaders of the world's great nuclear superpowers stared down the barrel of a gun. The US military was placed on a high state of alert to enforce the blockade and to be ready to invade Cuba if necessary, while Strategic Air Command maintained airborne alert with its B-52 Stratofortress heavy bombers.

To Beetham the crisis seemed to escalate very quickly. Initially there was not much media interest as the British government appeared to play down the state of affairs. As the situation deteriorated further he spent the height of the crisis in the underground operations room at High Wycombe and barely came out of the bunker except to eat and to catch up on some much-needed sleep at home. He was involved in regular meetings with the AOC-in-C and SASO, who were closely monitoring the situation and deciding on Bomber Command's next course of action while they waited for military direction from higher authority.

There were long periods when there was little information coming from America or, more importantly, there was little direction from the British government; this was either because the true gravity of the situation was not fully understood by the government or because of the government's continuing attempt to play down the situation. There was a strong feeling at High Wycombe that the whole nightmare could not possibly be happening for real. Was the world really on the verge of a nuclear holocaust?

In response to the worsening situation Bomber Command had recalled all of its aircraft and crews from overseas training sorties and recalled its personnel from leave. This was done discretely on Macmillan's instruction for fear of scaring the public, and the fact that Bomber Command managed to generate its aircraft and crews to a high state of readiness without raising national alarm through the media was great credit to those involved. Beetham was in regular contact with the groups and stations. As the week progressed the situation worsened and by the weekend there was a horrifying reality that it was looking increasingly likely that a nuclear war was about to start.

During his occasional short breaks above ground level, Beetham found the peace and tranquillity in the quiet countryside around High Wycombe to be completely at odds with the tension he was experiencing underground in the operations room. Although his wife clearly knew that something of major importance was happening, she was not aware of the true gravity of the situation; nor was

Beetham in a position to tell her. Furthermore, when watching the news on Saturday evening during one of his short breaks at home, Beetham was astonished to see that a football match took priority in the news bulletin over the rapidly deteriorating relationship between East and West that could have had such a devastating impact on the whole world; he simply could not believe it.

On 23 October the US Joint Chiefs of Staff instructed Strategic Air Command to raise its alert state to the unprecedented state of DEFCON 2, a measure of the activation and readiness level of the armed forces, just below the maximum readiness state of DEFCON 1, which, if declared, would most likely have preceded an all-out nuclear war. As a result of the declaration of DEFCON 2, Strategic Air Command dispersed its bombers within the USA and increased the proportion of aircraft maintaining airborne alert. The crisis deepened further when Khrushchev warned that the American 'pirate action' in enforcing the naval blockade of Cuba would lead to war.

As there was no sign of a slow-down in the development of the missile sites, Kennedy issued a security action memorandum that authorised the loading of nuclear weapons onto aircraft under the command of the Supreme Allied Commander Europe; these aircraft would have the responsibility of carrying out the first air strikes against targets in the Soviet Union.

The British government continued to monitor events as they unfolded. When Macmillan met with the Chief of the Air Staff, Air Chief Marshal Sir Thomas Pike, at Admiralty House during the morning of 27 October, the prime minister was clear that overt preparations should be avoided. Pike briefed his fellow Chiefs of Staff in the afternoon and then warned the AOC-in-C Bomber Command that he should place his forces on alert and that his key personnel should all be available on station, although, by then, the recall of personnel had already taken place. However, Bomber Command's request to disperse its aircraft discretely in accordance with its own dispersal plan – which required each squadron to disperse four of its aircraft to other RAF bases – was refused; the V-force squadrons would be required to operate from their home base.

During the afternoon of 27 October Bomber Command was placed on Alert Condition 3, its precautionary pre-dispersal state of preparedness. All key personnel were required to remain on station and operations rooms were prepared to be manned at short notice. Although there was no generation of aircraft ordered at this stage, preparations were made at the V-bomber squadrons to ensure a rapid generation if necessary. In addition, all available Thor missiles were placed at fifteen minutes' readiness and personnel were recalled to their respective bases. This in reality made no significant difference to the normal Thor readiness state but the escalation did mean that two launch crews were now to be available on base at any one time. All but one of the sixty Thor missiles were placed on fifteen minutes' readiness; the only missile not prepared was one used for training purposes, although the order would later be given to prepare this missile as well.

At fifteen minutes' readiness the Thor missiles lay horizontal in their shelters but they could be erected, fuelled and launched within fifteen minutes. Without fuel and liquid oxygen the missiles could maintain this readiness states for several hours, but once refuelled the missile would either have to be fired within less than twenty-four hours or de-fuelled and recycled back to standby, an operation that took six hours to complete. Also, given that the missile sites were in view of the public, raising the missiles would have been a visible sign of activity, which might have been seen as escalatory and would have been against the wishes of Macmillan.

On the following day, 28 October, the number of aircraft on QRA was doubled. The measures taken by Bomber Command were both discrete and consistent with the wishes of the prime minister, but, to ensure the QRA crews remained vigilant, Bomber Command occasionally exercised the higher readiness states of its crews. However, although everything was in place to generate more aircraft and to escalate the alert state further, the order was not officially given for fear of the effect it might have – should it become known – on the very tense negotiations between Kennedy and Khrushchev at the time.

Eventually, after days of negotiations between the two super-powers, and following a number of uncomfortable incidents in the waters off Cuba, the threat of all-out nuclear confrontation was averted. Khrushchev decided against prolonging the situation and ordered all Soviet supply ships away from Cuban waters and he agreed to remove the missiles from the island. In return Kennedy agreed to remove all American missiles in Turkey, although this was not initially made public as it was a secret deal between Khrushchev and Kennedy at the time. The world's perception of the outcome to the crisis was that Khrushchev had backed down from a situation that he had started and his fall from power just two years later can certainly be partially linked to his inept handling of the crisis.

The world breathed a sigh of relief. Bomber Command remained on Alert Condition 3 until 5 November, after which it gradually relaxed its alert state, although the US Strategic Air Command remained on DEFCON 2 for a further two weeks. The crisis had shown the real value of Thor as the missiles had been prepared ready for launch through simple communications and without any obvious visible sign to the public, but Thor sites were at a fixed, and known, location and the missiles could not have been recalled or immobilised if launched. In contrast, while it took time to generate a large percentage of the V-force to a high readiness state, and then a certain amount of effort to maintain it, the flexibility of having a V-force meant the bombers could have been dispersed and even once airborne could have been recalled if required.

Thor did not survive long after the Cuban Missile Crisis; the following year the missiles were withdrawn from the UK and returned to America. Although short-lived, Thor had satisfied a political rather than a military requirement and was an important and effective part of the national deterrent, but its departure from the UK was as low key as its arrival.

The events of October 1962 mark the closest the world has ever come to a nuclear war and left no doubt in Beetham's mind as to just how quickly things could escalate when the use of nuclear weapons is an option. Military doctrine at the time was one of massive retaliation, which could have led to Armageddon. He felt there was little that RAF conventional forces could have done when faced with overwhelming odds and the RAF would have been left with no alternative but to use tactical nuclear weapons on the battlefield.

Having also witnessed the nuclear tests at Maralinga in 1956 he was convinced that one small tactical nuclear explosion observed on the battlefield would be communicated back as something far more sinister and, from that point on, it would be very difficult to prevent a rapid escalation. In this context Beetham felt that many politicians did not fully understand or appreciate the implications of the very high states of readiness which nuclear forces required. It was rare for a minister to take any interest in RAF exercises, and so he wondered exactly how some of the most important political decisions would have been made without the key politicians having a firm understanding of what readiness states were all about.

With the Cuban Missile Crisis set to take its place in history, it was only a matter of days before Beetham and his colleagues at Bomber

Command faced another major problem, the origins of which had begun more than two years earlier. Following the government's decision to procure the Blue Streak IRBM to meet OR1139 for a ballistic missile, an increasing number of development problems, combined with escalating costs, had led to the cancellation of the Blue Streak programme in April 1960. By then the government had also abandoned its plan to develop Blue Steel 2, which was to have been an extended version of the air-launched stand-off weapon, and instead opted to procure the American Douglas GAM-87A Skybolt air-launched ballistic missile (to meet OR1149 – the development of a flying bomb with a range of 1,000 nautical miles), which it intended to mount on the V-bombers.

Britain had joined the Skybolt programme in May 1960 when Prime Minster Harold Macmillan agreed to purchase 144 Skybolt missiles for the RAF. However, since then, the Skybolt programme had suffered difficulties. Early launches had resulted in failure and by 1962 the value of Skybolt as an effective weapon system had been seriously questioned. The US Navy's Polaris submarine-launched ballistic missile had recently entered service with a military capability similar to Skybolt, and the development of the LGM-30 Minuteman land-based intercontinental ballistic missile for the US Air Force had shown improved accuracy over earlier land-based missiles which had reduced the need for air-launched weapons. The US defense secretary, Robert McNamara, publicly supported the Polaris and Minuteman programmes and had become convinced there was no need for Skybolt. Then, in November 1962 he recommended to President Kennedy that Skybolt be cancelled.

The information filtered down to Beetham at Bomber Command, although there had been rumours of this before and so he was not entirely surprised. Britain had cancelled its other projects in favour of Skybolt and there was no doubt that Skybolt offered Bomber Command a missile threat to targets well inside the Soviet Union and could be launched from outside the range of Soviet air defences. Beetham was aware that if two Skybolts were carried by each V-bomber an airborne alert could be maintained without flight refuelling due to the missile's long range; without Skybolt that capability would not exist.

The news did not go down well among British politicians as it potentially marked the failure of Britain's independent nuclear deterrent, and a political row soon broke out in the House of Commons. In December McNamara met with the British minister of defence, Peter Thorneycroft, and presented him with an aide-memoire, which set out the reasons that had led the US government to a tentative conclusion that the Skybolt programme should be cancelled. While it would be possible to produce the missile, McNamara explained that there were technical uncertainties and reliability issues that would take some considerable time to sort out and there were doubts that Skybolt would prove to be a really worthwhile weapon. Furthermore, the development and progress of other nuclear delivery systems meant that the US government had decided that the continuation of the Skybolt programme would not represent a good investment of money.

The aide-memoire suggested three possibilities for the British government to consider. First, the British government might wish to continue the Skybolt programme, either through a cut-back production programme in the USA, or through UK production employing US technology. Second, the American AGM-28 Hound Dog air-launched cruise missile might be adapted to British aircraft. Third, the British government might wish to participate in a sea-based medium-range ballistic missile force under multilateral manning and ownership.

Thorneycroft explained that Skybolt was central to British defence policy and agreement on it had formed part of a complex of decisions, which included granting the USA the use of facilities at Holy Loch in Scotland for its Polaris submarines. Thorneycroft also felt that of the three possibilities suggested only the first was a realistic option, but the cost of taking over the programme would be extremely high and, as he was quick to point out, the American conclusion that Skybolt was unlikely to be a really worthwhile weapon would give Britain little faith in taking the programme forward.

Beetham and group captain plans, Mike Le Bas, spent many hours attending a small committee at the Air Ministry to discuss the various options and in the end it seemed that the best choice, and to Beetham the only option, might be Polaris. However, Beetham also fully understood that an American decision to cancel Skybolt would leave the nation with a capability gap from the time when Blue Steel would cease to be a credible deterrent to the time when a replacement system, such as a British Polaris force, could become operational; this would most likely be about four years.

There was certainly scepticism in the Air Ministry and Bomber Command, where many people believed that the technical difficulties of Skybolt had been overstated and that it could be developed successfully. The option proposed by the US to adapt the Hound

Dog air-launched cruise missile to RAF aircraft had been considered by the RAF but turned down because major modifications would be required to fit it to the Vulcan and Victor, and because it could not be introduced into service in less than four or five years. Therefore, unless the US government could be persuaded to continue with Skybolt, the four realistic options available to Britain were: to acquire Polaris; to pay for completion of Skybolt in the USA; to complete Skybolt in Britain; or to join the French in producing a ballistic missile system. A paper including the likely costs of the different options was quickly drafted, which ended up concluding that the only weapon system of comparable effectiveness would be the Polaris submarine, and this effectively ended the concept of an airborne British nuclear deterrent.

As the crisis was fast coming to a political head, an emergency meeting was arranged between Macmillan and Kennedy in Nassau in the Bahamas. A brief prepared for Macmillan by the Air Ministry stated that none of the three options offered by McNamara in his talks with Thorneycroft was considered acceptable. It also urged that a strong case should be put to the president for continuing with Skybolt, or to make available an alternative submarine-based weapon system, because there was a strong belief in the House of Commons that Britain should remain an independent nuclear power.

The Nassau talks began on the evening of 18 December and the following day Kennedy and Macmillan reviewed the Skybolt development programme. Kennedy explained that the very complex weapon system would not be completed within the cost estimate or the timescale that had been projected when the programme had begun. Because of this, and because of the availability to the US government of alternative weapon systems, Kennedy said that he had decided to cancel plans for the production of Skybolt by the USA. He did, however, recognise the importance of the Skybolt programme for the UK, and expressed his willingness to continue with the development of the missile as a joint enterprise between the USA and the UK, with each country bearing equal costs of completing the development, after which the UK would be able to place a production order to meet its requirement. While fully recognising the value of this offer, Macmillan decided not to avail himself of it because of the doubts that had been expressed about the prospects of success for Skybolt and because of uncertainty regarding the date of completion and final costs of the programme.

Over the next few days the possibility of the US providing Polaris was discussed and the two leaders agreed that any decision must be considered in the widest context, both of the future defence of the North Atlantic Alliance and of the safety of the free world. The two leaders agreed that a start could be made by subscribing to NATO some parts of the force already in existence; this could include allocations from US strategic forces, from Bomber Command and from tactical nuclear forces already in Europe. Such forces would be assigned as part of a NATO nuclear force and targeted in accordance with NATO plans; British submarines developed under the Polaris agreement would be assigned and targeted in this way. The Polaris agreement stated that the USA would make available Polaris missiles on a continuing basis, less the warheads, for Royal Navy submarines constructed in Britain. The warheads would be provided by Britain without the dual-key system, which ensured that the UK would be able to retain its independent nuclear deterrent force.

The Nassau talks ended on 21 December and the Skybolt pro-gramme was officially terminated. The responsibility for Britain's strategic nuclear deterrent, which had been held by the RAF since the mid-1950s, was to be handed over to the Royal Navy. The politi-cal decision to opt for Polaris for the Royal Navy was not without its critics within the RAF, particularly because the decision implied that the credibility of Bomber Command's deterrent would decline from 1965 until Polaris was due to become operational in 1970.

The decision to cancel Skybolt had massive implications for Bomber Command and it raised many questions for Beetham and the air staff. Would more Blue Steels, either the present version or a stretched version, be required? Could TSR2, which was still under development at that stage, be used in a strategic deterrent role? Should the development of a long-range air-to-surface missile be considered as an insurance against the delay of Polaris? Would more advanced electronic counter-measures be required to extend Bomber Command's penetrative power, and would this then lead to more air tankers being required? It was, indeed, a busy period for Beetham.

Gradually the questions raised were answered by the air staff. There would be no value in procuring more of the current in-service Blue Steels, nor would a stretched version give value for money. Although TSR2 was considered to be a longer-term possibility, the development of a long-range air-to-surface missile called Pandora (a ram-jet missile project) was considered extremely expensive and was unlikely to be ready for another eight years. Electronic counter-measures would continue to be developed, so that the V-bombers could operate at low level, but the general decision was not to increase the Blue Steel order, or to develop it further, and not to attempt to maintain an airborne alert capability. Instead, it was decided to look at developing a lay-down bomb for the V-bombers and to study the possible merits of wider dispersal of the V-force.

The planned phasing out of Thor missiles from April 1963 meant that Beetham was involved in staffing proposals to compensate for the loss of capability, which resulted in Sir Kenneth Cross putting forward his proposal to the Chief of the Air Staff to increase the QRA force from 1 April to a total of seventeen Vulcans and Victors, plus the four Valiants of the NATO-assigned squadron, and to then increase the force to twenty Vulcans and Victors by 1 July, when the Blue Steel squadrons would be able to make their contribution. This plan would enable Bomber Command to maintain approximately 20 per cent of the V-force at permanent readiness and this would go some way to compensate for the loss of Thor.

Throughout 1963 Beetham was involved in staffing work that specifically addressed the deterrence from 1965 until 1970. Essentially, Bomber Command would need to maintain a front-line strength of seventy-two Vulcans and sixteen Victors; forty-eight of these aircraft would be armed with Blue Steel and forty armed with free-falling bombs, and of the forty non-Blue Steel aircraft, priority would be given for the development of a lay-down bomb with a yield in the megaton range, which could also be used by TSR2. One of the key issues was to make modifications to the navigation and bombing fit of the V-bombers to enable them to operate at low level. This also meant that electronic counter-measures had to be improved to increase the crew's chances of survival when operating at low level. Finally, the provision for wider dispersal of the V-force was considered, particularly through the use of overseas bases. Trials by Bomber Command had convinced the Air Staff that a low-level attack by V-bombers was practicable but it would require strengthening of the Victor airframe and, as previously expected, it would require the fitting of additional navigation and bombing equipment to both the Vulcan and Victor.

During 1963 much of the V-force converted to the low-level role, using their existing weapons in the short term, although it became increasingly important to continue the development of the lay-down bomb for the TSR2 and for use by the V-bombers. New tactics were developed by the squadrons, which were essentially based on a high-level transit outbound and then a low-level penetration into the target area. The type of weapon would then determine what the crew did next. For example, for an aircraft armed with Yellow Sun Mk 2 it was necessary to climb up to a release height of about 20,000 feet, during which the aircraft and crew were exposed to missile defences, after which the aircraft would either return to low level to make its escape or continue climbing quickly to high level, depending on what the threat was at the time.

Because of the aircraft's vulnerability to defences during the weapon-release phase of flight, it was decided to assess whether the Blue Steel missile could be modified for low-level launch. However, the problem of modifying Blue Steel was compounded by the fact that it was still being introduced into service. As Cross was due to hand over Bomber Command to his successor in September, he remained sceptical of the weapon's reliability and readiness potential. The time taken to generate a Blue Steel weapon system could not be reduced much below seven hours; in the case of any defects being detected this time could easily double. Nonetheless, if Blue Steel could be modified then it would undoubtedly increase the striking power of the V-force.

In September 1963 Cross handed over Bomber Command to Air Marshal Sir John Grandy. Just a matter of days before Grandy assumed command, the Ministry of Aviation gave clearance for the use of unfilled and unfuelled Blue Steels on Vulcan B2s on QRA. Blue Steel was then placed in the hands of Bomber Command and this was followed by the development of a comparatively simple and inexpensive modification for Blue Steel that would enable the missile to be launched at a height of no more than 1,000 feet and at a range of about fifty miles from the target.

Throughout the rest of his tour Beetham remained instrumental in further developing and maintaining the high readiness state of Bomber Command. An example of how far the command had developed in a relatively short period of time was demonstrated in Exercise Mickey Finn III, held in November, when all but one of the 103 aircraft available for the exercise were declared combat ready at their planned main base or dispersal airfield within twenty-four hours. He had also seen the introduction into service of the early-warning radars of the Ballistic Missile Early Warning System at Fylingdales in Yorkshire, which had become operational during 1963. These radars, covering an arc from the north to the south-east, provided the UK with a marginal four minutes' warning of an attack and also provided the USA with a warning time of about thirty minutes.

Although the V-force front-line strength was due to reduce in numbers to eighty-eight aircraft (made up entirely of Vulcan and Victor B2s), and although each aircraft could only carry one weapon instead of the two Skybolts that had originally been intended, Beetham was satisfied that Bomber Command still posed a significant threat and was capable of destroying a substantial number of major targets if required. While the development of Soviet defence systems would continue, he felt the deterrent effect of the V-force and Bomber Command would continue to be substantial until at least 1970.

Beetham completed his tour at Bomber Command at the end of July 1964, by which time he had personally given more than a hundred presentations to visitors at the headquarters and had supervised many others. The classification of his presentations depended on the rank and security vetting of the visitors, and ranged from general unclassified presentations on publicising why the nation needed a nuclear deterrent to the more secret presentations, such as those given to the Chief of the Air Staff or to other members of the Air Force Board, which included details of Bomber Command's targeting plans, where much of the detail was down to the work of Wing Commander Jack Furner.

Beetham had thoroughly enjoyed his time at Headquarters Bomber Command, in particular the last two years as group captain operations. It was a very busy and challenging period, when he had been right at the heart of what Bomber Command was doing, and he was able to leave well satisfied that he had done a good job.

CHAPTER 7

Trouble in Aden

For some time during early 1964 Beetham had been in discussions with his personnel officer to find out where his next appointment would be. He had made it clear that he wanted to command a station and, given his experience, a number of Bomber Command stations were discussed. However, what Beetham did not know at the time was that Air Vice-Marshal Johnnie Johnson, then Air Officer Commanding Air Forces Middle East, had personally asked for him to be the next station commander of RAF Khormaksar in Aden.

At the time Khormaksar was the RAF's largest overseas base, and its position in the Middle East was not only strategically important to the region but it was also a vital staging post for the Far East and East Africa. Because of its size and importance the intention had originally been to appoint a station commander in the rank of air commodore rather than a group captain, the normal rank of a station commander, but because Beetham had completed fewer than three years as a group captain he was not yet considered ready for further promotion. Moreover, the air secretary felt that Beetham did not have the wider experience required for such an important post; he was, after all, a Bomber Command man and Khormaksar operated many different types of aircraft in several different roles, none of which was a bombing role.

While this may have been a concern for the air secretary, it was not a concern for Johnnie Johnson, who had already discussed the opportunity with Beetham, and so he decided to keep the station commander post as a group captain so that he could get Beetham appointed. Johnson was determined to get his way and his naturally persuasive powers meant that, in July 1964, Beetham found out that he was to be the next station commander at Khormaksar. Not only did Johnson get Beetham but he also secured Air Commodore Mike

Le Bas as his SASO; Johnson certainly knew how to get the men he wanted for his organisation.

Understandably, Beetham was delighted at the news and he looked forward to renewing his acquaintance with his former senior officers as he got on very well with both Johnson and Le Bas. In particular, he thought that Johnson was a great character and leader who always seemed to raise the standards wherever he went. He had a more relaxed style than most other senior officers but he also instinctively knew if there was something wrong; Beetham had thoroughly enjoyed working for him before and Aden would be no different. As it was still some time before he was due to take over as station commander, Beetham took the opportunity to visit Khormaksar while still at Bomber Command and flew a Valiant from Gaydon to Khormaksar. He then spent two days viewing the station and meeting its people.

At the end of July Beetham left Bomber Command, but before he could assume command of Khormaksar he had to complete a conversion course on 242 OCU at Thorney Island, where he learned to fly the Argosy turbo-prop transport aircraft and the Beverley piston-engine transport aircraft. The course lasted just over a month, which he finished in mid-September. Having completed the handover from his predecessor, Group Captain Alec Blythe, Beetham assumed command of Khormaksar on 23 October.

Aden had been of interest to Britain as a link to British India since the nineteenth century, when Britain had first occupied the port and established Aden as a colony. A zone of alliances, known as protectorates, was then set up around Aden to act as a protective buffer. After the loss of British colonies following the Second World War and the Suez Crisis of 1956, Arab nationalism had spread to the Arabian Peninsula and anti-British groups with varying political objectives began to merge into larger organisations. The RAF base at Khormaksar was enlarged as Britain spread its own influence deeper into the Arabian Peninsula and to support British troops who had been sent to Aden to control inter-tribal rivalries and unrest.

The Aden Emergency that followed was an insurgency against British forces. It began in 1963 and would last for four years. When Beetham took over command of Khormaksar in 1964 the situation in the region had reached boiling point. The recently formed republican government of Yemen had started its anti-imperialist campaign, with Egypt taking every opportunity to support the Yemeni claim to South Arabia by stirring up subversion against British rule, and terrorists operating in and around Aden were being resupplied from the Yemen through the neighbouring British protectorate of Dhala. The British Army had set up a garrison at Dhala Camp to deter the resupply route, and the Radfan hills, sixty miles to the north of Aden, became the site of intense fighting.

The RAF command structure in the region had changed several times since Aden Command had first formed in 1928. The Middle East Air Force had formed after the Second World War and in 1955 was divided into a Southern Group, which covered Aden, and a Northern Group. The following year HQ British Forces Arabian Peninsula formed and had its headquarters at Steamer Point. It was unique as the first peacetime unified command with all three services controlled operationally, and to a certain extent administratively, by an inter-service headquarters. Then, in 1961, BFAP became Middle East Command, with the subordinate air element becoming Air Forces Middle East, commanded by Johnnie Johnson from October 1963.

The command's territory covered a vast area, from Bahrain in the Persian Gulf to the north, through the Trucial States (now the United Arab Emirates), Muscat and Oman, the South Arabian Federation and across the east side of Africa to Kenya; a distance of over two thousand miles. There were other RAF bases in the region – at Muharraq (Bahrain Island), Sharjah (Trucial States), Masirah Island and Salalah (Oman), Riyan (South Arabian Federation) and Eastleigh (Kenya) – but Khormaksar was at the heart of operations, with three-quarters of the command's aircraft based there.

Khormaksar had ten squadrons and flights, which operated eleven different types of aircraft. The airfield was situated on a thin neck of land that linked the Aden colony to the southern tip of Arabia. It had one main runway nearly two miles in length and a parallel perimeter track that could be used as a second runway in an emergency because there was no diversionary airfield in the local area. As well as being an RAF base, the eastern end of the airfield was used as Aden's civil airport and provided a number of services, such as meteorological, navigational and communications facilities for a number of civil airlines operating in the region. To the south of Khormaksar the Jebel Shamsan, an extinct volcano, dominated the landscape. Also to the south of the airfield within the Aden colony was the main harbour near Steamer Point, where the command's headquarters and Government House were located, and the towns of Maalla and Crater, where many of Khormaksar's service families lived. To the north of the airfield were the town of Sheikh Othman and the main road towards Dhala and the Yemen.

The Beethams lived in the station commander's residence on base, which came with staff to look after the house and to fulfil the essential duties when entertaining. Although living on base, the Beethams still ventured into the colony to go swimming and to sample the local shops when possible, although they generally restricted their movements off base to daylight hours. They also found that the climate took some getting used to. Between April and September it was extremely hot and very humid, but the weather was much more pleasant during the period between October and March, when it was cooler and less humid; rain was really quite rare.

Beetham's task as station commander was two-fold. First, on the tactical side, his squadrons and personnel were there to defend Aden and the protectorates from external attack and to help maintain law and order within the territory. The squadrons provided much-needed support for the British Army and could be called upon to operate anywhere in the region if required. Secondly, and strategically, he was responsible for making sure the airfield remained suitable for all air transport links.

Not only was Khormaksar the largest RAF staging post between the UK and Singapore; there were also scheduled air services to maintain as well as providing valuable supplies to other forces within the region. Beetham recognised very early on that security was a major problem, and this would remain his biggest concern. The station was bursting at the seams, the buildings on base were generally poor and overall Khormaksar lacked the resources that he had been more used to in Bomber Command. These problems would never go away and much of his time would be spent dealing with security matters.

One of his first tasks was to assess the proposed plan for the reorganisation of Khormaksar's command structure to obtain increased efficiency through greater economy of effort and improved span of control. While the familiar three-pronged station organisation was retained – Operations Wing, Administration Wing and Technical Wing – the flying and aircraft activities were conjoined in three largely autonomous operational wings: Strike Wing, Medium-Range Transport Wing and Short-Range Transport Wing. This meant that OC Operations Wing and OC Technical Wing became Beetham's staff officers, with responsibility for the co-ordination of all operational and technical matters. Completing the station's organisational structure was Supply Wing, the Station Medical Centre and 131 Maintenance Unit.

As far as the operational capability of Khormaksar was concerned, the most noticeable change was the renaming of the Tactical Wing to its new title of Strike Wing. The Strike Wing consisted of 8 and 43 Squadrons, equipped with Hunter FGA9s, and 37 Squadron, equipped with Shackleton MR2s, was used for maritime patrols although there were times when Beetham wanted to use these in the bomber role, but he would need government approval to do so.

The Hunters provided the wing with its fighter and ground-attack capability. The connection between 8 Squadron and Aden went back to 1927 when the squadron first took up residency at Khormaksar, and the squadron badge of an Arabian dagger sheathed commemorates the squadron's long sojourn in Southern Arabia and the policing role played by the squadron over so many years. The squadron had taken delivery of the Hunter in 1960 and these had become more frequently used in action against incursions from the Yemen across the ill-defined frontier of the Aden Protectorate. By contrast, the Hunters of 43 Squadron had only arrived at Khormaksar in 1963, having been moved from Cyprus in response to the increased tension in Aden. Completing the Strike Wing was a Fighter Reconnaissance Flight, 1417 Flight, which operated Hunter FR10s and T7s, which had been formed in 1963 using reconnaissance-trained Hunter pilots from 8 Squadron.

The Medium-Range Transport Wing provided support for the army in the Aden Protectorate and consisted of 84 Squadron, with Beverley C1s, and 105 Squadron with Argosy C1s. The Short-Range Transport Wing consisted of 26 Squadron, with Belvedere HC1 helicopters to provide helicopter transport support for the army in the Radfan, 78 Squadron, with Twin Pioneer CC1s, and a flight of Whirlwind HAR10 helicopters. There was also a communications flight operating Hastings, Andovers and Dakotas for general transport purposes.

The Technical Wing supported the flying wings and its task was made unusually complex by the number and variety of aircraft. The wing was divided into two sections: one for normal servicing of aircraft and the second, 131 Maintenance Unit, provided heavy repair facilities for all technical equipment within the command. In addition to the resident units at Khormaksar, there were always a number of different aircraft types from various army and navy units operating in and out of the base, as well as a steady flow of RAF transport and bombers transiting through Khormaksar en route to destinations

10. When Beetham took over command of Khormaksar in 1964 it was the RAF's largest overseas base. Seven Beverleys and two Argosies of the Medium Transport Wing, a Shackleton of 37 Squadron and a Hastings of the Communications Flight can be seen on the main aircraft apron, along with four visiting Britannia aircraft (furthest from the large hangars) that often visited or staged through Aden on the way to the Far East and Africa.

in the Far East, the Gulf and East Africa. Civil aircraft movements included aircraft from more than fifteen airlines, charter companies and private operators; among the aircraft types were DC-3s and Viscounts, as well as Boeing 707s of Air India and Comets of BOAC.

It took no time at all for Beetham to realise just how big Khormaksar was. In any one month the base would typically handle more than a hundred scheduled flights, totalling some four thousand passengers, and well over one million pounds of freight and ten thousand pounds of mail. In addition to the four thousand military personnel on the base, including two hundred British Army personnel and a handful of Royal Navy personnel, there were the Aden Protectorate Levies and a further two thousand local civilian personnel, who all travelled on and off base each day. The levies had been locally raised to protect the Aden Protectorate from infiltration by neighbouring states and to act in support of the RAF on the landward side of Aden, and the local civilians were employed on base as clerks, MT drivers, waiters and cooks, or were employed as labourers in family hirings and married quarters. Indirectly, Khormaksar also helped local trade and brought the remotest parts of the protectorate within easy reach of Aden.

Beetham was keen to fly with all his units so that he could get to know his personnel better and gain a greater understanding of the vital role that each squadron played. He first flew with 105 Squadron to Eastleigh in the suburbs of Nairobi in Kenya, which was the RAF's main operating base for the East Africa region, for a two-day visit. He was also keen to see the local area, including the Radfan, and first flew in a Hunter, then in a Belvedere helicopter and then a Twin Pioneer on a sortie lasting more than four hours that took him around some of the more remote landing sites at Thumier, Table Top, Paddys Field, Monks Field, Dhala, Khora and Mudia.

He soon familiarised himself with much of the region and, using an Argosy of 105 Squadron, visited Makhnuq, Riyan, Salalah, Masirah, Sharjah and Bahrain. However, closer to Khormaksar, the troubles further up country towards the border with Yemen had intensified, and the number of operational sorties flown by the Strike Wing increased month by month in response to an increasing number of requests for air support; these sorties were a mix of armed patrols, strike missions, armed reconnaissance sorties and general military presence over the ground, as well as providing airborne escort duties for the Communications Flight Dakota into and out of Beihan. Keen to further his experience of the operational situation in this part of the region, Beetham then flew on a Beihan patrol in a Hunter T7 of the Strike Wing.

Everyone at Khormaksar had to live with the constant threat of terrorism. Two days before Christmas a grenade was thrown into a teenager's party at the married quarters of Wing Commander John Teager, the commanding officer of 105 Squadron, which resulted in the death of sixteen-year-old Gillian Sidey, the daughter of the principal medical officer, Air Commodore Ernest Sidey. Gillian had only arrived in Aden two days earlier to spend Christmas with her family. Several more children were injured in the attack, including the son of the Commander-in-Chief Middle East, Sir Charles Harington.

It turned out that John Teager's batman, who had been away on leave in the Yemen at the time, was responsible. The police informed Beetham and also told him of their plan to arrest the batman on his return to the base. Beetham then informed Teager, who could not believe what he was hearing; as far as Teager was concerned, the batman had always been a loyal and reliable servant to his family. Nonetheless, Beetham told Teager that he was to assist with the plan and when the batman turned up for work he was to act as if nothing untoward was about to happen. By the time the batman returned to Teager's house the RAF Regiment had already surrounded the house and the batman was promptly arrested; he later confessed to carrying out the attack.

Another terrorist attack occurred during a formal dinner at the officers' mess at Steamer Point. Beetham was sitting at the top table and was being served wine when a bomb was thrown onto the table. The bomb landed in the soup plate of a squadron leader, who immediately shouted in a loud voice 'DOWN!' and everyone immediately took cover under the table. There was chaos in the dining room as the bomb went off but the squadron leader's warning meant that no one was killed or even seriously injured. This incident was traced to the receptionist in the officers' mess and resulted in an immediate review of the security arrangements in place at Steamer Point, particularly regarding the employment of civilians. After this attack the station commander was removed from post because there had been no extra security precautions put in place for the dinner.

These two incidents highlighted the problem of hitherto loyal servants who had families in the Yemen and gave the security forces a very difficult problem to deal with. Furthermore, the destruction of a DC-3 Dakota of Aden Airways on the ground at Khormaksar in May – almost certainly another act of sabotage – resulted in extra vigilance on the airfield with more security fencing installed around each of the aircraft pans to prevent any further sabotage taking place. Beetham also introduced new security regulations, which allowed native labourers only to work on aircraft when under strict individual supervision, but the base would always remain vulnerable to terrorist attack.

The risk of attack was largely held in check by the use of ground forces patrolling base areas and vantage points to the north of the airfield, as well as by frequent security patrols flown by helicopters. Beetham had appointed a security officer, Squadron Leader Mike Wright, whom he met with every day, and Beetham was always mindful of the fact that the combination of Khormaksar's location and the number of civilians working on the base meant that the best he could do was to deter, as best he could, any terrorist threat against the base.

As there was only one RAF Regiment squadron permanently established at Khormaksar, with the responsibility of covering a large area with so many vulnerable points, a second Regiment squadron was detached to Khormaksar on a four-month rotational basis. Eventually the RAF Regiment could no longer meet the commitment and so the detachment was later replaced by an army company, which for one detachment included a company from the York and Lancaster Regiment, his father's old regiment, which enabled Beetham to renew his acquaintance with the regiment and he was delighted and honoured to present regimental roses to the unit on its regimental day during a parade held at Khormaksar.

Beetham always carried a personal weapon when he travelled around in his Land Rover on base. He also introduced random searches by small teams of personnel, where an area would be cordoned off and everyone inside the cordon was searched. By doing this many times in different locations he sent a strong message to the civilian population that any potential terrorist faced the risk of being caught. Furthermore, he was also keen to ensure the guarding commitment was shared by all of his airmen on base – typically each airman would do a twenty-four-hour guard shift approximately every seven days. He also insisted that social functions ended at 11 p.m. Furthermore, if there was a social function in the officers' mess it was up to the officers on base to provide adequate guards; Beetham did not want his airmen guarding the officers while they socialised. Similarly, functions at other messes or clubs involving the other ranks, whether they were non-commissioned officers or airmen, would be guarded by personnel of equivalent rank.

While these may not have been popular decisions, they ensured that every serviceman at Khormaksar soon realised that security was everyone's responsibility. However, even with these protective measures in place, there was still a mortar attack on the base during Beetham's time as station commander, when a mortar fired from north of the airfield landed near a visiting Belfast parked in the centre of the main aircraft parking area, although fortunately the mortar landed in a sandy area nearby and there was no damage to the aircraft.

One horrific example of the continued threat against civil aircraft occurred the following year when another DC-3 Dakota of Aden

Airways was lost after crashing during a scheduled flight from Meifah to Aden. The aircraft was reportedly blown apart by an explosive device believed to have been carried in hand luggage; thirty passengers and crew were killed.

One of Beetham's key responsibilities as the station commander was to meet and act as host to the many senior officers and civilian dignitaries who were either visiting the region or passing through en route to other destinations. Some were more notable than others, but there would usually be at least one or two important visits per month. For example, during a short period in 1965 he hosted the air member for supply and organisation, Air Marshal Sir John Davis, the King and Queen of Malaya, the new Chief of the Defence Staff, Field Marshal Sir Richard Hull, a two-day visit from the C-in-C, Lieutenant General Sir Charles Harington, and the AOC, Johnnie Johnson, and then there was the farewell visit of the retiring Chief of the Defence Staff, Admiral of the Fleet Earl Mountbatten of Burma, followed the next day by a visit from the inspector general of the RAF, Air Marshal Sir Augustus Walker.

Beetham had no intention of being tied to Khormaksar, even during this eventful period, and so in between these high-profile visits he managed to visit Eastleigh, Salisbury, Bulawayo, Waterkloof, Embakasi, Habilayn, Ataq, Djibouti and Mombasa. It was an extremely hectic time for him, but he still managed to fly with all of his squadrons and units, and he managed to maintain his flying currency as aircraft captain on the Argosy, Beverley, Andover and Shackleton. It was also an extremely busy period for Khormaksar. In July alone the station handled twenty-two different aircraft types, a total of 117 visiting aircraft, which were all transiting through the base.

Because the RAF's scheduled Comet flight to Singapore staged through Khormaksar twice a week, Beetham was only required to meet and host the senior air officers, such as members of the Air Force Board, or ministers; for other visitors he could delegate the hosting responsibilities to other officers on base. When outbound from the UK to Singapore the Comet used to land at around 11.30 p.m. and depart at 1 a.m., and when inbound it would land at around 3.30 a.m. and depart again at 5 a.m. This meant that Beetham was often up during the night, and occasionally the aircraft's departure would be delayed, which meant that his hosting duties became even longer. Rather fortunately for Beetham, the Sudanese later banned over-flights and the Comet's route was then changed, which meant that it staged through Muharraq, Bahrain, rather than Khormaksar. Beetham was pleased.

In fact he rang the station commander at Muharraq to wish him good luck and from then on the amount of hosting he was personally required to carry out reduced significantly for the rest of his tour.

There was always much to do as the station commander, and many duties involved his wife too as she became totally immersed in her responsibilities. Serving overseas was a way of life and everything was provided for the servicemen and their families. There was the Aden Forces Broadcasting Association to provide entertainment and news from the UK and around the world. Much of the welfare work for the families was centred on the thrift shop, various wives' clubs and the youth club, and the children of the service families attended one of the three schools on base.

By October the troubles further up country had started to quiet down. Apart from a handful of operational sorties flown by the Strike Wing, for the rest of the month they concentrated on training sorties and a detachment to Masirah for two weeks to take part in an exercise. In November Beetham hosted an important visit from Lord Beswick, the parliamentary under-secretary of state for the colonies. As part of the work for Denis Healey's defence review, the Labour government had suggested that it was not essential for Britain's interests in the Middle East to maintain a British presence in Aden. This information was not public knowledge at the time, although it would be announced in the Defence White Paper that followed, and Lord Beswick was given the unenviable task of explaining Britain's decision throughout the region and to explain why Britain would be leaving Aden in 1968. As things turned out, the decision by the British government not to sustain a British presence in South Arabia led to the situation in the region deteriorating more than expected, resulting in the federation collapsing in less than two years and an earlier British withdrawal date of November 1967.

On 11 November 1965, Ian Smith unilaterally declared independence from the UK to become the first prime minister of Rhodesia under a white-dominated government. This created a major problem for the British government, and the prime minister, Harold Wilson, turned to the United Nations. The Security Council then imposed economic sanctions that involved British warships blockading the port of Beira in Mozambique and Shackletons from Khormaksar deployed to the French airfield at Manjunga in Malagasy to support the blockade in an attempt to cause economic collapse in Rhodesia.

In the UK, sections of public opinion demanded that the regime was toppled by force. Wilson, however, declined to use military force, believing that the British population would not support such action; besides, he could not have expected British forces to fight against the Rhodesians, given that many members of the armed forces, particularly those in the region, had friends in Rhodesia.

This period saw the start of much air activity at Khormaksar, including the arrival of a detachment of Javelins. Beetham went to visit the Shackleton detachment, but the political situation would remain unresolved and the detachment remained at Manjunga for the rest of his tour. In fact, the matter remained unresolved for several years and Ian Smith remained as prime minister during white minority rule until 1979, when, after a long civil war, Britain resumed control for a brief time before granting independence to the country in 1980, when the country became recognised as Zimbabwe.

The end of 1965 saw a change in senior appointments in the region. First, Sir Charles Harington made a farewell visit to Khormaksar before he departed the Middle East, and a week later the new C-in-C, Admiral Sir Michael Le Fanu, made his first visit to the base. Then it was the turn of the AOC, Johnnie Johnson, to leave. A formal dinner was held in the officers' mess at Khormaksar, led by Beetham, with the highlight of the evening taking place after dinner, when the AOC departed the mess in a large model Spitfire, painted in the 'JE-J' personal markings of the former fighter ace, pulled by the officers of the station as their goodbye to a most popular and legendary AOC. The following week Johnson carried out his final inspection of the station before leaving Khormaksar on 14 December. The ceremonial flypast was provided by eight Hunters of 8 Squadron that joined up to make the letter 'J'.

The following week, Johnson's successor, Andrew Humphrey, visited the station for his first formal visit as the new AOC. Operational activities now increased once more and the Strike Wing flew a number of supporting missions for 45 Royal Marine Commando during December around the areas of Dhala, Habilayn and Wadi Taym. Again, Beetham was keen to experience the roles played by his units in support of operations in the region. He had first flown up to Habilayn in a Wessex the previous month and he returned to Habilayn twice during the period of operations in December – first in a Twin Pioneer of 78 Squadron and then in a Beverley of 84 Squadron, when he landed at Dhala to spend some time on the ground with his personnel.

The operational tempo dropped off in the New Year and so Beetham managed to get away to Africa for a few days in an

11. Bidding farewell to the AOC and legendary fighter ace Johnnie
Johnson at the officers' mess at Khormaksar, 7 December 1965

Argosy of 105 Squadron. He first flew to Eastleigh and after a night
stop he flew on to Blantyre in Malawi, then to Matsapa Airfield at
Manzini in the British Protectorate of Swaziland, where he spent
two nights before flying back to Blantyre and Eastleigh once more.
After another night stop he flew on to Djibouti before making the
short transit back to Khormaksar. Also during early 1966 Beetham
faced one of the many diverse problems that he became involved
with as the station commander. A strike by Shell workers restricted
delivery of aviation fuel to a daily ration at the base, which had
an impact on the station's flying programme, but fortunately the
strike did not last long.

During his tour at Khormaksar Beetham worked almost every
day and rarely took time off, but he did enjoy a game of golf.
Whenever the opportunity arose he would fly the weekly Argosy
schedule to Eastleigh, flying in the left-hand seat of the aircraft
but always making sure there was another captain on board to
complete the routine clearances. Once at Eastleigh he would go
straight to the golf club and play a round of golf and after a night in
the officers' mess he would get up the following morning and play
a further round before returning to Khormaksar later that day. It
was the perfect combination of flying, golf and a night in Nairobi!

For his annual leave he chose to travel down to Kenya with his family rather than return to the UK. They would fly to Nairobi and then hire a car and drive down to Malindi on the east coast, just to the north of Mombasa, where they stayed at a leave centre for servicemen in Aden run by the NAAFI, from where they explored the coastline and the national parks, spending hours observing the fantastic wildlife, as well as spending time in Nairobi. The Beethams also got on extremely well with the Johnsons and Le Bas and the three couples would occasionally get away for a weekend together. All this provided a wonderful break from life in Aden and gave Beetham the opportunity to spend more time in Africa, a continent he had grown to love.

During his final six months as station commander Beetham took every opportunity to fly with his units as often as he could. He returned to Africa twice more during the spring and continued his visits by helicopter and Twin Pioneer to the more remote areas of Dhala, Habilayn, Monks Field, Wallan and Awahbil. The operational intensity had increased once more, just as news of his promotion to the rank of air commodore was announced.

There had been a period of relative quiet, but the Hunters of the Strike Wing flew more than two hundred operational sorties during August – more than in any month since the Radfan operations had first commenced over two years before, following a border infringe-ment and the strafing of the Nuqub border area by Yemeni-based Migs. These attacks occurred about two hundred miles to the north-east of Khormaksar, but patrols by the Hunters soon put an end to border infringements and nothing more of the Migs was seen.

The Aden Emergency would last for another year until British forces eventually withdrew from South Arabia and the independ-ent People's Republic of South Yemen was proclaimed. There was never a moment when Beetham took his eye off the operational situation in the region. Nor was there ever a rest from the seem-ingly never-ending number of visits that he had to host, or from the numerous ceremonial parades and activities he was required to take part in.

In his final weeks as station commander he hosted a visit from the Imperial Defence College, which coincidentally was to be his next destination as he had just been informed that he had been selected for the next course starting in January, and he then started to prepare to hand over to his successor, Group Captain Desmond Browne. The Beethams were then dined out from the officers' mess during a formal guest night held on 19 October with the AOC, Andrew Humphrey, the senior guest.

It had been a truly memorable tour, and Beetham's last duty was to unveil a plaque at the Provost and Security Flight's Club to mark the opening of the club's extension dance floor. During the ceremony the station security officer, Squadron Leader Mike Wright, presented him with a portrait cartoon drawn by one of the senior non-commissioned officers in commemoration of the occasion. An unexpected diversion occurred when a kilted piper from the 1st Battalion Cameronians mounted the wall of the club and, silhouetted against the night sky, played haunting old 'Highland Pibroch'. It was a most fitting farewell. The piper then descended to the dance floor and played 'Strathspey' and other reels while guests and members of the club joined in some spirited dancing. The Beethams left the club in a car that was towed in the traditional style by stalwart members of the Police Flight, headed by the piper playing 'Bonnie Prince Charlie's Farewell'. It was yet another night to remember.

12. Beetham stands on the dais as nine Hunters from the Strike Wing fly past in a letter 'M' as Khormaksar says goodbye to him, 1 November 1966.

On 1 November it was time to leave Khormaksar. After saying their goodbyes, the Beethams went down to the airfield ready for their departure. A flypast of nine Hunters from the Strike Wing, led by Squadron Leader Des Melaniphy of 8 Squadron, formed up in the letter 'M' and flew over the airfield with Beetham standing to attention on the dais, dressed in civilian attire for the journey home, as Khormaksar said its final goodbye to Air Commodore Michael Beetham.

Beetham had enjoyed a very good tour as station commander of the largest station in the Royal Air Force, which was also the most diverse. He was faced with a major security situation on the station and much turbulence with the war in the Radfan and the political crisis in Rhodesia. It was certainly demanding but he enjoyed the challenge and he always believed that being a station commander was the most satisfying tour of an RAF officer's career.

CHAPTER 8

To the Stars

Having returned to the UK, Beetham had a few weeks to find
somewhere in London to live and to get settled before his course
at the Imperial Defence College. Fortunately, a member of the
Foreign Service, whom he had met on the previous course visiting
Khormaksar, had been posted to the Far East and had a house on
Kew Green that he wanted to let. It suited the Beethams perfectly.
Facing the green and backing onto Kew Gardens, it was in a lovely
position. It was only two hundred yards from the main entrance
to the gardens and they could enjoy an evening walk there for just
three pence. Furthermore, it was only two miles from the Royal
Mid-Surrey Golf Club, a very prestigious and well-known club that
Beetham was only too glad to join. Travel too was easy, a fast train
service from Richmond to Victoria Station and then a short walk to
Belgrave Square.

Not only was it good to be back in England; Beetham soon found
out that he was to be appointed as a Commander of the Order of the
British Empire in the New Year's Honours list for his work as station
commander at Khormaksar during what had been a very turbulent
time. The announcement came as a complete surprise to him and
a few weeks later he was presented with his CBE by the Prince of
Wales at Buckingham Palace.

Located at Seaford House in Belgrave Square, the Imperial
Defence College was an internationally renowned institution that
prepared senior military officers of the UK and other countries
– as well as non-military future leaders from other sectors and
countries – by developing their knowledge of defence, international
relations and security, and strategic vision. Only one course was
run each year, with up to eighty students on each course. When
Beetham joined the 1967 course in January he found himself among
some familiar faces. The other members of the course were from a

variety of backgrounds, including the Royal Navy, the British Army, the Ministry of Defence, the Diplomatic Service, the Ministry of Overseas Development, the Ministry of Technology and the Board of Trade; the overseas students were from the USA, Australia, New Zealand, Canada, India, Pakistan, Malaysia, Jamaica, Nigeria, Sierra Leone and Ghana.

The commandant was General Sir John Anderson, the former military secretary, and he was supported by two-star directors from the other services. Beetham found the lectures and discussions both fascinating and rewarding. It was also a more relaxing working environment than that he had experienced at Khormaksar during the Aden Emergency. The course was conducted in three terms, with the focus being on defence and international relations, but everything Beetham encountered was at a much more strategic level than he had encountered before. During the early weeks there were daily lectures and presentations from senior British military officers, senior civil servants and even government ministers. These sessions ranged enormously, from lectures on global instability and how to prevent armed conflict to general discussions on the more familiar national defence and political issues at home in the UK. Beetham found that he gained most from the course during the questions and discussion periods that followed each presentation, in particular by listening to the views of the presenters as well as his colleagues on the course.

During the spring term there was a tour of various military establishments of all three services, including a trip at sea on a submarine, and visits to a number of industrial and political establishments as well as a three-day visit to Northern Ireland. In the summer term the course discussed international issues from a strategic perspective, after which the course was divided into three smaller groups for an overseas visit during August and September. Although a visit to either the USA or the Middle East was on offer, Beetham instead elected to go to Europe; he had, after all, spent so much time in both of the other regions and he personally felt he had more to gain from a visit to northern Europe.

The tour of northern Europe lasted a month and took him to West Germany, Norway, Sweden, Finland and Poland. Beetham found the visit to Poland the highlight of the tour. Not only was it his first visit to the country, it was the first time that a military visit of this type had been allowed behind the Iron Curtain. While in Poland the IDC students were given a fair amount of freedom; it felt to Beetham that their Polish hosts were a little unsure of exactly what to do with them. They were certainly free to wander around Warsaw, although the students were warned that certain areas where they were staying might well have been bugged.

One interesting discussion followed a presentation to the course by a young Polish lieutenant colonel about Poland's involvement during the Second World War and the country's subsequent relationship with Russia. What made it particularly fascinating was that many of the course members had fought alongside the Poles during the war, whereas the young Polish officer was too young to have served in the war and his views seemed somewhat clouded by the post-war influence of Russia on Poland.

While there were no visits to any Polish military bases, the IDC students did visit the beautiful old city of Krakow and then the former Nazi concentration camp at Auschwitz. This was to be Beetham's one and only visit to a concentration camp; he found it to be an unforgettably horrific and quite sickening experience. The infamous long wrought-iron sign above the entrance to the camp with the words *Arbeit Macht Frei* (translated to mean 'Work Sets You Free'), a collection of personal belongings such as shoes, spectacles and false teeth, and the buildings and the chimneys, were all stark and very sad reminders of the atrocities that had taken place there during the Second World War. It had an extremely strong impact on Beetham, but not only on him: on the Argosy flight back to the UK it was obvious just how much the visit had affected all the other students as well. It was a sombre way to end the tour.

The students returned to Belgrave House for the final term. There were further lectures and discussions on leadership in a strategic environment, followed by a visit from the Queen and Duke of Edinburgh towards the end of the course when they attended a discussion period on 'Britain in Europe', during which the Duke of Edinburgh made some pertinent points. For Beetham the course passed very quickly and he found it had been a most enjoyable and valuable year, and a great sabbatical after the challenges of Aden. He had gained an important insight into strategic thinking at home and overseas, and he had built a good network of contacts, both military and civil servants, from the UK as well as from overseas nations. He had found the IDC course to be conducted at a leisurely pace, rather as he imagined university to be, and he had made many friends – particularly those from overseas who liked to play golf, whom he had managed to introduce to the Royal Mid-Surrey Golf Club during the course.

Like Beetham, many students on the course would go on to achieve senior appointments and he would meet up again with many of them throughout the rest of his career. He always took his IDC tie with him whenever he travelled overseas as he found it was often recognised at social functions and it always provided a good introduction to any conversation.

Beetham's next appointment was at the Ministry of Defence and, for the time being at least, he was able to continue living at Kew. It was January 1968 when he walked into Main Building to start his appointment as director of Operational Requirements 3, but this was not a position he had particularly asked for because he had always preferred to be in front-line appointments rather than in a headquarters or at the MOD. Nonetheless, he had enjoyed a good Christmas break after finishing IDC and he now felt ready for the next challenge.

It had been twelve years since Beetham had left Whitehall at the end of his squadron leader tour as OR1a in 1956, and so much had happened since. One major change had occurred in 1964 when the Air Ministry merged with the Admiralty, the War Office and the Ministry of Aviation to become the Ministry of Defence. The final piece of the jigsaw would not be completed until 1971, when the function of the Ministry of Aviation Supply also merged into the MOD organisation.

The formation of the Ministry of Defence meant that the RAF was no longer administered by its own ministry and it now came under the Air Force Department of the MOD. What had previously been the Air Council had now become the Air Force Board, which was the single-service element of the Defence Council that was given responsibility of the day-to-day running of the RAF.

In a period of financial savings and changing policies, there had been a number of other organisational changes and reductions in manpower and equipment overseas. Furthermore, a number of major equipment programmes had been cancelled, such as the TSR2 and then later the F-111. Then, following the Defence White Paper of 1966, came the most significant change to the organisational structure of the RAF when it was announced that in April 1968 Bomber Command and Fighter Command were to merge into a single command, Strike Command, with its headquarters at High Wycombe. From then on the units previously under Bomber Command would come under 1 Group and the former units of Fighter Command would come under 11 Group.

The merging of Bomber Command and Fighter Command into Strike Command was not the only change in command structure. Transport Command, in existence since 1943, was renamed Air Support Command in August 1967 and Flying Training Command and Technical Training Command were to merge to become Training Command in June 1968. The RAF was getting smaller in terms of number of aircraft and manpower, and by the end of 1968 its strength would be around two thousand aircraft and 120,000 personnel. This meant that its equipment had to be of the highest quality for the service to maintain its capability in all roles, and it was against this background that Beetham began his appointment as DOR 3, taking over from Air Commodore John Downey.

Beetham was one of three air commodore directors working in Operational Requirements for the Assistant Chief of the Air Staff (OR), Air Vice-Marshal Derek Hodgkinson. As DOR 3 Beetham was responsible for 126 new equipment programmes, an extremely complicated task, and although he had three deputy directors working for him, he soon became totally immersed in the highly complex world of technology and equipment capability, working closely with industry and dealing with a myriad of companies on a daily basis in an attempt to understand fully the complex equipment programme. As always, he worked very hard in his new appointment, but he did not overly enjoy it. He was also frustrated by continuous attempts to further strengthen the Ministry of Defence's 'centre' at the time, which had originated during Mountbatten's time as the Chief of the Defence Staff just a few years earlier. From the OR perspective things had certainly changed from his previous tour at the Air Ministry during the mid-1950s when he had been looking after the RAF's programme without the need to report to a central staff. Now he had to write papers to persuade the centre, and this entailed much greater effort and required more staff.

Although Beetham fully expected to complete his tour as DOR 3 he did not remain in the appointment very long. He was extremely fortunate when another one-star appointment came his way following the posting of the director of Strike Operations. Although it had never occurred to him that he could change appointments at the MOD, he was delighted when the Deputy Chief of the Air Staff, Sir Peter Wykeham, informed him that he was to move across into Strike Operations. The reason was quite simple: Beetham had vast operational experience whereas the new air commodore posted in, Air Commodore J. A. Allan, had more technical experience, and so it was decided that Allan would move into the DOR 3 post so that Beetham could be released to take over as the director of Strike Operations.

In November Beetham moved offices and took over his new appointment. He was delighted at his change of post but also felt the need to apologise to all the industrialists who had spent the last ten months getting to know him and, quite rightly, had expected more continuity in the post. This rather fortunate, and completely unexpected, move within the MOD was probably another one of those defining moments in his career. His new appointment was certainly higher profile than his previous one and he felt far more comfortable in the operational arena than in operational requirements. The change in appointment also coincided with a domestic move to Latimer House in Notting Hill as the Beethams had to give up their rented accommodation in Kew following the return of the owner to London, and his new appointment meant that it was now necessary for him to be closer to the MOD's Main Building.

As director of Strike Operations, Beetham worked for the Assistant Chief of the Air Staff (Operations), Air Vice-Marshal Peter Horsley. Although Horsley had been in his appointment for just a matter of six months he immediately showed complete trust and confidence in Beetham's ability and delegated his responsibilities accordingly. This suited Beetham perfectly.

It was an exciting time and one of the most significant dates was 30 June 1969, when the responsibility for Britain's strategic nuclear deterrent passed from the RAF's V-force to the Polaris submarines of the Royal Navy. The year also saw the introduction into RAF service of some new, and very capable, combat aircraft. In May the two-seat American McDonnell Douglas Phantom FGR2, which could be used in fighter, ground-attack and reconnaissance roles, was introduced into service at Coningsby, followed soon after by the Phantom FG1 at Leuchars in Scotland. In July the single-seat Hawker Siddeley Harrier GR1, which could take off vertically from very basic operating strips, entered service at Wittering, and then in October the two-seat Blackburn Buccaneer S2B low-level maritime strike aircraft entered service at Honington. It was not only the new combat aircraft that had enhanced the RAF's capability towards the end of the 1960s. Brize Norton in Oxfordshire had become home to the RAF's new transport aircraft, the Vickers VC10 and Short's Belfast, which operated under Air Support Command's 38 Group. Coastal Command had already been subsumed into Strike Command, as 18 Group, and 1969 saw the first Hawker Siddeley

Nimrod MR1 maritime patrol aircraft enter service at St Mawgan in Cornwall. Keen as always to fly whenever possible, Beetham managed to get his first flight in the Nimrod in November.

There were also more new aircraft on the way. The Anglo-French Jaguar, which had initially been designed in response to Britain's requirement for a two-seat supersonic jet trainer, had first flown in September 1968 and would eventually enter service with the RAF as a single-seat ground-attack and reconnaissance aircraft. In March 1969, the three countries involved in the Multi-Role Combat Aircraft project – Britain, Germany and Italy – announced the formation of Panavia GmbH to manage the project; this would eventually lead to the two-seat Tornado, which entered service with the RAF ten years later. Both aircraft design and technology were moving at a pace and the RAF had come a long way since Beetham had first flown the Lancaster a little over a quarter of a century before.

One of Beetham's main responsibilities as director of Strike Operations was operational policy. Plans were emerging for Air Support Command to merge into Strike Command to form a single UK-based operational Strike Command by the early 1970s (this would eventually happen in 1972) and the RAF was in the process of withdrawing from a number of overseas bases following the Labour government's announcement in 1967 to withdraw British forces deployed east of Suez. The RAF had already withdrawn from Beetham's former base at Khormaksar and in Singapore had started withdrawing from its bases at Changi, Seletar and Tengah as the Far Eastern Air Force began to wind down towards its planned disbandment date of October 1971.

As the commitments in the Far East and Middle East reduced, the RAF's commitment to NATO and the defence of Western Europe steadily increased – in particular the expansion of RAF Germany, a separate command of the RAF under Air Marshal Sir Christopher Foxley-Norris. In June 1970 the first Harriers moved in to Wildenrath and within a few weeks the first Phantoms moved in to Bruggen.

Beetham worked closely with all the commands, in particular Strike Command, and during his tour he was fortunate to visit America, Australia and New Zealand to attend various conferences. Then, after nearly two years as director of Strike Operations, it was time for him to move on once more. He had worked tirelessly to ensure that the RAF retained its capability in all its roles at a time when the political focus was on efficiency and financial savings.

Having been an air commodore for four years, at the age of forty-seven, he was now being looked at for further promotion.

Beetham knew there were two-star appointments about to become available – at Air Support Command, as SASO, and at Bracknell as the commandant of the RAF Staff College. He was sure in his own mind that, if promoted, his next appointment would be as SASO at Air Support Command because his colleague, Neil Cameron, who was already an air vice-marshal, was also due for a change in appointment and was interested in becoming the next commandant of the Staff College. Beetham believed that Cameron was the most likely successor at Bracknell and so it came as a complete surprise to him when he was sent for by the air secretary, Air Marshal Sir Gareth Clayton, and told that he was to be promoted to the rank of air vice-marshal and appointed as the next commandant of the RAF Staff College at Bracknell.

Having completed his own staff training at Andover in 1953, the RAF Staff College at Bracknell was essentially new to him. He had been there before but it was a proud moment when he took over as commandant in September 1970. He and his wife moved in to the commandant's residence of Brookham House, named after Robert 'Henry' Brooke-Popham, the first commandant of the Staff College at Andover. Now they had their own staff and it was a vast difference from the residence they had just vacated in Notting Hill.

Beetham relished the challenge ahead. He now enjoyed the benefit of having an ADC, Flight Lieutenant Peter Jones, for the first time in his career to assist him with his daily administrative tasks. Bracknell had by this time absorbed the elements of the RAF's other Staff College at Andover, which had closed the previous year after it had been decided that there was no need to retain both colleges. As the commandant, Beetham reported directly to the air member for personnel and to the Air Force Board, and was responsible for the policy of the course, setting and maintaining its high standards and for managing Bracknell's directing staff, or 'DS' as they were known to the students. His deputy commandant was initially Air Commodore Bob Freer and then Air Commodore Jock Kennedy.

The course essentially followed the same format that Beetham had undergone several years before: the organisation and structure of the RAF; lectures on all aspects of warfare, including land and naval warfare; staff work focusing on written and oral communication skills; the role of NATO within the modern world, and in particular its relationship with Eastern Europe during the Cold War; the study of previous conflicts and various discussions on political and economical relationships, plus many more lectures and presentations that would all help the students to become a competent staff officer in their own organisation.

There was one course per year, and the first of the combined Bracknell/Andover courses in 1970 had 180 students in total, including the overseas students and the students from the other services. The course started in January and ended in December, which meant that when Beetham took over as commandant in September the course in residence at the time was entering its final term. This was a UK-only part of the course, when the content was at a higher security classification, which meant that the overseas students had now left Bracknell and had been replaced by the incoming overseas students for the next course; these arrived around the same time as Beetham so that they could conduct their introduction to the UK during the final months of the year before starting the next course in January.

Beetham sat in on all the main lectures and presentations, hosting the guest speaker and summing up each discussion period at the end. Once the 1971 course started in January he was able to sit through the whole course and observe it closely for himself. He knew that the new Chief of the Air Staff, Air Chief Marshal Sir Denis Spotswood, was keen to shorten the Bracknell course to six months. The course had been shortened before, during the Second World War – when it had been little more than two months – and it was felt by some members of the Air Force Board that the course should be reduced once again. Many of those who had completed their Staff College training during the war felt that it was good enough for them in the 1940s and so it should be good enough for the students of the 1970s. Beetham categorically disagreed and he personally favoured the course as it was. The Air Force Board decided that a study was required to look into the length of the course and its content, and it was commissioned and directed to look at the feasibility of a course lasting six months. Beetham could not stave off the study team and he knew that the existing course of twelve months could not last, so he proposed a course of nine months instead, which retained all the essential elements of the course. He also proposed the establishment of a shorter Basic Staff Course, which would be completed earlier in an officer's career, and these proposals would later be adopted.

Beetham very much valued the course and its content. His primary aim was to teach the students to think logically and to express themselves in good English while broadening their own knowledge and understanding of the services. He fully appreciated what it had taught him some twenty years earlier and felt that the fact that he had become a better staff officer was very much down to what he had learned during his training at Staff College. He also enjoyed spending time with the students, whether it was in the lectures and presentations as part of the course or during the many social functions he was required to attend or host; with 180 students on the course there were numerous functions hosted by the Beethams at Brookham House. Many of his students went on to achieve high rank within the service, most notably Michael Graydon and Richard Johns, who both went on to become Chief of the Air Staff.

The time spent at Bracknell proved to be a most settled way of life for Beetham's family. For once they could plan their holidays well in advance and he only spent short periods away from home on visits. The best were the exchange visits to the staff colleges in America and Canada. So settled were the Beethams that after eighteen months at Bracknell they decided to get a dog as a family pet. Beetham did not expect a move for at least another year and, having discussed his likely future with the air secretary he found out that there were no plans to post him overseas again and so he bought a West Highland terrier.

With hindsight he should have known better and ironically his decision to buy a dog was followed by an overseas posting soon after. As soon as the West Highland terrier had settled in to Brookham House the Chief of the Air Staff, Sir Denis Spotswood, called for Beetham. During their brief meeting, Spotswood explained to him that for some time he had wanted a senior RAF two-star officer presence in the Supreme Headquarters Allied Powers Europe at Mons in Belgium, and that a new post for the RAF had just come available as Assistant Chief of Staff (Plans and Policy). It was a post that had previously been held by the Canadian Army but Spotswood did not want to let the opportunity go and felt that Beetham was the right man to fill the post, and so with just three weeks' notice Beetham was posted to SHAPE and the dog stayed behind with friends!

NATO is a military alliance that was established by the signing of the North Atlantic Treaty on 4 April 1949. A year earlier the UK had signed the Treaty of Brussels with four other nations – Belgium, France, Netherlands and Luxembourg – but following the Soviet blockade of Berlin later that year it was felt that a new alliance that

included the USA was required to deter any likely expansion of
Soviet military power. This led to the North Atlantic Treaty, which
included the five nations of the Treaty of Brussels plus Canada,
Denmark, Iceland, Italy, Norway, Portugal and, most significantly,
the USA. Following the signing of the treaty the Allied nations
asked the USA to designate an officer to become the Supreme Allied
Commander Europe and in 1950 General Dwight D. Eisenhower was
appointed as NATO's first SACEUR. He set up his headquarters,
known as SHAPE, at Rocquencourt, near Paris, in April 1951.

The principle of the Alliance has always been a system of collective
defence where its members agree to mutual defence in response to
any attack made by an external aggressor. In the early years NATO
was little more than a political association, but the member states
were galvanised during the 1950s following the Korean War, and
soon afterwards Greece, Turkey and West Germany joined the
Alliance. In response, the Warsaw Pact, which was led by the Soviet
Union, was signed in 1955 by seven other nations: Albania, Bulgaria,
Czechoslovakia, East Germany, Hungary, Poland and Romania.

NATO's unification was to be tested by the French president,
Charles de Gaulle, during the late 1950s and early 1960s as France
pursued an independent deterrent. In 1966 France removed its
military forces from NATO's integrated command and, although
France remained a member of the Alliance and committed to the
defence of Europe, all non-French NATO troops were asked to leave
France by April 1967. General Lyman Lemnitzer, SACEUR at the
time, had hoped that SHAPE could be located near to the NATO
headquarters in Brussels but because it would be a major wartime
target the Belgian authorities decided that SHAPE should be at
least fifty kilometres from Brussels and so offered Camp Casteau, a
Belgian Army training camp near Mons, instead.

Having left the Staff College at Bracknell in the capable hands of
the deputy commandant, Jock Kennedy, Beetham made the journey
across the Channel and took over his new appointment in August
1972. He and his wife took over their house in Chemin Fer, about a
mile from SHAPE, from the outgoing Canadian Army major-general.
Their children, Lucinda and Alexander, then aged fourteen and eleven
respectively, remained in boarding school in the UK but took every
opportunity to travel to Belgium during the school holidays so that
the family could be together and spend time exploring Europe.

Working in a senior NATO appointment was unfamiliar territory
for Beetham but he quickly adapted to his new surroundings and

he enjoyed being overseas once more. As Assistant Chief of Staff (Plans and Policy) he was involved in just about everything within the headquarters that involved planning for any potential conflict or war. He worked for the three-star Deputy Chief of Staff, Lieutenant General Karl Schnell of the German Army (who would later be replaced by Lieutenant General Josef Schultz) who, in turn, worked for the four-star Chief of Staff, General Russ Dougherty of the US Air Force, and ultimately for SACEUR, General Andrew Goodpaster. Goodpaster had been SACEUR since July 1969 and was often referred to as the soldier scholar having studied at Princeton University in New Jersey, where he received an MA in Engineering, after which he went on to receive his PhD in International Affairs. Deputy SACEUR was a British general, Sir Desmond Fitzpatrick, who had previously commanded the British Army of the Rhine and the Northern Army Group, and had been in post as DSACEUR since December 1970.

Although Beetham worked for the German three-star DCOS, he was considered the policy and plans expert and he soon found that his day-to-day working relationship was direct to COS, General Dougherty, and to SACEUR. Beetham had a deputy, Rear Admiral George Steel, a US Navy officer who had been the first Polaris submarine commander to surface at the North Pole. Beetham quickly realised that Steel was an extremely high-calibre officer and a man he would get on with very well; Steel would often keep him informed of the outcome of the many US-only meetings that took place in the headquarters. Beetham also had an executive officer, Lieutenant Colonel Carl Smith of the US Air Force, another extremely high-calibre officer who would eventually reach the rank of lieutenant general.

The North Atlantic Alliance periodically conducted major reviews, from which it would adapt its policies to accord with the changing circumstances of the times. When Beetham took up his appointment in 1972 he inherited NATO's integrated defence policy for the 1970s following the Defence Planning Committee's decision to examine NATO's integrated defence in depth for the next ten years. The outcome was that NATO's approach to security in the 1970s would continue to be based on the twin concepts of defence and détente, and the principle was reaffirmed that the overall military capability should not be reduced except as part of a mutual reduction in forces. Although there was evidence of the Soviet Union increasing its military capability and strengthening its political power during the late 1960s and early 1970s, there was a mood of optimism regarding relations between the North Atlantic Alliance and the Warsaw Pact as it was genuinely felt there was a real possibility of a relaxation of tensions between the two powers.

The transition from a period of confrontation in East–West relations to a period of negotiation meant that it was even more essential to preserve the cohesion between the member countries of the Alliance. Beetham realised that the Alliance was facing the need to adapt to a changing international scene, and Europe would have to make a larger defence effort in order to relieve the USA of much of the burden. He was also aware that the Soviet Union had more or less achieved strategic nuclear parity with the USA, and this would have a bearing on the defence of the European continent.

At the time that Beetham took up his appointment it was hoped there would be continued success in the Strategic Arms Limitation Talks. An increasing number of missiles were being deployed with multiple independently targetable re-entry vehicle warheads, which made anti-ballistic missile defence difficult and extremely expensive. This led to SALT 1, which froze the number of strategic ballistic missile launchers at existing levels and provided for the addition of new missile launchers only after the same number of older launchers had been dismantled. Talks that had started in Helsinki in November 1969 concluded in Moscow in May 1972 when US President Richard Nixon and the leader of the Soviet Union, Leonid Brezhnev, signed the Anti-Ballistic Missile Treaty and an interim agreement between the USA and the Soviet Union, which limited strategic offensive weapons to help improve relations between the two superpowers.

SALT 1 was a significant step forward but it was felt in NATO that the position of the Alliance during any continued period of negotiation regarding security in Europe and mutual force reductions would be weakened if NATO reduced its forces, particularly those in Western Europe. Therefore, the NATO strategy of deterrence and defence, with the concept of flexibility in response, remained valid and required an appropriate mix of nuclear and conventional forces.

Strategic nuclear capability remained a key element in the security of the West throughout the rest of the 1970s, but the situation in respect of conventional forces was considered less satisfactory regarding the imbalances between NATO and Warsaw Pact capabilities. Warsaw Pact forces were estimated to total more than five million men, and the estimated strength of the Soviet Air Force was about 12,500 aircraft, of which 7,000 were fighters and nearly 3,000 were bombers of various types.

NATO possessed adequate conventional strength, but Beetham was aware that the member nations had varying trends in expenditure and costs, as well as major re-equipment programmes to consider, which meant that careful consideration was needed to determine how to improve NATO's conventional forces over the next few years, with priority being given to the defence of the Alliance in terms of deterrent effect. The important areas in NATO's conventional defence posture included better mobilisation and reinforcement capabilities, enhanced communications, further improvement in the defence of NATO's flanks and the peacetime deployment of ground forces. Beetham also realised the importance of close collaboration among the member nations to ensure NATO adopted the most cost-effective defence posture and that each nation should make an appropriate contribution to maintaining the necessary military strength.

The activation of some Soviet and US forces as a reaction to the Arab–Israeli War of October 1973 provided a timely reminder that the danger of a sudden crisis was still very real, and also provided justification that NATO should not relax its defence efforts. There had, however, been some very positive developments in Europe, such as the recognition of the German Democratic Republic by the Allied nations, the normalisation of relations between the Federal Republic of Germany and Czechoslovakia, Bulgaria and Hungary, as well as visits by Brezhnev to Berlin and Washington.

For Beetham, these were exciting times. He shared the view that the commitment of substantial US forces in Europe was essential for effective deterrence, both politically and militarily. He also felt that NATO's move away from massive retaliation, which had been its previous policy since the early 1950s, to the policy of flexible response, which NATO had adopted as its strategy in 1967, was correct. Having the policy of flexible response meant that NATO could call upon any, or all three, of its main options available – a conventional response, a tactical nuclear response or a strategic nuclear response – depending on the size and nature of any attack. However, conventional capacity had to be built up, which meant that national targets had to be set, but help was given to the smaller nations for their equipment programmes.

The post of policy and plans was undoubtedly a major one in the headquarters. Every meeting attended by SACEUR that involved Beetham's area of responsibility meant that Beetham went too; he would usually sit immediately behind SACEUR at the meeting table so that he could easily provide comment or advice when required. His close working relationship with SACEUR meant that he got to know Goodpaster very well, and he was fortunate to be present during many top-level discussions, where he gained a valuable insight into decisions being made at the highest level within NATO.

The Alliance marked its twenty-fifth anniversary in 1974 with the adoption by ministers of a Declaration on Atlantic Relations, which reaffirmed the commitment of all members to the Alliance and set its course in the light of new perspectives and challenges of a rapidly changing world. The essential elements had not changed but the effects of the energy crisis generated by events in the Middle East the year before had become increasingly pronounced, with a four-fold increase in the exported price of oil coinciding with a shortage of certain raw materials. In December, ministers met in Brussels and discussed the implications of the economic situation for the maintenance of Allied defence and reaffirmed their determination to seek appropriate solutions through co-operation.

It was also in December 1974 that Goodpaster was replaced by General Alexander Haig, who would remain as SACEUR until 1979. A veteran of the Korean and Vietnam wars, Haig had previously served as the Vice-Chief of Staff of the Army, the second-highest appointment in the US Army, and had also served as the White House Chief of Staff during the Watergate Affair. He was widely credited with playing a key role during the time President Richard Nixon was preoccupied with Watergate, and then during the subsequent transfer of power from Nixon to Gerald Ford. Having remained at the White House during the early days of the Ford administration, Haig was then replaced by Donald Rumsfeld in September 1974. After the Nixon debacle, and the appointment of Ford as president, Goodpaster was removed abruptly as SACEUR and Haig was appointed his successor.

When news of Haig's appointment circulated around SHAPE there were some concerns because Goodpaster was considered to be a very capable commander and was extremely well liked by his staff. Haig, on the other hand, was less well-known among senior military staff, and there were concerns about his experience and ability to command NATO forces in Europe. Somewhat unusually, there was to be no great change of command ceremony because Goodpaster did not want to be involved in one and so his departure was relatively low key. The deputy SACEUR, General Sir John Mogg, a British Army officer who had replaced Sir Desmond Fitzpatrick, then assembled the senior staff and emphasised the importance of showing loyalty to the new SACEUR, General Haig, and to put to one side any rumours they had heard or personal thoughts they might have about his experience or ability to command.

Beetham had no prior knowledge of Haig and so he had no preconceived thoughts one way or the other, but he did wonder what sort of man Haig would prove to be and he was not sure how well he would be received in his new appointment. However, he did not worry for long. When Haig arrived at SHAPE he addressed his staff and spoke for fifteen minutes, without reference to any notes. His address went down extremely well, particularly amongst those who had doubted his ability to be SACEUR; it was a quite brilliant opening address. After Haig's opening address Beetham spoke to one of the interpreters, whom he knew quite well, and who had been translating Haig's speech into French. A copy of Haig's opening address had been given to the various interpreters and his colleague made the point that Haig had spoken almost word perfectly for the fifteen minutes, without any reference to his speech or notes whatsoever. Such was Haig's ability as a speaker.

During the next few weeks Haig visited all his staff, including those at the lower levels who did not normally get the chance to meet SACEUR. Everywhere he went Haig would listen to what people had to say and he communicated to them in a way they understood. Haig was immediately seen as a very personable individual and he took no time at all to win over his staff. Beetham personally witnessed Haig's performance at several meetings during his early days as SACEUR and he was in no doubt of his ability; Haig was very knowledgeable and extremely sharp, and he took no time at all to settle into his new appointment. He was helped enormously by his deputy, Sir John Mogg, whose sound common sense and even temperament tended to balance the more direct approach of Haig.

As far as Beetham was concerned, the change in SACEUR made little, if any, difference to his daily responsibilities and commitments. He was glad that Haig understood the importance of the plans and policy post and, like his predecessor, Haig took Beetham with him whenever his input or advice was required; Beetham had, after all, been in post for more than two years and was by then one of the most experienced and knowledgeable officers in the headquarters.

By the end of his tour Beetham had gained a valuable insight into the daily workings of the Alliance at the very highest levels. Much had been done to build up NATO's conventional forces in accordance with the strategy of flexible response and much had been achieved, not least in the hardening programme of NATO's airfields and the considerable improvements in communications. This had involved many visits and meetings during which he had gained valuable experience of working with many senior officers of the other nations within the Alliance. Despite the fact that his appointment had been made particularly busy because the Americans worked such long hours – including Saturday mornings, which Beetham felt did not mean that any greater efficiency was achieved – and even though most nations tried to push their own national interests, Beetham still believed that NATO planning worked well.

Beetham found his NATO tour to be an enjoyable and interesting experience. He found that most of the staff work was done by the Americans and British because of the language factor, but there were many capable officers from other nations – the Germans and Dutch in particular. He found working with many of the Mediterranean and Scandinavian nations to be very interesting and also enjoyed the social side of serving with NATO when each nation, on their national day, would give a most enjoyable party.

Some years later Beetham met up with General Russ Dougherty in Washington and, talking over dinner about their time together at SHAPE during the 1970s, Dougherty informed him that Sir Denis Spotswood, then the Chief of the Air Staff, had visited him at a time when he was keen to secure the transfer of the ACOS (Plans and Policy) post to the RAF. During their conversation Spotswood had told Dougherty and SACEUR that he was sending him a top-quality man called Beetham who was destined to be the future Chief of the Air Staff. This had helped secure the post for the RAF but had been completely unknown to Beetham at the time and Dougherty never told him of this during their time together at SHAPE – but Spotswood would prove to be right.

CHAPTER 9

RAF Germany

————

Beetham returned to the UK in the spring of 1975 ready to take up his next appointment as Deputy Commander-in-Chief Strike Command on promotion to the rank of air marshal. He had been informed of his promotion by the air secretary during his final months at SHAPE and was naturally delighted. He had certainly hoped to be in with a chance of a three-star appointment, but he had wondered whether he might instead be considered for the appointment at the Air Headquarters in Cyprus or in RAF Germany. What came next, though, was even better news. The Chief of the Air Staff, Sir Andrew Humphrey, then informed Beetham that he would not be at Strike Command very long, probably only about six months, because he was being lined up to be the next Commander-in-Chief RAF Germany. This was excellent news as it was the appointment Beetham really wanted, but for the time being the news about Germany had to remain quiet as the formal announcement would not be made until later in the year.

As news of the new Deputy C-in-C circulated around Strike Command, the Beethams initially moved into married quarters at Bradenham Beeches. However, this was only a temporary arrangement as the Deputy C-in-C's official residence, Merton House, had just been refurbished, although it would be three months before they were able to move in. Their children were still at boarding school and the move to High Wycombe meant that the family would be able to spend more time together, at least for the time being. They were also reunited with the family West Highland terrier who had been looked after by friends during their time away at SHAPE.

In June Beetham took over as DCINCSTC from Air Marshal Sir Peter Horsley. By the time Beetham took up his appointment Strike Command had completed its amalgamation with Air Support Command to form a single operational command. Strike

Command was the fighting element of the RAF and had the operational responsibility for all RAF units at home and overseas, apart from RAF Germany. It was also an integral part of NATO to the extent that the AOC-in-C Strike Command, Air Chief Marshal Sir Denis Smallwood, was a major subordinate commander under SACEUR and held the NATO title of C-in-C UK Air Forces, known as CINCUKAIR.

Essentially, Strike Command's two main tasks were to defend the UK's airspace and to provide combat-ready forces for NATO in accordance with approved plans or as directed by SACEUR. As the deputy commander, Beetham effectively acted as the Chief of Staff to Smallwood and to assist him he had a personal staff officer, Squadron Leader Roger Sweatman.

For the time being Beetham put thoughts of Germany to one side and began a tour of Strike Command bases. This period gave him the opportunity to become up to date on the RAF's front-line activities and, in particular, to familiarise himself with aircraft such as the Jaguar, Phantom and Harrier, all of which would soon operate under his command in Germany. He first flew in a Jaguar T2 during a visit to Coltishall, then a Phantom FGR2 during a visit to Coningsby, and he flew a Harrier T2 during a visit to Wittering. He also managed a nostalgic flight in the Lancaster of the Battle of Britain Memorial Flight during a visit to Coltishall in November. It was the first time he had flown a Lancaster for nearly twenty-five years and the first time he had flown PA474 since 1951 when he served with 82 Squadron in Africa. When he landed, the crew chief asked him how it had felt to fly the Lancaster again after so many years, to which Beetham replied that he had noticed two things in particular. First, there were no coffee stains in the cockpit and everything was immaculately clean and, second, when he had pressed the starter button the engines had started immediately!

Beetham thoroughly enjoyed his visits to the Strike Command bases but he personally found it rather awkward as he knew the arrival visit at each base was also his farewell visit, although he could not say anything at the time. While he managed to visit as many stations as he could during his six months as DCINCSTC, his main responsibility was to stand in for Smallwood when he was out of office and so Beetham spent most of his six months in the headquarters at High Wycombe.

At the end of the year there was more good news when Beetham found out that he was to be appointed as a Knight Commander of the Order of the Bath in the New Year's Honours List of 1976. He was now Air Marshal Sir Michael Beetham KCB CBE DFC AFC. Then, on 19 January, and having handed over his responsibilities at Strike Command to Air Marshal John Stacey, he boarded an Andover VIP transport aircraft at Northolt that had just returned his predecessor, Air Marshal Sir Nigel Maynard, to make the short flight to Wildenrath to take up his appointment as Commander Second Allied Tactical Air Force and Commander-in-Chief RAF Germany. Travelling with Beetham on the flight was his wife and his new ADC, Flight Lieutenant Mike Winning, and on arrival he was met by his deputy commander, Air Vice-Marshal Bill Bailey and the station commander, Group Captain Leech.

The appointment of Commander 2 ATAF was invested in the C-in-C RAF Germany. The origins of 2 ATAF date back to the end of the Second World War, when the RAF's Second Tactical Air Force became the British Air Forces of Occupation. After a post-war reduction in the RAF's commitment in Germany the situation changed in the early 1950s following the breakdown in relations between East and West, and the RAF went through a period of expansion in Germany once more as part of its commitment to NATO. 2 ATAF was formed to direct its air forces operating in support of the Northern Army Group, NORTHAG, and then RAF Germany was formed in 1959 as a peacetime command; in time of war the RAF assets would be allocated to 2 ATAF. In addition to units of the RAF, 2 ATAF was made up from the air forces of Belgium, Netherlands and West Germany. Its operational area of responsibility extended from Denmark in the north, south-west across the North Sea, then south-eastwards along the Franco-Belgian border to the northern point of Luxembourg, then north-eastwards to Kassel and then northwards along the eastern borders of the Federal Republic of Germany.

Understanding exactly where 2 ATAF fitted into the organisation of NATO during the mid-1970s is not helped by a rather over-complicated NATO command structure. Responsibility for providing central control of all the NATO air forces operating in the Central Region of Europe was that of Allied Air Forces Central Europe, AAFCE, with its headquarters at Ramstein in Germany. AAFCE's task was to co-ordinate the two air headquarters of 2 ATAF at Rheindahlen, in the northern part of the Central Region, and 4 ATAF at Ramstein, responsible for the south. AAFCE was a subordinate command of Allied Forces Central Europe, AFCENT, with its headquarters at Brunssum in the Netherlands, which in turn reported to Allied Command Europe, ACE, with its headquarters at SHAPE in Belgium, responsible for the land area extending from the North Cape to North Africa and from the Atlantic to the eastern border of Turkey, but excluding the UK and Portugal, whose defence did not fall under the responsibility of any single major NATO command. Overall responsibility for the defence of the Allied countries within his area of command was that of the Supreme Allied Commander Europe, SACEUR, under the general direction of NATO's Military Committee, the highest military authority in the Alliance. Also reporting to SACEUR under the NATO command structure was CINCUKAIR, at High Wycombe, the Commander of the Allied Command Europe Mobile Force (Land) at Seckenheim in Germany, and the two other principal subordinate commanders – the Commander-in-Chief Allied Forces Northern Europe, AFNORTH, with his headquarters at Kolsas in Norway, and the Commander-in-Chief Allied Forces Southern Europe, AFSOUTH, at Naples in Italy.

From a national perspective, HQ RAF Germany was responsible for the operational training of its units and for providing them with administrative and logistical support. In 1976 the RAF had four main operating bases in Germany, all in North Rhine-Westphalia. RAF Gütersloh was the furthest east and the other three, known as the 'Clutch' airfields, were all located along the German–Dutch border – RAF Bruggen, RAF Laarbruch and RAF Wildenrath.

Because of the nature of Beetham's dual appointment, he would often have to give priority to his NATO commitments and so the responsibility for the daily running of RAFG was delegated to his deputy commander, Bill Bailey, whose responsibilities were essentially those of an AOC as the number of stations and squadrons in RAF Germany were broadly comparable to those under the command of a two-star group commander in the UK. Bailey knew Germany very well, having previously commanded Wildenrath and having been SASO at Rheindahlen before he was promoted and appointed as the Deputy C-in-C, but he was not due to remain in Germany much longer and he would soon hand over to his successor, Air Vice-Marshal Tim Lloyd. As Commander 2 ATAF Beetham had additional staff led by the Deputy Chief of Staff, Air Commodore C. Gaiger Broad, which consisted of a Joint Secretariat (Air), an Exercise Plans and Operations Analysis Division, Offensive and Defensive Operations Divisions, a Plans and Policy Division, a Communications and Electronics Division, a Logistics Division, a Personnel and Administrative Division and a Budget and Finance Division.

Understandably, there was much media interest in Beetham's appointment as the new C-in-C, particularly because his arrival coincided with that of General Sir Frank King, the new Commander-in-Chief of BAOR and Commander NORTHAG. As Commander NORTHAG King was in a four-star NATO command appointment but, as far as King and Beetham were concerned, this made no difference whatsoever. Right from the start the two men got on extremely well together as they generally shared the same views when it came to matters of British military policy in Germany and both held the same strong views when it came to Britain's support to NATO.

The day after Beetham's arrival in Germany there was an official parade at the Joint Headquarters to mark his and King's arrival. As Beetham was in the car on his way to the parade Winning received a message to say that one of the eight flights, formed from four different nations as a guard of honour, was missing. Beetham was keen to find out which formation was absent and so Winning had to inform him that it was the RAF flight that was missing! Beetham was not impressed and, although the absence of one flight from the guard of honour did not detract from the occasion, once the event was over those involved with the arrangements were invited to Beetham's office to explain exactly why the RAF flight was missing. It turned out to be a matter of timing. The RAF flight had not been formed up at the right time and had been starting to gather around the corner when the parade had started. It had been a simple, but somewhat embarrassing, error of mistaking local time with Zulu time (GMT): the one-hour time difference meant the RAF flight had thought they still had another hour to go before the parade!

Beetham's office was in the Joint Headquarters at Rheindahlen, near Monchengladbach, although wartime operations would be conducted from the Joint Operations Centre at Maastricht just across the Netherlands border. Rheindahlen was a large non-flying base established after the Second World War as the military support centre for the Second Tactical Air Force, and within the headquarters there were both NATO and national staff. Although there was a common entrance to the headquarters, the building was configured so that the army was on one side, with the multinational staff of NORTHAG working on the top floor directly above the national staff of the British Army of the Rhine, and on the other side of the building was the staff of 2 ATAF, working directly above the staff of RAFG. Beetham and King had adjoining offices, with a small sitting room in between where they could host their visitors either together or separately as required. While there might have been occasions in the past when the two commanders in post at the time had not got on particularly well, and the adjoining doors had been kept locked, this was not the case for Beetham and King: their excellent working relationship was evident for all to see. They took it in turns, on a six-monthly rotational basis, to act as the senior hosting or briefing officer whenever the occasion required and there was a small baton which passed between them when the responsibility was transferred from one to the other.

Adjoining Beetham's office was the deputy commander's office and Beetham's outer office, where his PSO and ADC were located, and there was also a small team of RAF administrative staff led by a flight sergeant. His PSO was Squadron Leader Peter Harding, a Canberra and Vulcan pilot, who had been in post eighteen months, having already been PSO to Sir Nigel Maynard. His experience as PSO would provide valuable continuity during Beetham's early weeks in command. Beetham's approach was more formal and meticulous than what Harding had been used to with Maynard but he found Beetham to be extremely personable. One thing that stood out straightaway was how quickly Beetham could grasp detail and gain an understanding of any particular issue, and one of Harding's main responsibilities was to make sure that Beetham was thoroughly prepared ahead of any meeting or occasions when he was asked to speak, and so he soon got used to preparing many speeches and briefing notes.

The ADC, Mike Winning, was thirty-two years old and was only the second RAF Regiment officer to become an ADC. His main responsibilities were to make sure that Beetham was in the right place at the right time and in the appropriate uniform or civilian attire. This involved booking the necessary transport and accommodation, and to make sure that Beetham was as well briefed and prepared as possible. These responsibilities also extended to Beetham's wife, who often accompanied her husband on many official engagements as well as performing other duties on her own, and Winning's responsibilities included making the domestic arrangements for the many social engagements that took place at the Beethams' residence, Air House.

Air House had been provided by the Germans under war reparations and had first been occupied by the RAF more than twenty years earlier when Air Marshal Sir Harry Broadhurst was the C-in-C Second Tactical Air Force. Beetham had a staff of seven – three RAF stewards, two German house maids and two cooks. There were enough rooms to host three VIP couples at any one time and during their time in Germany there would be many occasions when the Beethams would be required to entertain visitors at Air House as well as to host many dinner parties and other social gatherings.

Just three days into his tour Beetham hosted his first visit – a two-day visit to RAFG by the leader of the Conservative opposition, Margaret Thatcher. Thatcher had risen to political power after the Conservative Party had lost the general election of October 1974. This was the first of many meetings with her and it was immediately obvious to Beetham what a strong leader she was and how much she would support the armed forces if elected as prime minister. During her stay at Air House Beetham took the opportunity to find out her views on military policy, both in Germany and elsewhere. Thatcher was very much aware that even after a period of détente the armed forces of the Soviet Union were still increasing with no sign of reductions. She believed that Western Europe needed to stand united and its armed forces should be strong enough to deter any aggression, and through NATO and the USA it should

13. Enjoying an informal moment with the Conservative Party leader, Margaret Thatcher, during her visit to RAF Germany on 22 January 1976, *just* three days after Beetham assumed command

drive towards a common purpose – the pursuit and preservation of liberty. Thatcher's vision differed from others who believed the Cold War could not be won and that the future lay in détente between the superpowers, but her vision was not one of eternal stalemate. She believed the foundations of communism, particularly in the modern day Europe, were at fault and that communism would eventually be forced to recognise its own failure. She would be proved right.

Later in the week Beetham conducted his first official visit to Wildenrath. Located just six miles to the south-west of Rheindahlen, Wildenrath had been the first of the RAF's 'Clutch' airfields to open in 1952 as part of the expansion of RAF and NATO forces in Germany. It was now home to three squadrons of Harrier GR3s, although two of the squadrons would soon move to Gütersloh and be replaced by two squadrons of Phantoms, and the third squadron would re-form at nearby Bruggen with Jaguars. Also based at Wildenrath were a handful of Pembrokes that were used as communications aircraft and for transporting senior officers around RAF Germany. As the C-in-C Beetham had the use of a Pembroke and one of the squadron's pilots whenever required, and he would fly the Pembroke many times throughout his tour. The Pembroke was not his only form of air transport and he often used a Wessex or Army Scout helicopter when travelling from Rheindahlen when he had many engagements in one day or if the Pembroke was not suitable for the task.

Already conversant with much of the German scene from his years at SHAPE, Beetham was now in charge of one of NATO's main air forces, and much of his early period in post was spent attending to his NATO responsibilities. Whenever possible during their early weeks in their respective commands Beetham and King would call on the other NATO commanders in the region together. These included a visit to the Commander-in-Chief Allied Forces Central Europe, CINCENT, General Dr Karl Schnell, and his Chief of Staff, Lieutenant General van Ardenne, at Brunssum in the Netherlands. For Beetham there were many other office calls and meetings with his NATO colleagues, notably the Deputy CINCENT, Air Chief Marshal Sir Peter Le Cheminant, the Commander Allied Forces Baltic Approaches, Lieutenant General Veggars, and the Commander Allied Air Forces Baltic Approaches, Major-General Brodersen.

Berlin, seen by Beetham under somewhat different circumstances more than thirty years before, required regular visits too as he was also the air commander of the British Sector. Unlike the RAF's four main operating airfields in Germany, RAF Gatow in Berlin did not operate any combat aircraft and its use was limited to supporting transport aircraft in and out of the city. As the C-in-C, Beetham had a second residence in Berlin, High House, situated high up on a hill overlooking the suburbs of the city, provided by the Germans at no cost to the British taxpayer. All the food was provided but not the drink, and the facility came complete with German staff and a Mercedes car including driver.

Beetham made his first visit to Gatow within his first month in Germany and met with the general officer commanding Berlin (British Sector), Major-General Roy Redgrave, and then returned to Berlin at the end of March to meet the Berlin mayor, Herr Klaus Schutz; he also took the opportunity to fly in a Chipmunk with the station commander to view Berlin from the air. During his visits to Berlin Beetham would often find the time to go across to the Eastern Sector to go to the opera with his wife and friends. Dressed in his formal mess uniform, there would be silence as they passed through 'Checkpoint Charlie', and once on the Eastern side he could not help but notice the stark difference between West Berlin, which was a thriving, busy, modern and prosperous city, and East Berlin, which seemed run-down, dirty and with very few new buildings; the only people who seemed to be smartly dressed were the orchestra and conductor at the opera in their gleaming white tie and tails.

Although Beetham's NATO responsibilities would take up much of his time he was keen to visit his RAFG bases whenever he could. The command's overall effectiveness had been considerably improved by the introduction of aircraft such as the Phantom FGR2 and the Buccaneer S2B, which had initially taken over the roles of the Canberra, and the introduction of new aircraft such as the Harrier and Jaguar. Having already visited Wildenrath, Beetham now visited the two other Clutch airfields close to his headquarters at Rheindahlen. Laarbruch, about thirty miles to the north, had been the last of the Clutch airfields to open in 1954 and was now home to two squadrons of Buccaneer S2Bs and a squadron of Phantom FGR2s. He then visited Bruggen, ten miles to the north-west of Rheindahlen, which had already taken delivery of its first Jaguar GR1s and within the next year the total number of Jaguar squadrons at Bruggen would be four.

One reason why Beetham always enjoyed visiting Bruggen was because it had a magnificent golf course, the vision of Harry Broadhurst while he was the C-in-C twenty years before. His driver was a top-class and well-known golfer, and Broadhurst had wanted a golf course at Bruggen, but because any new construction on RAF bases in Germany was provided by the host nation he could hardly ask for a golf course; instead he asked for the construction of eighteen emergency landing strips with areas of sand along each strip to put out any fires!

Beetham also visited Gütersloh, about a hundred miles to the north-east of Rheindahlen. Gütersloh was the only RAF airfield east of the river Rhine and was about a hundred miles from the East German border. It was home to two squadrons of Lightning F2s, although both of these squadrons would leave Gütersloh at the end of the year to make way for Harriers. Also at Gütersloh was a squadron of Wessex HC2 helicopters and from the end of 1976 the main role of the Gütersloh squadrons would be to support the British Army and HQ 1 (British) Corps at nearby Bielefeld. Beetham also took time to visit the RAF Support Unit at Decimomannu in Sardinia, which came under the responsibility of RAF Germany, and many of the other smaller units under his command as part of RAF Germany.

As Commander 2 ATAF, Beetham had an indigenous offensive force of just over four hundred aircraft, with a fairly even contribution from each of the four member nations. In the ground-attack role there were the RAF's Harriers, Jaguars and Buccaneers as well as German Phantoms and G91s and Dutch NF5s, which all offered varying operational capabilities. In the reconnaissance role there were RAF Jaguars, Belgian Mirages and Dutch F104s. During any time of conflict Beetham could expect reinforcements of RAF Jaguars and Phantoms, and augmentation from the US Air Force, including A10s, Phantoms and F-111s, some of which would operate permanently under 2 ATAF while others would be allocated for specific periods by COMAAFCE. This would bring the total number of offensive aircraft available to just over seven hundred, which would give 2 ATAF the ability to initially mount up to fifteen hundred offensive sorties per day. However, there was one major weakness in the inventory: a lack of significant indigenous night all-weather capability in either ground-attack or reconnaissance, and this would remain the case until the Tornado Multi-Role Combat Aircraft became available at the end of the decade.

While 2 ATAF was a formidable force, it faced a significant threat from the Warsaw Pact. Beetham was fully aware of the recent dramatic increase in performance, range and striking power of the new generation of tactical combat aircraft with which the Warsaw Pact had been steadily re-equipping in the forward area; these included the Mikoyan-Gurevich Mig-21 Fishbed J, which was the first aircraft to have a demonstrable capability in both offensive and defensive roles; the Mig-23 Flogger, of which there were estimated to be 350 in the forward area, all possessing an offensive capability; the Sukhoi Su-17 Fitter C; and the Su-24 Fencer, which was similar to the F-111, with an estimated fifty aircraft already facing the region.

Despite its capabilities Beetham also believed the Warsaw Pact had its limitations. Its pilots generally flew significantly fewer hours per month and flew to far higher weather minima than NATO's pilots. The Warsaw Pact also did little or no training at low level and its command and control structure was more rigid; if it were to be degraded, as it would in time of war, there was little evidence of much inherent flexibility. Furthermore, he was in no doubt that 2 ATAF had a higher standard of training, quality and skill.

One of Beetham's initial concerns was how to co-ordinate the operations of his own force with those of 4 ATAF under US command further south. He believed it was essential for his own forces to be able to operate in 4 ATAF's area as well as their own and vice versa, and to exploit the reinforcements and other resources which he hoped would be made available during a time of conflict. However, there appeared to be a fundamental difference between his and US thinking when it came to employing air power. This was possibly due to the large number of air assets available to 4 ATAF: from Beetham's perspective there always seemed to be US forces available in significant numbers, often with greater capability than those assets available to him. However, he was always adamant that 2 ATAF should remain under a British commander, with the RAF influencing the tactics and procedures rather than the Americans. For Beetham and 2 ATAF it was a matter of prioritisation, but he also felt it was essential that there should be better co-ordination and co-operation between the two air forces, which meant regular visits to his US counterpart at Ramstein.

Close links were necessary with NORTHAG too, and this was helped by the very close friendship that Beetham had developed with Frank King, who had repeatedly impressed Beetham during joint exercises with his strong leadership and firm grasp of tactics at every level, ranging from NATO's strategy in Europe to the tactics employed on the battlefield at unit level. Beetham knew a number of army generals and in his own mind always assessed them on how he thought they would have performed on the battlefield against a general such as Rommel during the Second World War, and he had so much respect for King that Beetham was convinced he would have seen off Rommel, or any other general for that matter.

While Beetham was satisfied at 2 ATAF/NORTHAG headquarters level, and that true joint planning of the land/air battle had never been so well integrated, he felt there were some who had yet to be truly converted, and that in some quarters there still existed an underlying cynicism that the army and RAF would prefer to go their own separate ways. He also felt that the term 'air support' was still regarded by some in the army as 'close support', but – as virtually every type of air action would see 2 ATAF operate in support of NORTHAG – he was keen for the army to understand there was a wide range of air options available under the heading of 'air support'. While the priorities were unpredictable, each option would have an immediate or near-immediate effect on the land battle. In other words, the forward air-controlled close-support mission was not the only valid form of air support, nor was it necessarily the most effective use of the limited tactical air resources.

Beetham gave a presentation to 1 (British) Corps on 'Air Support for NORTHAG', during which he was able to dispel some myths about what air support meant, brief the audience on the wide range of air options available under the heading of 'air support' and reinforce his own message of the importance of 2 ATAF's support to the army. He always welcomed such opportunities as both 2 ATAF and NORTHAG had far fewer resources available than he believed were required, and it was more important than ever that there was a clear understanding of each other's intentions, capabilities and problems while at the same time being honest about their limitations. He was also keen to manage the expectations of the army in terms of response times when requesting air support as he sensed that some in the corps had come to regard the RAF's Harriers as their own dedicated air force.

Having briefed the audience on the capabilities of 2 ATAF and the threat it faced from the Warsaw Pact, Beetham concluded by emphasising three points. First, it was vital to make every sortie count and so selection of the type of air support mission had become increasingly critical. This required considerable flexibility to be able to respond quickly and effectively to a whole range of threat options, none of which could be certain. Secondly, 2 ATAF and NORTHAG should not fall into the trap of planning options and tactics without knowing how vulnerable they would be to large-scale air action because NATO could not afford the luxury of general air superiority and could not neutralise the Warsaw

Pact air threat completely. Thirdly, concerning the fundamental attitude towards the basic roles of the army and the RAF, and their interaction, Beetham stressed the importance of joint planning and consultation and the importance of the co-ordinated and integrated approach to the land/air battle. 'Jointness' did not imply a one-way street but an appreciation of the complete interdependence of the two sides of the battle that may have to be fought.

2 ATAF's lack of night-reconnaissance capability had remained a concern for King, which Beetham fully understood. Although in time of conflict 2 ATAF would be allocated US night reconnaissance, the response time between the aircraft's 'time on target' and the arrival of its mission report, known as the MISREP, was still too long – to the point that the information was of little use to the ground commander. This, again, had highlighted the need for better co-operation between 2 ATAF and 4 ATAF; during exercises it had become only too evident that the request for timely night reconnaissance had not received high enough priority. Beetham was, however, now in a position to reassure King and the matter was given more urgent attention. Various measures were being put in place, ranging from improving the communications between both air forces to looking at the possibility of 4 ATAF and UK-based US reconnaissance aircraft landing at 2 ATAF bases for sensor exploitation and a much more rapid receipt of the MISREP at NORTHAG and corps level.

There was also the important issue of airspace management or, to use its official NATO title, 'airspace control'. HQ AAFCE was in the process of finalising an Airspace Control Plan for the Central Region to give greater recognition to the problem and to make proposals for airspace-control measures within high-density airspace. This was important because it allowed combat operations, whether on land, sea or in the air, to be conducted without undue restrictions and with minimal adverse effect on the capabilities of the other air and/ or ground forces involved. Beetham was fully aware of the army's occasional frustrations, and indeed fully understood their point of view, but the problem was quite simple in that aircraft needed to operate safely and effectively in and through the battle area and at the same time allow ground forces maximum freedom to engage the enemy. It was vital, therefore, that procedures were put in place to make sure that friendly air assets were not shot down by the very people they were trying to assist.

As Commander 2 ATAF and C-in-C RAFG Beetham was a powerful figure in Germany because of the strong influence of the military at the time. Although there were the inevitable difficulties over low flying, which would necessitate regular contact with the various local communities, things generally were going very well. The RAF had improved its infrastructure in Germany during the mid-1970s, and the protection and hardening of its airfields, which had largely been paid for through NATO funding, were almost complete after a long programme that had seen the construction of fully equipped and hardened aircraft shelters, hardened operation centres and other key installations.

Beetham found that moving into the new hardened sites had improved morale on the squadrons, particularly among the ground crew, who could now, once again, work on their own squadron's aircraft in the hardened shelters rather than having to carry out aircraft maintenance through centralised servicing. There had also been improvements in other key areas, such as communications systems and the general toning down of all runways, taxiways, hard standings and buildings, in an attempt to blend the airfield in with the surrounding landscape. Effort had also been directed at defending the Clutch airfields with Bloodhound surface-to-air missiles at Bruggen, Wildenrath and Laarbruch, and the role of the RAF Regiment and its Rapier squadrons had also been developed to provide low-level air defence of all three airfields and for Gütersloh further east.

In addition to defending the airfields and the completion of the improved infrastructure and hardening programme, the tactical evaluation system, known as TACEVAL, was working well, although it was resource intensive. TACEVAL was NATO's way of testing the ability of its forces to transition from peacetime to wartime conditions and then to operate during a war. An evaluation team would descend on a station without any prior notice and during the TACEVAL – which could last several days – the team would simulate as many incidents as possible to disrupt the station's task progressively, such as obstructing or destroying part of the runway, disrupting communications or removing key personnel by simulating injury or death. At the end of the evaluation an assessment would be made of the station and each unit. While TACEVALs may not have been popular among station personnel, they did much for maintaining NATO's operational readiness. Beetham was not involved with the running of TACEVALs, nor would he visit a base during a time of TACEVAL because the station personnel would have enough to worry about already, but he was always interested in the results of each evaluation. He simply wanted the RAF to be the best when it came to evaluations and assessments within NATO, and this was often the case as the RAF always performed very well.

As well as the TACEVALs, there were many NATO exercises to increase the effectiveness and combat capability of the armed forces and to further the spirit of co-operation between the different nations. These were planned some months in advance to ensure the necessary forces were available and to give member nations the chance to co-ordinate national exercises with those of NATO. There were many different types of exercises and the number of forces participating varied from no live forces in the case of command post exercises, which were used to familiarise commanders and staff officers with likely wartime scenarios, to major exercises involving large numbers of forces from many nations.

Beetham used to spend much time thinking about Soviet intentions and capabilities and he and Frank King had the opportunity under a scheme called BRIXMIS to meet one of their Soviet counterparts, Army General Ivanovski Yevgeni Filippowich, the Commander-in-Chief Group of Soviet Forces Germany. BRIXMIS was short for the British Commanders'-in-Chief Mission, which had been set up after the Second World War as an agreement for a reciprocal exchange to foster good relations between the British and Soviet forces in occupied Germany. Each side took it in turns to host the visit every six months, at Rheindahlen or Potsdam, where the commanders would exchange pleasant conversation and gifts, which would usually include an exchange of whisky and vodka. Beetham would try to get his Soviet counterpart to talk openly during discussions but he rarely got very far and most of the time he would reminisce about his times flying Sturmoviks during the Second World War, talking with great animation and demonstrating his great hatred for the Nazis. While these visits were somewhat superficial, Beetham recognised their importance, given that NATO was working hard towards improving East–West relations.

It was now time for Beetham's PSO, Peter Harding, to move on as he was delighted to have been promoted and given command of 12 Squadron (Buccaneers) at Honington. Harding had thoroughly enjoyed his time as PSO and recognised how much he had developed while in Germany. He had got to know Beetham very well during the past nine months and, despite their great difference in rank, Beetham would often consult with him on various matters and ask his opinion. For Harding this was an invaluable part of his tour and this close working relationship helped him develop his own thinking, particularly on NATO strategy. He had been fortunate to accompany Beetham on the majority of his 2 ATAF visits and meetings, and this had given him a valuable insight into decision making at the highest levels.

Harding was replaced as Beetham's PSO by Squadron Leader Ian Macfadyen. The son of an air marshal, Macfadyen had flown Lightnings and Phantoms, and had just finished a tour as a flight commander at Leuchars in Scotland. Although he did not previously know Beetham, he knew Peter Harding quite well and recognised that a tour as a PSO would be a good opportunity to enhance his own career. He had obviously done enough to impress Beetham during his interview at Rheindahlen the previous month and he was now facing the challenge of being in his first ground tour as a staff officer. He needed not have worried. Macfadyen quickly settled in to life in Germany and he found working for Beetham to be quite straightforward. While he felt that Beetham was quite formal, it was always made clear to him what was required, and Macfadyen always knew where he stood.

Each morning there was a short briefing in the headquarters starting at 9 a.m. and lasting about twenty minutes. Occasionally Beetham would attend the briefing but it was usually run by the deputy commander, Tim Lloyd, and included the routine matters of weather, intelligence and any other matters of importance for the day. After the briefing Lloyd would update Beetham on any specific matters and then Macfadyen or Winning would be called into the office to receive any new tasks or to provide him with any staff work or briefings required for the day. After that Beetham generally left his staff to get on with their work and he would usually leave the office at the end of the day by 6 p.m. so that his staff could get away, and his evenings would depend on whether there were any planned social events to attend or if he had any additional work to attend to at home.

Macfadyen soon found there were some very helpful and extremely capable people around him in the headquarters. On 2 ATAF matters he was able to turn to the very capable Squadron Leader Dick Joyce, the PSO to the deputy commander, and to Wing Commander John Burns, who led the Secretariat, for all international matters and protocols. For matters involving the army he was ably assisted by General King's staff, in particular Lieutenant Colonel Dick Mundell and Mark Cook, the military assistant to the Chief of Staff BAOR.

Macfadyen soon realised just how meticulous Beetham was, with handwritten notes on all the actions that needed to be taken; this was all good experience for himself.

Beetham's winter leave during the Christmas break of 1976 was spent at the NATO establishment at Oberammergau in Bavaria, where his family enjoyed the excellent skiing conditions and other facilities on offer. There was to be no extended leave because early in the New Year Sir Andrew Humphrey made his first visit to Germany as the new Chief of the Defence Staff. During Humphrey's short stay in Germany Beetham entertained him at High House in Berlin, where they could reminisce about their time together in Africa and Aden as well as look forward to the future. Humphrey then went on to visit a number of army units and viewed the border with East Germany as well as visiting the Headquarters Allied Forces Central Europe at Brunssum. Although everything had gone well during the visit, the weather had been extremely cold and within days of leaving Germany Andrew Humphrey was taken ill. He was immediately admitted to the RAF Hospital at Halton but sadly died of pneumonia on 24 January at the age of fifty-six.

This tragic and premature death of one of the RAF's finest post-war leaders sparked a change in the higher appointments that would eventually lead to Beetham reaching the pinnacle of his career but, at the time, that never crossed his mind. He had lost a good friend. Humphrey's death led to the First Sea Lord and Chief of the Naval Staff, Sir Edward Ashmore, being temporarily appointed as the Chief of the Defence Staff to allow the RAF time to find a successor to Sir Neil Cameron, who had only recently succeeded Humphrey as the CAS, so that Cameron could be appointed as the next CDS to complete the remaining two years of the RAF's term; at that time the CDS appointment was a rotational post between the three services.

Understandably, thoughts turned to who might succeed Cameron as the next Chief of the Air Staff. While Beetham clearly hoped to become the CAS at some point in the future, he wondered whether he lacked the right experience, particularly at the Ministry of Defence, and thought he might have been considered a bit 'junior' in terms of rank and seniority. At that point he thought he might be in line to become the next air member for personnel and that it was probably too early for him to be a strong contender to be the next CAS. There were certainly other contenders to be the next Chief, and Beetham would occasionally discuss the subject with his good friend, Peter Le Cheminant. During one telephone call between them

Le Cheminant told Beetham that he felt it was a matter of whether the service would go for the 'old dog' (referring to himself) or the 'young lion' (referring to Beetham), and as far as Le Cheminant was concerned he clearly felt it would be the 'young lion'.

Then, during a very brief and private meeting with Cameron at Wildenrath, Beetham was informed that Cameron was putting his name forward to the secretary of state, Fred Mulley, to become the next CAS. Beetham was naturally delighted but Cameron also informed him that, although Mulley was in favour, there might be some objection from the parliamentary under-secretary of state for defence for the RAF, James Wellbeloved. This lack of support from Wellbeloved could only have followed his earlier visit to Germany when, despite the best efforts of Beetham, the two men had not warmed to each other. This was evident when Wellbeloved was due to visit Laarbruch one afternoon but during lunch he was informed that he would have to return to London early instead. While he might have shown some concern at having to cancel the rest of his visit to Germany, particularly given the amount of prep-aration that had gone into his visit at Laarbruch, which would now prove nugatory, he instead seemed more concerned about whether he would get his duty-free before boarding his flight home; this disappointed Beetham.

Soon after Beetham's meeting with Cameron, Mulley was visiting Germany and during a dinner party hosted by the British ambassador in Bonn, also attended by Beetham, Mulley took Beetham to one side and informed him that his name had been put forward by Cameron to be the next CAS, although Wellbeloved was not convinced. Mulley suggested to Beetham that he should 'butter up' Wellbeloved on his next visit to Germany in order to gain his support. In the end Well-beloved did not go to Germany and if he did formally object then it clearly had no bearing and Beetham was appointed as the next CAS.

On Wednesday 2 March 1977, *The Times* newspaper announced: 'Air Chief Marshal Sir Michael Beetham is to be the next Chief of the Air Staff from 1 August in succession to Air Chief Marshal Sir Neil Cameron who had been appointed CDS.' That same afternoon Beetham received a signal from SACEUR, General Alexander Haig, which read: 'Delighted to learn of your appointment to succeed Neil Cameron as CAS. Your steady leadership at Two ATAF had had a marked effect on the progress of the Alliance, for which you have my deep gratitude. You also have my warmest best wishes and solid support as you face the difficult challenges that lie ahead.'

Further letters of congratulations followed, not only from colleagues in the RAF but also from across the world. Beetham was naturally delighted at the news, but it would mean leaving Germany early and there was still work to be done. Jaguars now replaced the Phantoms in the ground-attack and reconnaissance roles so that the Phantoms could replace the ageing Lightnings for air defence. By April two Phantom squadrons had been established at Wildenrath, replacing two Harrier squadrons that had moved to Gütersloh; this move saw the development of new and highly mobile procedures for the Harrier force. With the ability to take off vertically, or with a very short take-off run, the Harrier offered NATO a unique capability, particularly when providing valuable support to ground forces. Without the need for a permanent airfield, the Harrier could operate on hastily prepared strips in woodland or dense forest, which made its operating site almost impossible to detect and meant that the Harrier force was less susceptible to attack from the air. The introduction of the Harrier GR3, with its uprated engine, radar-warning receiver and a revised nose design to accommodate a laser-ranging and marked-target seeker, was a significant improvement over the earlier GR1 and proved to be the ultimate development of the first-generation Harrier at the time.

Overseeing the move of the Harrier force to its new base at Gütersloh was among the last of Beetham's tasks as C-in-C. Mac-fadyen had noticed a change in him – he now seemed more relaxed, and Macfadyen found that he got to know Beetham very well during those final weeks in Germany. For Beetham the last weeks passed very quickly. In April he attended the NATO Chiefs of Air Staff visit to Ramstein and he then went on a NATO Air Chiefs Tour of the USA. During the visit the Chiefs visited the Headquarters Tactical Air Command at Langley, Virginia, where they were welcomed by the C-in-C, General Bob Dixon, and there were visits to the air force bases at Eglin (Florida), Tinker (Oklahoma), Nellis (Nevada) and Andrews (Maryland). There were also industry visits to General Dynamics at Fort Worth in Texas, where the Chiefs were given an up-to-date brief on the F-16 fighter, and to the Douglas Aircraft Company at Long Beach in California. Beetham was most impressed by the immense power and capability of the USAF, and Beetham was particularly impressed by the drive and dynamism that was being put into improving combat effectiveness and the measures being taken to exploit new technology. While he was disappointed not to catch up with General Russ Dougherty, who was now C-in-C Strategic Air Command at Offutt Air Force Base in Nebraska, he was pleased to meet up for a game of golf with his former executive officer at SHAPE, Colonel Carl Smith.

Back at Rheindahlen, Beetham hosted a two-day visit by the prime minister, James Callaghan. The first day of the prime minister's visit involved a trip to Bruggen with the chancellor of West Germany, Helmut Schmidt, before Callaghan visited JHQ at Rheindahlen, where he was taken through the decision-making processes that would need to take place in certain scenarios leading up to war, particularly those difficult decisions that would have to be made in the event of nuclear conflict. It became increasingly apparent to Beetham that the prime minister had either not been particularly well informed or had not previously appreciated the decisions that he would personally be required to make in any time of conflict, and during further discussions over dinner at Air House that evening Beetham sensed that the prime minister's eyes had now been well and truly opened wide regarding the nature and gravity of some of the decisions that he might have to make.

Beetham's residence, Air House, was marvellous, but it was inevitable that its existence would come under financial scrutiny from Whitehall as the Ministry of Defence continued to search for economies, and towards the end of Beetham's tour in Germany a team of civil servants visited Rheindahlen to assess whether the retention of Air House as the C-in-C's residence could be justified. The first question Beetham was asked was whether the C-in-C needed to live in such a luxurious home, to which he replied 'no', and he explained that his children were away at boarding school and that his wife and he had quite modest requirements. Beetham could see the gleam in the eyes of the inspectors at the prospect of a saving as they asked him what his requirements were. Beetham then explained that he had a large number of official visitors. For example, the prime minister, James Callaghan, had recently stayed there and the leader of the opposition, Margaret Thatcher, had also stayed at Air House. There had also been a continuous stream of members of Parliament, NATO delegations and senior government officials, as well as a number of foreign dignitaries, and he was also expected to do a considerable amount of official entertaining locally. The inspectors then asked how these requirements could be met, to which Beetham explained that it would need a similar-sized residence to Air House. Furthermore, Air House was comparatively secure for VIP visits and if there was no official residence on base then the cost of accommodating visitors elsewhere, including the security measures that would need to be put in place, would all need to be taken into account. When discussing the staff requirements Beetham explained that one additional staff member would be required to be in overall charge, probably of squadron leader rank with experience of catering and hotel management, which was currently performed by his wife at no cost to the British taxpayer. After the civil servants had returned to London, Beetham received a telephone call saying they had returned satisfied and that he should not hear any more about justifying the retention of Air House!

Beetham was promoted to the rank of air chief marshal on 21 May and the last weeks in his appointment were very busy. There were many social events to mark his departure from 2 ATAF and RAFG, and there were office calls in Monchengladbach, Brussels, London, The Hague and Bonn. Beetham also attended the BAOR Royal Review at Sennelager to mark the Queen's Silver Jubilee. By now the PSO, Ian Macfadyen, had been busy liaising with the Chief of the Air Staff's outer office in London to establish Beetham's commitments once he had taken over as the new CAS. Finally, it was time for Beetham to hand over to his successor, Air Marshal Sir John Stacey. This was their second handover in just eighteen months as Stacey had previously taken over from him at Strike Command. It was then time to leave. On 22 July there was one final guard of honour at Wildenrath as the Beethams boarded the same Andover aircraft that had brought them to Germany eighteen months before.

The following week Beetham received a personal letter from General Sir Frank King that thanked him for the past eighteen months. King stated that it had been a very happy period and commented on the joint approach that he believed Beetham had so firmly espoused. There were further pleasantries in the letter, including a reference to the golf course and comments on the similarities between their wives on just how they approached their military duties, which all provides clear evidence of how close the working relationship and personal friendship was between the two commanders.

Although some might have seen Beetham as a hard man during his time in Germany – and there were certainly times when he was justifiably so – he was also perceived as an extremely positive commander who always made it absolutely clear what he wanted and he was certainly respected by those who served under him. There is no doubt that the operational effectiveness of RAF Germany had been greatly enhanced by the introduction of some high-quality equipment and by its training and operational standards, and there had also been an improvement in relations between the Allied air forces in NATO. The procedures put in place during the 1970s would stand the test of time as both 2 ATAF and RAFG would remain in existence until 1993, when they were both disbanded following the reduction of military forces in Europe at the end of the Cold War; 2 ATAF was disbanded as part of a major reorganisation of the NATO command and control structure, its role being taken over by Allied Forces Central Europe, and RAFG was disbanded when its units were absorbed by Strike Command.

There is no doubt that the untimely death of Sir Andrew Humphrey was the final defining moment that shaped Beetham's career and accelerated his appointment to be the next Chief of the Air Staff. While it is probable, but certainly not definite, that he would have become the CAS anyway, because he appears to have been the front runner to replace Cameron in the fullness of time, things could have turned out differently. It was also fortunate that Sir Neil Cameron was an extremely worthy successor to Humphrey as the Chief of the Defence Staff. The RAF could not have foreseen Humphrey's death and so the situation could well have been different had there been a lesser man than Cameron as the CAS at the time. This might seem an unusual suggestion to make, but each service knew the rotational post of the CDS lasted three years and each service would always ensure it had a Chief lined up who was capable, and politically acceptable, of becoming the CDS in turn. It would have been the mid-1980s before the RAF would have expected to provide the next CDS after Humphrey, and so Cameron was given an unexpected opportunity, which in turn saw Beetham given his.

Beetham was now about to climb the final rung on the ladder and reach the very top. There had been several defining moments throughout his career and the last piece of the jigsaw had now been put in place.

CHAPTER 10

The Chief

———

Beetham arrived back in the UK amid national celebrations for the Queen's Silver Jubilee year, which marked the twenty-fifth anniversary of Queen Elizabeth's accession to the throne. He soon moved into his official residence in London, a flat on the third floor of Kingston House overlooking Hyde Park, which he took over from the departing CDS, Sir Edward Ashmore. The flat in Kingston House was quite luxurious, but it was small when compared to Air House that he had left behind in Germany. As part of the Silver Jubilee celebrations there were many events taking place across the country and the last formality that his predecessor, Sir Neil Cameron, had to fulfil was to attend the Royal Review at Finningley. Beetham, now within a few days of taking over as the CAS, was also invited as a guest.

Beetham's appointment as the CAS was formally announced in the *London Gazette* and there were two entries, which read:

> Air Chief Marshal Sir Michael Beetham KCB CBE DFC AFC is appointed Air Aide-de-Camp to the Queen in succession to Air Chief Marshal Sir Neil Cameron GCB CBE DSO DFC on the latter's promotion to Marshal of the Royal Air Force, 31st July 1977.

> Air Chief Marshal Sir Michael Beetham KCB CBE DFC AFC is appointed Chief of the Air Staff in succession to Marshal of the Royal Air Force Sir Neil Cameron GCB CBE DSO DFC, 1st August 1977.

The Chief's office was on the sixth floor of the MOD's Main Building, on the south side of Whitehall and directly opposite Downing Street. Beetham's first day in office, Monday 1 August, was memorable for a number of reasons, one of which was because on his desk when he arrived was a letter of apology from the secretary of state for defence, Fred Mulley, who had infamously drifted to sleep at the Royal Review at Finningley three days earlier in the presence of the Queen. This was not at all what Beetham would

1   As the commandant of the RAF Staff College at Bracknell, Beetham hosted the royal visit on 6 June 1972. Also in the front row is Lord Elworthy (second left), the former Chief of the Defence Staff, who was then the constable and governor of Windsor Castle, and on the extreme left is a former student of No 1 Course. Standing far left is Murillo Santos from Brazil, the senior overseas student, with whom Beetham would meet up again later in his career.

2   With SACEUR, General Alexander Haig, in 1975 during Beetham's NATO tour as ACOS (Plans and Policy) at SHAPE (NATO)

3 Sir Michael Beetham with his family at Buckingham Palace following his appointment as a Knight Commander of the Order of the Bath in the New Year's Honours List of 1976

4 Among Beetham's early visits as the new CAS was one to Warton, where he flew in the rear seat of the Tornado prototype 'P03' on 26 September 1977 with the manager of flight operations, Paul Millett (British Aerospace).

5 Arriving at RNZAF Base Okahea during his visit to New Zealand in March 1978 (RNZAF)

6 Meeting of the Defence Council, 20 August 1978. From left, clockwise around table: General Sir Dwin Bramall (Vice-Chief of the Defence Staff (Personnel & Logistics)), Marshal of the RAF Sir Neil Cameron (Chief of the Defence Staff), Dr John Gilbert (Minister of State for Defence), Fred Mulley (Secretary of State for Defence), Sir Frank Cooper (Permanent Under-Secretary of State), Sir Clifford Cornford (Chief of Defence and Procurement), R. Facer, Prof Ronald Mason (Chief Scientific Advisor), Patrick Duffy (Parliamentary Under-Secretary of State for Defence for the RN), Admiral Sir Terence Lewin (Chief of the Naval Staff), Robert Brown (Parliamentary Under-Secretary of State for Defence for the Army), James Wellbeloved (Parliamentary Under-Secretary of State for Defence for the RAF), Beetham. At the far end of the table are the Secretariat, W. Reeves and Air Commodore J. Duxbury

7   Beetham greeted at Komatsu Air Base during his visit to Japan in October 1978 (JASDF)

8   Climbing into the cockpit of a Mirage F1CG of the Hellenic Air Force during a visit to Greece in March 1979 (HAF)

9   The three service Chiefs at the funeral of the Earl Mountbatten of Burma, 5 September 1979, following his assassination by the Provisional IRA

10 During a visit to the Royal Saudi Air Force, October 1979 (RSAF)

11 The Chiefs of Staff during the Falklands conflict of 1982. From left to right: Beetham, Sir Henry Leech (First Sea Lord), Sir Terence Lewin (Chief of the Defence Staff) and Sir Dwin Bramall (Chief of the General Staff)

12 With his former PSO, Peter Harding (right), the station commander at Honington, before his last flight in a combat aircraft as the CAS, 31 August 1982

13 On appointment to the supreme rank of marshal of the Royal Air Force in October 1982. Having served as Chief of the Air Staff for over five years, Beetham remains the second longest-serving CAS in the RAF's history. He was the twenty-second MRAF and is now one of only four men still holding the rank and the most senior of the three former Chiefs.

14 Escorting the Queen Mother at the unveiling of the memorial to Bomber Harris outside the RAF Church of St Clement Danes, 31 May 1992

15 Because five-star officers in the armed forces retained the rank for life, defence cuts during the 1990s meant that general service promotions to the rank ceased. HRH the Duke of Edinburgh decided to invite all those still holding the rank to Buckingham Palace on 27 May 1998 for a formal gathering; Beetham is in the second row, far right.

16 Pictured with his family

have expected to face on his first day as the CAS, but the apology was duly accepted and the matter was closed, although the media had made much of the story.

In an adjoining office were his personal staff, led by his private secretary, Andrew Ward. Ward was a principal in the Civil Service and a product of its fast-track scheme. He had previously served as PS to Cameron and had remained in post to retain continuity in the outer office during the change-over of Chiefs. Beetham's PSO was Wing Commander Mike Stear, a Phantom pilot who had previously commanded 17 and 56 Squadrons and had also served under Cameron. The division of responsibilities between the PS and PSO was reasonably straightforward in that Ward was responsible for routine MOD matters, and getting the right advice from the various departments and committees, whereas Stear would deal with all military and operational matters specific to the RAF and prepare all the briefings and speeches for the Chief.

The RAF was the only service to appoint a PS to the CAS; the Army's Chief of the General Staff had a military assistant and the Royal Navy's First Sea Lord and Chief of the Naval Staff had a secretary and a naval assistant. Beetham felt it an advantage to have a private secretary as it provided him with a strong connection with the Civil Service and he was also mindful that two key civil servants at the time had both been a PS to the CAS earlier in their career: Sir Frank Cooper, the permanent under-secretary of state and one of Whitehall's more outspoken characters, had been private secretary to Sir William Dickson, and Michael Quinlan, the deputy under-secretary (policy), a man of great esteem who would later become permanent under-secretary of state, had been private secretary to both Sir Thomas Pike and Sir Charles Elworthy. This meant that both Cooper and Quinlan had a firm understanding of the RAF at the highest level, which Beetham would often find worked to the RAF's advantage.

As it was the beginning of August, and therefore the middle of the summer break for politicians, Beetham initially focused much of his time on his service responsibilities and was keen to get out of the office to find out more about parts of the service he was less familiar with. His first official visit as the Chief was to Headquarters Strike Command and he flew to High Wycombe in a Gazelle helicopter from Battersea. Beetham started as he intended to go on and whenever possible he would fly as the first pilot or co-pilot during transits, but never as the designated aircraft captain: as the CAS he would have to be blameless should there ever be an incident in the air.

The following day he visited Valley on the island of Anglesey. As this was his first visit to a flying station since taking over as the Chief there was much media interest. Beetham flew to Valley in an Andover from Northolt in the morning and during his visit he flew the RAF's new jet trainer, the Hawk T1, which had entered service just the year before. It was his first flight in the Hawk and he was most impressed. Flying in the front seat, with OC standards, Squadron Leader Roy Gamblin, in the rear seat, Beetham was able to fly the aircraft for most of the sortie. During the one-hour training flight he experienced the excellent performance of the aircraft at low level over Anglesey and Snowdonia before he climbed high above North Wales to carry out aerobatics and spinning. Having experienced almost all the aircraft's flight envelope, Beetham was instantly convinced that the Hawk would be an outstanding jet trainer for the RAF for many years to come. He would prove to be right.

A week later he visited Gibraltar, flying first from Northolt to St Mawgan in Cornwall and then on to Gibraltar with the station commander, Group Captain Duxbury, in a Nimrod maritime patrol aircraft. During his brief visit Beetham met the flag officer Gibraltar, Rear Admiral Stacey, before returning to the UK the following day. During the next few weeks there were further overseas visits to the bases at Malta and Cyprus, as well as to Northern Ireland, so that he could fully understand their roles and responsibilities and be brought up to date with the current issues.

There were several other visits to RAF bases during Beetham's first weeks as the Chief. These were essentially fact-finding visits and to get feedback direct from the station personnel. Beetham would take every opportunity to get among the people, not just the aircrew and officers, and he particularly valued his time with the senior non-commissioned officers. While he expected every station commander to have a firm grip on all the issues and welfare matters on his station, he believed that it was only by listening to the views of the experienced senior non-commissioned officers on the station that he would best understand the issues at the time.

Among his many early trips was a visit to the RAF Staff College at Bracknell where, as part of the course programme, the CAS briefed the students. As a former commandant, he proudly addressed the assembled audience as their professional head of the service. His address included his vision for the RAF over the coming years and also highlighted his awareness of some of the challenges faced by the service due to recent political and service decisions on issues such as cutbacks, pay and conditions of service. He also listened with interest to the views of the students in the discussion period at the end of his address.

For these visits Beetham was usually accompanied by both his PSO, Mike Stear, and his ADC, Mike Winning, if the workload back in the outer office permitted; if not, then only one would go. The ADC looked after all the domestic and travel arrangements, and the PSO was generally responsible for recording any actions; if travelling by air to and from Northolt, it was usually during the return transit that Stear or Winning, or both, would write up their notes from the visit and then start writing the many thank-you letters from the Chief.

In addition to Beetham's visits, there was also a weighty programme of office calls during his early weeks, which included the secretary of state for defence and other key politicians, the other service Chiefs of Staff, General Sir Roland Gibbs and Admiral Sir Terence Lewin, the Chief of Personnel and Logistics Air Chief Marshal Sir Ruthven Wade, the Chief Executive of the Procurement Executive Clifford Cornford, the Chief Scientific Adviser Professor Sir Hermann Bondi, the Head of Home Civil Service Sir Douglas Allen and the Permanent Under-Secretary of State to the Foreign and Commonwealth Office Sir Michael Palliser.

There were also many introductory calls to Beetham's office by senior air force officers and their two-star staffs, in particular from those working directly for him in the Department of the Chief of the Air Staff such as the Vice-Chief of the Air Staff, Air Marshal Peter Terry, and the three Assistant Chiefs – Air Vice-Marshals John Sutton (policy), David Craig (operations) and Donald Hall (operational requirements). There were also many other duties to perform as the Chief, such as attending the Battle of Britain Service at Westminster Abbey in September, when he read the second lesson, and as the new CAS and ADC to the Queen, he went to Buckingham Palace for an audience with the Queen. There were also visits from foreign or Commonwealth Chiefs of Staff.

Beneath Beetham's office in Main Building was the conference room where the Chiefs of Staff would meet. The Chiefs of Staff Committee system was set up in 1923 with a collective responsibility for advising government on defence policy as a whole. The Chiefs generally met with colleagues and advisers once a week to discuss matters of military importance, not only to the armed forces but also to the nation as a whole, although meetings would be more frequent if required. Heading the Chiefs, and chairman of the committee, was the Chief of the Defence Staff, the principal military adviser to the government, who sat at the head of a long table. On his right was the CGS and to his left sat the First Sea Lord. Beetham's seat was alongside the First Sea Lord, and next to the CGS was the permanent under-secretary, the civilian head of the MOD, who also acts as the adviser to the secretary of state for defence on financial, political and parliamentary matters. The remaining seats around the table would be taken by various senior advisers, depending on the nature of the meeting. The responsibilities of the committee have varied over the years but essentially it is the forum for discussion and decision making in order to advise the CDS, and therefore the government, on the capabilities, activities and issues of each of the armed forces while taking into account the political direction given by ministers accountable to Parliament, and any financial constraints.

As the CAS, Beetham was required to sit on many senior political and military groups and committees. The senior departmental committee of the MOD was the Defence Council, which provided the formal legal basis for the conduct of defence in the UK, and meetings were generally held once a month. It was chaired by the secretary of state for defence, Fred Mulley, and included senior politicians, senior military officers and other senior officials heading the armed forces and the department's major functions. Beneath the Defence Council was the Air Force Board of the Defence Council; again this was chaired by Fred Mulley and included John Gilbert and James Wellbeloved as the two nominated vice-chairmen. Beetham soon got used to his other regular commitments such as the Chiefs of Staff Informal meetings, known as COS(I)s, which would be arranged as the need arose, and his other service commitments such as the Air Force Board Standing Committee and the CAS's Policy Review Meeting, both of which usually met once a month.

While his many early meetings and visits were important, it was clear to Beetham that there were more important issues to address and he was keen to provide some stability to the service, which had suffered a period of change. From his visits to RAF bases and his meetings around Whitehall, he was certainly aware that the Chiefs of Staff were in the middle of an extremely difficult political and economic climate. In the defence review two years earlier, the previous secretary of state for defence, Roy Mason, had found himself under extreme pressure from the chancellor of the Exchequer, Denis Healey, to reduce defence spending from 5.5 per cent of the gross domestic product to perhaps 4 per cent over the next ten years. This political approach was considered unacceptable by the Chiefs of Staff at the time but, rather than create a shopping list of reductions, the service Chiefs instead established a 'critical level of forces', below which the reduction in Britain's contribution to NATO would be called into question. Commitments such as defending the UK and defending NATO's central front by maintaining BAOR and RAF Germany, remained relatively unscathed, but there were other commitments that came under the spotlight.

One of these was maintaining Britain's nuclear deterrent but, although this was the most politically sensitive issue of all, the future of Polaris was secured when, after much debate, it was decided that the disbandment of Polaris early would produce a relatively small financial saving in proportion to its immense contribution to NATO's strategic nuclear capability. The two other areas that came under immense scrutiny were Britain's contribution to the defence of NATO's northern flank and the British presence in the Mediterranean. Britain's military contribution to the defence of the northern flank was successfully defended because it was relatively easy to argue that the alternative option of not protecting the northern flank would significantly increase the threat to the UK; it was less easy, however, to defend Britain's military contribution to the southern flank and the Mediterranean. This led to the decision being made to end the British presence in Malta in 1979, which would reduce the nation's military presence in the Mediterranean to Gibraltar and the sovereign base areas in Cyprus. Otherwise, the Chiefs of Staff had successfully defended Britain's contribution to NATO, for the time being at least, but they were nonetheless instructed to make short-term savings, amounting to more than £500 million over the next three years.

Although the reduction in overseas commitments would inevitably result in a reduction of RAF transport aircraft, Beetham at least knew that the RAF's multi-role combat aircraft, the Tornado, had survived the round of potential cutbacks. On 26 September he visited what had until recently been the military division of the British Aircraft Corporation but had now merged with other companies to become British Aerospace at Warton, near Preston in Lancashire. He was met on arrival by the chairman, Harry Baxendale, and the legendary former wartime pilot, Roly Beamont, now the company's director of flight operations. After a short briefing Beetham flew the prototype aircraft 'P03' with the manager of flight operations, Paul Millett. It was Beetham's first flight in the Tornado and from the rear seat he experienced the aircraft's superb handling characteristics at low level over North Wales before rapidly climbing to 25,000 feet for subsonic and supersonic handling, which included aerobatics, before landing back at Warton to experience the aircraft's reverse-thrust landing capability.

His visit had attracted much media attention and after the flight he emphasised the Tornado's fine handling qualities and, as a weapons system, operating in the low-level European environment, it would provide its crew with an exciting challenge. In answer to a question about the recent Labour Party defence study group's report titled 'Sense about Defence', which had recommended that Tornado should be cancelled, Beetham was quick to explain that he felt that the study group did not understand the great importance to the RAF and to NATO of an aircraft that can operate effectively at low level and high speed, day or night and in bad weather conditions. Furthermore, with its unique multi-role capability, he explained that the Tornado was scheduled to replace five of the RAF's front-line aircraft types that were coming to the end of their service life and that the Tornado would provide the RAF with its main offensive and defensive capability throughout the 1980s and 1990s.

The Tornado programme had survived, but further defence savings could only be made by reducing military activity and delaying other equipment programmes. If this was not enough to concentrate the minds of the Chiefs of Staff, they also faced another serious problem, which would undoubtedly have a significant impact on the capability of the armed forces. For some time the problems of service pay and quality of life had been bubbling away beneath the surface. Successive pay freezes meant that recommendations made by the Armed Forces Pay Review Body, which existed to ensure comparability with civilian rates of pay, could not be implemented in full without breaching government guidelines. As a result, service pay had continued to lag behind comparable civilian rates and the number of applications from servicemen wishing to leave the armed forces early was rising beyond all expectations.

The general problem of service pay had not been particularly evident to Beetham in his previous appointment as C-in-C RAF Germany. The overseas allowance was good and there were further benefits for service personnel living in Germany, such as an absence of duty on items such as alcohol and cigarettes, as well as tax benefits when buying new cars and when buying petrol. These benefits meant that the cost of living in Germany, when compared to the cost of living back in the UK, was relatively cheap. Now back in the UK, Beetham could better understand the problems faced by the vast majority of service personnel. However, the increase in numbers of service personnel wishing to leave the armed forces early could not be entirely attributed to pay. Successive cuts in defence spending over recent years had resulted in frustration, and the continued reduction in activity and deployments, combined with an increasing failure of equipment and the lack of spares, were all evidence that morale in the services was low.

The increase in numbers leaving the armed forces, together with the difficulty in recruiting, had resulted in manpower shortages across all three services. These shortages were particularly felt in critical areas such as pilots and tank crews, and the number of ships that the Royal Navy could fully man was at the lowest level ever. Beetham had first become aware of the severity of the issue just days after he took up his appointment as the CAS when he was copied in on a minute from the CDS, Sir Edward Ashmore, to the secretary of state. Before handing over as the CDS, Ashmore had felt it right to inform the secretary of state of his concern regarding the worsening pay situation in the armed forces and asked, as a matter of some urgency, for an official government announcement to show commitment to restoring full pay comparability. This, he felt, would go a long way to reassuring and sustaining servicemen and women whose morale and discipline could not be taken for granted when they were aware of a considerable and growing loss of pay comparability.

By the end of October there had been no sign of the government resolving the issue and the national press now picked up on the story. One national paper ran the headline – 'Who'd be a Soldier in Fred Mulley's Army?' The article that followed suggested that the pay and conditions of Britain's fighting services were nothing less than a national scandal. It went on to say that much had been heard recently about a 10 per cent pay rise for the police, with the promise of further investigation of their grievances, and pointed out that servicemen had no union and so could not send representatives to heckle Fred Mulley, much as they no doubt would have liked to. Another paper pointed out that a soldier serving in Northern Ireland was earning less than the police and civilians he was working alongside, and another made comparisons between a Jaguar pilot earning less than a police constable, suggesting that if the government gave way to the police or miners then the effect on recruiting and wastage rates in the three services might be severe. Another paper reported on how servicemen were frustrated at having fallen behind civilian workers during two years of pay controls. And so it went on.

The issues of pay and the quality of life in the armed forces might, from a political perspective, have remained on the back burner, but the matter started to come to a head in November 1977 when the country's firemen went on national strike. The strike started when the government rejected the Fire Brigade Union's demand for a substantial increase in pay, of up to 30 per cent, and a reduction in the working week so that firemen could earn considerable amounts of overtime pay. Talks between the union leaders and the government broke down when the government insisted there was to be no breach of its 10 per cent ceiling on public-sector pay increases. Servicemen were brought in to provide emergency cover, although there was concern within the armed forces about their lack of training and shortage of modern firefighting equipment. At the same time, the Chiefs of Staff made it quite clear to the prime minister and government ministers that to make an improved offer to the firemen without implementing the recommendations of the Armed Forces Pay Review Body would be totally unfair and it would destroy any faith the servicemen had in the government.

The national press were again quick to point out that a member of the armed forces who was working an eighty-four hour shift while standing in for a striking fireman was earning just 50 per cent of the hourly gross rate of pay of the fireman he was replacing. On 29 November one leading national newspaper ran the headline, 'Misunderstanding on Soldiers' Pay, Says Mulley', and in the article that followed the secretary of state was quick to point out that there was an 'enormous misunderstanding' about the pay of Britain's armed forces. He went on to add that he had no objection to servicemen 'moonlighting' with other jobs to supplement their income, provided that it did not interfere with their service jobs. Mulley also confirmed that there was concern about overstretched or simply too few servicemen chasing too many commitments. Referring specifically to the firemen's strike, the secretary of state added that the situation was serious in all three services, particularly for those who were not involved in providing fire cover as they had to carry out all the jobs that their colleagues would normally have done.

By now Beetham and the other Chiefs of Staff were extremely concerned at the impact on morale of the armed forces and were anxious for the government to issue a statement to reassure the services. There was none. The only words that came from the government acknowledged the disappointment felt within the services and recognised that there had been much publicity given recently to large pay claims, including those of miners, police and firemen. The government also pointed out that the annual review for the armed forces was on 1 April and the review body would report directly to the prime minister. The government line was that any recommendations significantly outside its pay guidelines might have to be phased in over a period but, subject to this, the government and Defence Council were determined to ensure that the military salary was brought up to date and full pay comparability restored at the earliest opportunity.

For the time being the situation hung in the balance and in his first Christmas message as the CAS, Beetham wrote:

> I have been personally aware of the problems you all face with such patient goodwill in these financially difficult times. Those of you who have already met me or heard me speak will be aware of my personal involvement in the negotiations to improve our pay situation. I cannot, I regret, offer you a specific message of cheer yet, but I can assure you that I and my colleagues on the Air Force Board are personally doing all in our power to ensure an early return to pay comparability and, at the same time, to alleviate the burden of some of our charges.

He went on to add:

> As I look forward to 1978, I am looking to a period of consolidation and increased stability. Our Nation's economic performance is already on the upswing and we can, I am sure, look forward with confidence to playing our full part in that by continuing to provide the National security on which it must be based.

Beetham insisted that all members of the Air Force Board should visit some of the RAF personnel who were providing continuous fire cover at various local establishments on Christmas Day. Accompanied by Winning, he personally visited RAF personnel at a local drill hall in West Ham in East London. He arrived just before lunch and was met by the detachment commander, Flight Lieutenant Mark Fulford, and spent an hour touring the premises and speaking to the men. He learned that the period before Christmas had been relatively quiet but during the last few days there had been a number of incidents, including a large fire in a shop at night and a fire at a granary warehouse at the East India Docks the day before. Not only had the RAF personnel provided fire cover for the local area, they had also laid on a special Christmas outing to the theatre for local handicapped children, which was followed by a party back at the drill hall, with one of the corporals arriving at the party dressed as Father Christmas in one of the RAF's emergency fire tenders, known as a 'green goddess'. Not one to miss out on a good public relations opportunity for the benefit of the armed forces, Beetham was accompanied during the visit by the local press and he was quick to point out the vital role being carried out by members of the RAF and that the public could see how essential public services across the country had been kept going by members of the armed forces.

The firemen's strike lasted for nine weeks into January 1978 but essentially only the firemen were on strike and not the support staff, which meant that the strike was undermined by the union leaders and Trades Union Congress and was ultimately defeated. At its peak some twenty thousand members of the armed forces manned emergency fire tenders, dealing with nearly forty thousand incidents during the strike.

In the New Year's Honours List Beetham was appointed a Knight Grand Cross of the Most Honourable Order of the Bath, the highest of the three classes in the military division of the Order of the Bath. He then went on an overseas tour that would take him around the world. Accompanied by Stear and Winning, the first leg of the tour took Beetham to Sri Lanka by VC10 for a one-day visit, where he met the commander of the Sri Lankan Air Force, Air Marshal Harry Goonetileke, at the air headquarters in Colombo. The SLAF had originally formed as the Royal Ceylon Air Force in 1951 with the assistance of the RAF, and Beetham was made extremely welcome. The day included a trip up country in a helicopter and the visit proved very congenial.

Having left Sri Lanka, Beetham flew on to Hong Kong for a short stay before arriving in Australia. During his time in Australia he visited Canberra and the RAAF base at Amberley, near Brisbane in Queensland, where he enjoyed a flight in the F-111 swing-wing strike aircraft. He then flew on to New Zealand in an Andover of the RAAF, where he was met at the RNZAF Base Auckland by the RNZAF Chief of the Air Staff, Air Vice-Marshal Cyril Siegert, a former pilot with Bomber Command during the Second World War. Beetham then visited Whenuapai and Hobsonville, which had been integrated into RNZAF Base Auckland, and during his stay in New Zealand he also visited the strike base at Ohakea, near Bulls, and the training base at Wigram, Christchurch, which was home to the RNZAF's Central Flying School, where he took the opportunity to fly in a CT-4 training aircraft.

The tour then moved on to the USA, via a refuelling stop in Fiji and a night stop in Hawaii, where Beetham was able to meet up with many old friends from the US Air Force. He first visited the headquarters of Strategic Air Command at Offutt Air Force Base in Nebraska, where he also had the chance to meet up with his former NATO colleague, General Russ Dougherty, who had recently handed over as Commander-in-Chief of Strategic Air Command on his retirement from the United States Air Force. From Offutt, Beetham flew to Washington DC, where he met with US officials at the Pentagon and the British defence staff in the British embassy before returning to the UK.

The overseas tour had provided Beetham with a welcome break from Whitehall but as his memories of the tour faded into the past, he again focused on the problems back home. The biggest issue of pay had yet to be resolved, despite the fact that the armed forces had provided essential emergency cover during the firemen's strike. At the end of February the Chiefs of Staff met to discuss the handling of the Armed Forces Pay Review Body Report, which was due to be issued within the next few weeks. It was agreed that the best strategy for discussion of the pay award would be to have it conducted on a broad political front, rather than on points of detail, and, given that the principle of restoring comparability was accepted, it could be portrayed as absurd to allow the services to fall further behind. It was also pointed out in discussion that the use of the X-factor – an adjustment to military pay in recognition of the special conditions and demands of service life experienced by members of the armed forces compared to those in the civilian sector – could be significant in allowing the government to agree to a pay rise of more than 10 per cent. The Chiefs also agreed that it would be advantageous if Cameron could brief the prime minister on the strength of feeling in the armed forces concerning pay before the Armed Forces Pay Review Body Report was issued; in the event of a delay in the announcement of the pay award it would be necessary to advise the services of the reasons for the delay.

The prime minister did agree to meet with Cameron and during their meeting held on 16 March Cameron made clear the concerns of the Chiefs of Staff about service pay and explained that the situation had now reached a point where there seemed to be no realistic sign whatsoever of the government making any improvements. In the following weeks the Chiefs of Staff continued to make their views known to Fred Mulley and, as he was the secretary of state for defence, these views must have become known to the prime minister.

Beetham was fully aware of just how desperate the situation had become for the RAF. As far as retention was concerned there were 450 officers waiting for premature voluntary release from across all branches, although the waiting time to leave varied depending on the branch; in the case of a junior officer pilot, the longest waiting time was eight and a half years! Furthermore, 60 per cent of pilots approaching their optional retirement date were exercising their option to leave. The situation was not much better across the ground branches and the overall position for the service was that 40 per cent of officers approaching their optional retirement date had made the decision to leave and the number of senior officers refusing to accept command tours, particularly in ground appointments, was a growing concern. Previous recruiting targets for officers had been artificially depressed as a result of the 1974 defence review to bring the officer strength down to the new establishment, but the recruiting position had also become critical. This combination of serious recruiting shortfalls, coupled with the high outflow of trained officers, had now led to substantial deficits, particularly for pilots, where only 168 had been recruited in the past year against a target of 260; unless the trend was reversed the RAF anticipated a shortfall of more than two hundred front-line pilots by 1980. Recruitment of navigators, fighter controllers and air traffic controllers was just as serious – where recruiting achievement was just 48 per cent, 37 per cent and 27 per cent of target respectively – and there was also a shortfall in the number of engineering officers recruited. Furthermore, the fact there had only been an uptake of 40 per cent of university cadetships available was evidence that the RAF had lost its influence in schools. This deterioration in officer recruiting had occurred following a series of cuts in the RAF's recruiting organisation and with its current establishment the organisation could not be expected to meet its aims. While recruiting targets for airmen had been largely met, the targets themselves had been artificially low during the past few years and the climate of civilian employment could hardly have been more favourable for recruiting. However, the numbers of enquiries was falling, especially for trades requiring a higher calibre of entrant, and the target of a 32 per cent increase in airmen from the previous year had presented a formidable task.

The RAF's manpower shortages, especially for pilots, and the need for an immediate strengthening of its recruiting organisation, had been an issue for Beetham and the Air Force Board for some months. A critical situation had now been reached and there was a need for urgent action. The shortfalls would have to be made good and because of the large deficits in some branches – particularly those concerned directly with the front line – recruitment targets in the following years would have to be substantially higher. Therefore, the recruiting organisation required strengthening in two areas. The first was to restore RAF influence in schools and to attract academically well-qualified young people needed to man the front line, and the second was to increase the size of the recruiting organisation to attract a 40 per cent increase in the number of enquiries. There was certainly no shortage of evidence for Beetham to continue the political fight for additional pay in order to reduce the outflow of experienced personnel from the service and to attract more enquiries for recruitment; in the meantime a number of measures, including an examination of how best to effect improvements in the training wastage, were put in place.

By the middle of April it had become increasingly apparent to the Chiefs of Staff that nothing further was happening regarding the pay issue, certainly as far as the government was concerned, and they were now faced with a conflict of loyalty between their responsibility to the government and, more importantly, their responsibilities as the professional heads of their services. They could no longer sit back and watch the exodus of highly trained and highly skilled servicemen from the armed forces and, having met in one of their COS(I) meetings, the Chiefs of Staff decided to release details of the numbers leaving the armed forces to the national press.

Rarely have Chiefs of Staff had to revert to such desperate measures, but Beetham was absolutely convinced it was the right thing to do in the position he and his colleagues found themselves in, and because service pay was fast approaching 40 per cent less than civilian comparability. The Chiefs of Staff were fully aware that the news was unlikely to come as a big surprise to the press, given the numbers that were already seen to be leaving the armed forces, and Beetham felt sure there would be strong public support if information was made publically available. Avoiding any political comment, the Chiefs gave the authority for the factual information to be released to the Press Association on 18 April. That same afternoon Beetham sent a signal to his Commanders-in-Chief, group commanders and station commanders, which read:

> The Armed Forces Pay Review Body's strongly worded report has been with the Prime Minister since 1 April and has been under consideration, together with supporting MOD representations, at cabinet level since 6 April. Ministers have difficult issues to resolve and a decision on our pay is unlikely therefore before late April. The delay is frustrating, but it is not in our interests to push for an early decision so long as our representations, which the Chiefs of Staff are pressing strongly, seem likely to influence the outcome.

That same afternoon of 18 April, and after the figures had been released to the Press Association, the disclosure of the numbers released was put to the prime minister in question time. Callaghan was reported to have reacted with irritation but in answer to one question said he understood that recruiting was going well.

In response to the prime minister's answer in the House of Commons, Beetham sent a minute to the secretary of state the following morning, detailing the recruiting and outflow figures for the RAF and stated that the most worrying shortfall was pilots. He also emphasised the projected shortfall of over two hundred pilots by 1980, and that the outflow figures reinforced the need for a substantial increase in pay. That same day the Chiefs of Staff formally asked to see the prime minister, as they are entitled to do when they cannot get a satisfying outcome by any other means to a matter which they believe to be of essential military importance. In response to the request from the Chiefs of Staff, the prime minister's office offered a meeting on 25 April, but that would be five days after the cabinet were due to meet to decide the government's policy on service pay and on the actual day that the outcome of the cabinet's decision was due to be announced in public.

The cabinet then met as planned on 20 April and decided to endorse a 14 per cent policy. Having seen that a decision had already been made, the Chiefs of Staff saw little point in holding a meeting with the prime minister and so decided to withdraw their formal request for a meeting. Under increasing pressure from the press and opposition, Callaghan described the release as 'malicious' and 'mischief making' by the MOD and he ordered an inquiry into the leak.

The Chiefs then received a visit from the government's most senior civil servant, the permanent under-secretary of state, Sir

Frank Cooper, who explained that the government had found out that General Dwin Bramall, the Vice-Chief of the Defence Staff (Personnel and Logistics), had been the source of the leak and asked the Chiefs what they intended to do about it. The Chiefs informed Cooper that they had authorised the leak and accepted full responsibility. Through the PUS the prime minister asked the Chiefs to make a public apology, but after another COS(I) meeting the Chiefs instructed the PUS to inform the prime minister that they were not prepared to do so. The Chiefs were then asked if they were prepared to let the government publicly reprimand them and, after another COS(I), the Chiefs agreed.

The national press covered the story in some detail. From a senior politician's point of view the fact that the Chiefs of Staff had dared to tell the truth to the public was something of a serious 'offence'; furthermore, the figures released were seen politically as 'somewhat selective'. On the other hand, and certainly from the public's point of view, the Chiefs of Staff were seen to be campaigning for a fair pay deal for the armed forces. There was strong support for the action taken by the Chiefs of Staff, not only from within the armed forces but also from the public and other senior politicians. In an article in one leading national newspaper by the opposition party's defence spokesman, Sir Ian Gilmour, it stated that it was quite right to publicise the facts. In the same article Fred Mulley said that the Chiefs of Staff should have sought the authority of ministers in this matter, but had they have done so it is unlikely that the Chiefs would have been given the authority to release any figures to the national press.

On 28 April Beetham sent a signal to his Commanders-in-Chief, group commanders and station commanders to publish the following message in all routine orders:

> You will all now have seen the outcome of the pay review and no doubt everyone will have calculated what it means to them individually. You will also have seen the main features of the Armed Forces Pay Review Body Report and the amounts by which it recommended that our pay should be increased. There will be some natural disappointment that the Government have not made a larger award this year but they have felt constrained by the terms of their income policy and, in what they regard as the wider national interest, they have felt unable to restore full pay comparability immediately. The Government have however given a firm guarantee of full comparability by 1980. Half the gap will be closed next year and the remainder in 1980. Both pay

awards will be fully adjusted to reflect the improvement of civilian wages and salaries in the meantime. This is of course nothing less than our due but it is nevertheless a step of immense significance and a guarantee that it is important for everyone to understand. The last few months have been unsettling ones in which the subject of pay has dominated everyone's thoughts. We must now put this back in its proper place in our minds – not forgotten but no longer dominant – and get on with our normal day-to-day business. Meanwhile in Whitehall, I and my fellow Chiefs of Staff will be continuing to press for further improvements in our conditions of service which we regard as essential to the well-being of the Forces.

The gratitude within the RAF and the support for Beetham and the other Chiefs of Staff for deciding to make public the severity of the situation within the armed forces was evident when he arrived at Northolt to make a routine visit to Leeming. It was just days after the newspapers had reported that it was the Chiefs of Staff who had released figures to the national press and on arriving at Northolt the station commander greeted Beetham and explained to him that the station's personnel had wanted to come out and cheer him as a mark of their gratitude for his stand against the government. Then, when Beetham arrived at Leeming he went to meet the senior non-commissioned officers in the sergeants' mess, as he usually did on all his station visits, where he was greeted with a round of applause.

The issue of service pay was the biggest challenge faced by Beetham during his first months as the Chief. The outcome of the Chiefs of Staffs' action was a substantial phased pay award for the armed forces, which was well received by the services and significantly reduced the outflow of men and women from the armed forces. The matter was now closed, but the story received some rather comical press coverage in the 'Mac' cartoon in the *Daily Mail* on 18 May, which showed the Chiefs of Staff cleaning the kitchens in the House of Commons with the prime minister, James Callaghan, standing outside the kitchen next to the secretary of state for defence, Fred Mulley, with both men looking into the kitchen and Callaghan saying to Mulley, 'All right Mulley – that's enough jankers but tell them not to do it again.' It was a rather light-hearted conclusion to the incident.

The Royal Air Force celebrated its sixtieth anniversary on 1 April 1978. The night before, Beetham attended a formal dinner to mark the occasion given by the Lord Mayor, Air Commodore the Right Honourable Sir Peter Vanneck, at the Mansion House in London.

'All right, Mulley—that's enough jankers. But tell them not to do it again.'

14. The Mac cartoon in the *Daily Mail*, 18 May 1978, showing the Chiefs of Staff cleaning the kitchens at the House of Commons with the prime minister, James Callaghan, and the secretary of state for defence, Fred Mulley, looking on (*Daily Mail*)

The principal guest was the Duke of Edinburgh and there were many other notable guests, including seven marshals of the Royal Air Force: Sir Arthur Harris (AOC-in-C Bomber Command 1942–5); Sir William Dickson (CAS 1953–5, chairman of the Chiefs of Staff 1955–8 and the first appointed CDS in 1959); Sir Dermot Boyle (CAS 1956–60); Sir Thomas Pike (CAS 1960–3); Lord Elworthy (CAS 1963–7 and CDS 1967–71, and then constable and governor of Windsor Castle 1971–8); Sir Denis Spotswood (CAS 1971–4) and Sir Neil Cameron (the current CDS at the time). In addition to Beetham there were two other air chief marshals, Sir David Evans (AOC-in-C Strike Command) and Sir Douglas Lowe (Controller Aircraft), and also attending were many other senior RAF officers and politicians.

It was a grand affair to mark a truly historic occasion and throughout the meal the guests were entertained by the Salon

Orchestra of the Central Band of the RAF. The RAF had come a long way since its formation in 1918 when the Royal Flying Corps and the Royal Naval Air Service had amalgamated to form a single service, and it would have been a proud day for its original architects, Winston Churchill and Lord Trenchard. Trenchard, in particular, had the vision to recognise the need for an independent air force and had the courage and tenacity to translate that need into an organisation that had withstood the test of time, including the ravages of war and several radical changes in defence policy. As a reminder to those attending the sixtieth anniversary dinner that the RAF in 1978 bore a remarkable resemblance to Trenchard's original vision, inside the menu card there was a copy of the Air Force Memorandum No 3, which had been issued by the Air Council on 18 March 1918. It read:

> The Royal Air Force comes into existence on 1st April and the Air Council have confidence that the whole of the personnel, officers and men, will do their duty in the new Air Force as they have done so in their Services from which they have come, and will be animated by the same spirit. The development of the Royal Air Force will undoubtedly be watched by critical eyes in the older Services, and this is an additional reason why the newly-formed Service should be especially alert in questions of discipline. There is nothing that shows so much the state of order that exists in a Corps as smartness on the part of the personnel, good order in materiel, and the making and returning of proper salutes by officers and men alike. The Air Council wish to impress on all ranks the necessity for urgent attention to these matters.

For Beetham it was the start of a busy week of events to mark the anniversary. The following day, 1 April, he read the lesson at a service of thanksgiving at Westminster Abbey, attended by the Queen and the Duke of Edinburgh, and he then attended a Diamond Jubilee Concert in aid of the RAF Benevolent Fund at the Royal Festival Hall, which was attended by the Queen Mother and included music presented by Yehudi Menuhin, the Royal Philharmonic Orchestra under the baton of Sir Charles Groves, and the RAF's own Central Band. To round off a month of close connections with the royal family he presented the Prince of Wales with his parachute wings at Brize Norton after the prince had made eight jumps.

Because of an increasing amount of paperwork passing through Beetham's office, and because it was deemed necessary to provide another level of supervision and assistance for the outer-office staff, Squadron Leader David Davies was appointed as staff officer to Beetham. It was now time for Winning to move on, as he had been ADC for more than two and a half years, and in May he handed over to Flight Lieutenant Warwick Woodhouse and took command of 51 Squadron RAF Regiment at Wittering on promotion.

Recognising that the combination of the heavy cuts his predecessors had been compelled to impose and the issue of service pay had affected morale in the RAF, Beetham saw the restoration of some stability and the further improvement of communication within the RAF to be among his immediate priorities. His many visits to stations, combined with regular station commanders' conferences and the part played by the RAF Presentation Team, all helped to achieve this, and the wider dissemination of the message about the importance of air power.

He also remained concerned about the increasing capability of the Soviet Union and believed there was a formidable and recognisable threat to the UK of air attack, which was greater and far more deadly than Britain had ever faced before. In the event of a period of conventional warfare it was essential for the UK to have a strong defensive capability and it was in this area that he wanted to see more expenditure committed. His plan included increases in the capabilities of aircraft, missiles and radar systems and, because the UK's strategy for air defence was closely aligned to the NATO Alliance, he was keen for other NATO nations to contribute more financially. Furthermore, while there was the obvious danger of direct confrontation in Europe, the expansion of Soviet capability in Africa also presented a disquieting picture. Not only did Beetham voice his concerns in the UK and NATO forums in Europe but he also took the opportunity to raise his concerns about increasing Soviet global capability during his overseas visits to the USA, Australia and New Zealand.

During the summer of 1978 Beetham continued his round of RAF airfields and took the opportunity to fly whenever he could. During a visit to Finningley in South Yorkshire he had his first flight in the new Sea King HAR 3 Air Sea Rescue helicopter, which then entered service and would later be dispensed as single flights at various coastal airfields to replace the Whirlwind and Wessex. He then visited Cranwell, Leuchars, Brampton, Marham, Aldergrove, Lossiemouth and Kinloss. During the visit to Marham he flew in a Victor K2 air-to-air refuelling aircraft, which carried out in-flight refuelling of a Phantom, and then in Aldergrove he flew

in a Puma helicopter to view parts of Northern Ireland from the
air. At Lossiemouth he flew in a Jaguar, carrying out a low-level
strafe and lay-down attack in the range, and the following day he
flew a maritime patrol exercise in a Nimrod from Kinloss. Having
returned from Scotland, he visited the Farnborough International
Air Show in September, which was the first year it had been titled
as an 'international' air show, and one of the attractions was a
specially constructed ski-jump for the Harrier to demonstrate its
short take-off and landing capability. The following week Beetham
visited RAF Germany, first flying from Northolt to Wildenrath in
an Andover, and on to Gütersloh, before flying back to Wildenrath
in a Harrier and then visiting Bruggen the following day.

Beetham travelled to the Far East for official visits to the Republic
of Korea and Japan. Travelling throughout the tour in a RAF VC10,
and accompanied by his wife and Mike Stear, he initially flew to
Hong Kong, where he paid his first visit to the RAF base at Sek
Kong and met with the Commander British Forces, and his former
colleague from his days in RAF Germany, Major-General Roy
Redgrave. During his brief visit he flew in a Wessex and inspected
a guard of honour before being conducted around the base by the
Commander RAF Hong Kong, Group Captain Dan Honley. During
the tour of Sek Kong Beetham was able to observe the new facilities
that had been provided by the Hong Kong government for the RAF
as a replacement for the former RAF base at Kai Tak, which was
one of the major provisions of the 1976 defence costs agreement
following the defence review the previous year.

After his short stopover in Hong Kong, he travelled on to South
Korea. During his five-day visit he was hosted by the ROKAF's
Chief of Staff, General Choo Young Bock, and the visit provided a
marvellous opportunity to establish close ties between the two air
forces. On 1 October Beetham represented the Chief of the Defence
Staff at the Armed Forces Day celebrations, which marked the day
when South Korean forces broke through the thirty-eighth parallel
in 1950 during the Korean War, and honoured the military forces
of the Republic of Korea. The standard of drill was so high that
even the RAF's own Queen's Colour Squadron would have been
impressed. It was a wonderful occasion and provided Beetham
with a rare opportunity to meet senior officials of South Korea
including the prime minister, Choi Khu-hah. Beetham found the
South Koreans to be extremely friendly and very keen to develop
a good rapport with Britain. During his stay Beetham also took

time to travel to the Imjin River where, in 1951, the Gloucestershire Regiment had made its historic last stand despite being surrounded and outnumbered by Chinese forces during the Korean War.

Beetham flew on to Yokota Air Base, in Fussa near Tokyo to start his five-day visit to Japan. Under the Treaty of Mutual Cooperation and Security between the USA and Japan, signed in 1960, the USA has been committed to defending Japan in close co-operation with the Japan Self-Defence Force, and Yokota has been the Headquarters US Forces in Japan and home of the US Fifth Air Force. The Japan Air Self-Defence Force, or JASDF, is the aviation branch of the Japan Self-Defence Force and is responsible for the defence of Japanese airspace. The following day Beetham had briefings and meetings with senior officials of the JASDF at the Air Staff Office in Tokyo, which included a meeting with the chairman of the SDF's Joint Staff Council, General Takashina Takehiko. After the meetings Beetham had time to visit the Imperial Palace, the main residence of the emperor of Japan, and to walk round the large grounds.

That evening there was a formal dinner hosted by General Takeda of the JASDF to mark the occasion of Beetham's visit, and the following day he visited the Headquarters Air Defence Command at Fuchu Air Base and then Komatsu Air Base, which was home to the F-4EJ Kai Phantoms (built by Mitsubishi under licence) of the Central Air Defence Force. With the formalities over, the Beethams were able to enjoy a day of sightseeing in Kyoto, formerly the imperial capital of Japan, where they visited a number of local sites, including the Old Imperial Palace, before travelling back to Tokyo by bullet train. Finally, after a farewell lunch, it was time to return home. The ten days had been a most unforgettable visit. Although the Japanese had been extremely polite and courteous, and the hospitality excellent, there was not quite the same rapport with the Japanese as Beetham had so much enjoyed with the South Koreans.

The past few months had been both enjoyable and valuable for Beetham. In addition to the wonderful overseas visit to the Far East, he had been able to concentrate almost totally on service matters rather than having to deal with some of the more political issues that seemed to dominate much of his first year as Chief of the Air Staff. During his many visits to RAF bases he had been able to see for himself the significant advances that were being made in technology, many of which had been introduced into service to make the RAF a far more capable force.

*　　*　　*

The politically sensitive subject of Britain's nuclear deterrent came to the fore again at the end of 1978 following a study by the MOD's chief scientific adviser, Professor Ronald Mason, and the deputy under-secretary in the Foreign Office, Sir Anthony Duff. The study addressed whether or not Britain needed to maintain a national nuclear deterrent and, if so, what options were available to a future government for the replacement of Polaris – the critical factor was the life of the submarine hulls. This was another potentially thorny subject, given the Labour government's policy at the time not to continue Britain's nuclear deterrent once Polaris came to the end of its life.

The study recommended that Polaris should be replaced with Trident submarines and C4 missiles, which meant that a change would be required in the government's long-term policy regarding Britain's nuclear deterrent, and this came at a time when there were concerns among European leaders about the SALT 2 negotiations between the US president, Jimmy Carter, and the Soviet premier, Leonid Brezhnev. These talks were a continuation of the progress made during SALT 1 earlier in the decade and sought to reduce the manufacture of strategic nuclear weapons and the Soviet deployment of the latest SS20 intermediate-range missiles that had been targeted at Western Europe.

In January 1979 Callaghan attended a meeting on the island of Guadaloupe with US president, Jimmy Carter, the French leader, Giscard d'Estaing, and the German leader, Helmut Schmidt. The result of the meeting was a plan to deploy American cruise missiles in Western Europe in response to the threat from the SS20 missiles and at the same time to negotiate with the Soviet Union for the elimination of all intermediate-range missiles. During the meeting Carter also suggested to Callaghan that the USA could provide Trident to the UK should the British government decide to replace Polaris in the future. However, political events during the next few months would mean that the Callaghan government would not have to address further the politically sensitive issues of deploying American cruise missiles on British soil, or the replacement of Polaris with Trident.

At the end of February, Beetham, accompanied by his wife and Stear, visited the Hellenic Air Force in Greece. The HAF had recently undergone a period of modernisation and had taken delivery of the Dassault Mirage F1CG and F-4E Phantom II. The visit was hosted by the Chief of the Hellenic Air Force General Staff, Lieutenant General Demetrios Papageorgiou, and during the four-day visit Beetham held talks with the HAF's Air Staff and visited the Headquarters

Tactical Air Command at Larisa as well as visiting Tanagra Air Base to view the Mirage F1CG.

The visit to Greece was to be Mike Stear's last event as PSO as it was now time for him to hand over to Wing Commander John Thomson, who had just completed his tour as OC 41 Squadron following the squadron's recent conversion to the Jaguar at Coltishall. Stear had clearly done well as the PSO and Beetham wanted to ensure he was given the best possible appointment next. Having confirmed that Stear was to be promoted to the rank of group captain, Beetham asked Stear whether he would prefer to return to the Phantom and become station commander at Leuchars in Scotland or whether he would prefer to go to the Harrier force in Germany as the station commander at Gütersloh. For Stear it was a great choice but he was keen to opt for the Harrier at Gütersloh because he had previously flown the Phantom in all its roles, including an exchange tour in the USA, and he now felt ready for a new challenge.

During his eighteen months as PSO to Beetham, Stear had worked extremely closely with the Chief and held the highest respect for him. Beetham's reputation was probably harder than Cameron's before him, but it was not unreasonably so and Stear had found Beetham to be very fair. His instructions were always clear and meticulous in every way, and the Chief was appreciative of Stear's efforts. From his perspective, the reason that Beetham stood out as such a good CAS was because he was a great 'street fighter' and would not let things go when fighting to ensure he always got the best for the service. He would fight every possible corner that he could for the RAF and would always hold his line about what equipment the RAF should have. While this might have meant, at times, that he was not popular with the other Chiefs of Staff, it did not seem to bother Beetham, although he always came across as good friends with them. Stear also believes that Beetham's strong character stemmed from his wartime operational background. The same of course could be said of Cameron, although he was perhaps more academically minded, but within the RAF there was certainly no doubting Beetham's credibility as the Chief. Stear also felt there were times when some of the most senior RAF officers seemed to be scared of Beetham; to them he was made of steel and he was certainly not afraid to tell them what he thought. But Stear firmly believes the RAF was extremely fortunate to have a man like Beetham at the top during what was a difficult period, particularly when it came to some of the more politically difficult and emotive issues such as pay.

Stear handed over to Thomson on 12 March and his departure from Beetham's outer office completed a change-over of personnel as Andrew Ward had already been replaced by Tony Pawson as private secretary some months before. Attention now turned to the general election of 1979. Callaghan could have gone to the country during the previous autumn, when the economy was seen to be showing signs of improving and the government appeared to have regained some of its popularity, but he decided instead to carry on and face the country when the economy had improved further still. However, when he returned from his January meeting in Guadaloupe he found that many workers were involved in industrial action and the country was in the middle of a period being labelled a 'Winter of Discontent', which severely damaged the government's economic policy and its standing in the polls. Callaghan was accused by the media of being out of touch with the mood of the country, which led to the infamous 'Crisis? What Crisis?' headline on the front page of one leading tabloid newspaper. Callaghan was then forced to go to the country after his government lost a vote of confidence.

On 3 May the Conservative Party under the leadership of Margaret Thatcher defeated Callaghan's government. It was to be the first of four general election victories for the Conservative Party and was seen by many to be a pivotal point in twentieth-century British politics. The overall swing of 5.2 per cent was the largest since 1945 and marked a change in government that would last for eighteen years.

CHAPTER 11

A Change of Government

———————

When Margaret Thatcher became Britain's first woman prime minister in May 1979 it marked a most remarkable rise to political power. Thatcher had first become a Conservative MP in the 1959 general election when she won the seat for Finchley in North London just days before her thirty-fourth birthday. That election had been a third successive victory for the Conservative Party led by Harold Macmillan, and, having later served under Edward Heath as secretary of state for education and science, Thatcher had become leader of the Conservative Party in 1975. Her victory over James Callaghan's government was the largest political victory since the war and her tenure as prime minister would last until November 1990; she would be the longest-serving prime minister since Lord Salisbury and held the longest continuous period in office since Lord Liverpool.

Like the majority of the country, the Chiefs of Staff welcomed the change in government. For several years the armed forces had suffered significant cutbacks as a result of a number of defence reviews but Beetham now felt more optimistic about the future. In her general election manifesto, Thatcher had stated that her government would seek value for money in defence expenditure, as elsewhere, but the government would not hesitate to spend what was considered necessary on the armed forces, even when cutting public expenditure elsewhere. As her deputy prime minister and home secretary she appointed the vastly experienced Willie Whitelaw, as her secretary of state for defence she appointed Francis Pym and Geoffrey Pattie, a former army officer, became the parliamentary under-secretary of state for defence for the RAF.

Thatcher's hard line against trade unions at home and the Soviet Union abroad soon earned her the nickname 'The Iron Lady' but as far as the armed forces were concerned she was a shining light.

She was quick to ensure the immediate payment of the balance of the phased pay award of 32 per cent, agreed the year before by the Callaghan government following the firemen's strike, and then took a second key decision to raise defence spending by 3 per cent for the next seven years.

Confirmation of the service's pay rise would help provide a turning point which would boost morale. Furthermore, the RAF had stopped running down and had now entered a new period of selective expansion. However, air defence of the UK remained a problem. The shortage of pilots and the long lead time for training limited how far the RAF could contemplate increasing the number of air defence aircraft in the short term. Apart from an outright foreign purchase, the first opportunity to add significantly to the fighter force would be the mid-1980s when the Phantom squadrons could be run on as the Tornado entered service. The Phantoms could then be replaced in due course by procuring extra fighters, such as the Tornado F2, at the end of the production run in the late 1980s. The Air Force Board endorsed the general requirement for a minimum of three extra fighter squadrons for the defence of the UK and it was also agreed in principle that the Phantoms should be run on to sustain an expanded front line, although a decision on the choice of aircraft to meet the long-term requirement, particularly the acquisition of Tornado F2, should be deferred for the time being.

As far as increasing aircraft numbers in other roles was concerned, the assumptions used for the financial planning of LTC 79 (Long-Term Costing 1979 – the RAF's bid for its share of the annual defence budget) allowed for the retention of thirty Buccaneers for ten years following their replacement in the strike/attack role in 1985. Various other roles for the Buccaneer after its replacement by Tornado IDS were in the early stages of consideration, with the main proposal retaining a squadron in the maritime strike/attack role. The air staff was also considering the desirability and implications of acquiring a sideways-looking radar reconnaissance capability, which would imply running on a dedicated force of about six aircraft – probably Canberras. All other plans generally assumed the one-for-one replacement of existing assets, such as the Puma for the Wessex helicopters. Further options were being looked at, including top-up purchases of Harrier and Jaguar, Harrier and Jaguar improvement programmes, additional Rapier surface-to-air missile squadrons, a war role and top-up buy of Hawk, and the rationalisation of the airborne early-warning and maritime fleets.

Replacing aircraft was fine but unless the service could improve its manning situation there was little room to manoeuvre. The earlier reduction of the RAF to a critical level followed by the unprecedented outflow of skilled servicemen had reduced the RAF's ability not only to operate normally but also to expand or to meet unexpected commitments. From the aircrew perspective, manning plans were based on 'into productive service' targets, and the requirement had now increased from 160 pilots in the previous year to 192 in the next. Beetham knew that the RAF would not be able to overcome its manpower shortages overnight but he firmly believed the foundations had now been laid. He was also committed to building up the RAF's reserve strength and in an address to nearly 3,500 delegates at the RAF Association's annual conference in Blackpool he announced the formation of three regiment field squadrons of the Royal Auxiliary Air Force for the defence of the UK's airfields in time of war.

The problems and major options he and the Air Force Board were now considering were essentially long-term ones, and the pro-gramme within the LTC period was manageable, given some modest growth. He also felt that a period of stability and consolidation was essential to sustain the morale and confidence of the service. This was not to say he was seeking to maintain the status quo, but he believed he should avoid giving the impression that there were mili-tary, political or financial pressures to make fundamental changes or take difficult decisions in the near future.

In July there were changes to the two other Chiefs of Staff appointments. Gibbs was replaced as the CGS by Sir Dwin Bramall and Lewin was replaced as the First Sea Lord by Admiral Sir Henry Leach, who stepped up from his previous appointment as C-in-C Fleet and Allied Commander Channel and Eastern Atlantic; Lewin then succeeded Cameron as the CDS in September.

It was a sombre day on 5 September as the Queen led the nation in mourning at the funeral of Earl Mountbatten of Burma, who had been assassinated by the Provisional Irish Republican Army while on holiday at Mullaghmore on the north-west coast of Ireland. The uncle of the Duke of Edinburgh, Mountbatten had a long and distinguished career in the Royal Navy; he was a former First Sea Lord and was the second CDS to be appointed. On the day of his assassination, 27 August, the IRA had also killed eighteen soldiers of the British Army at Warrenpoint in County Down. Mountbatten's funeral marked a day of pageantry in London that saw members of

Britain's armed forces joined by representatives from overseas. The funeral procession went from Wellington Barracks, near Buckingham Palace, to Westminster Abbey. Beetham and the other service Chiefs marched behind Mountbatten's coffin as thousands lined the route. The memorial service at Westminster Abbey, conducted by the Archbishop of Canterbury, was attended by royalty, leaders and politicians from all over the world and afterwards the coffin was taken to Romsey Abbey near the family home in Hampshire, where Mountbatten was buried at a private service.

Beetham then made a short visit to Goose Bay in Canada, flying in a Vulcan from Waddington. Because of the lessons learned from the Vietnam War and the increasing capability of Soviet radar and surface-to-air missile technology deployed in Europe, NATO turned more and more to low-flying tactics to avoid detection. The densely populated areas of Europe meant there were few places where low flying was permitted and even fewer places where military aircraft could fly down to heights of around a hundred feet. The location of the Canadian Forces Base at Goose Bay in Labrador, with its large area and sparse population, made it an ideal location, and Goose Bay would soon become the primary low-level tactical training area for several NATO air forces, including the RAF.

The following month Beetham made a goodwill visit to the Royal Saudi Air Force. The RSAF had been formed with British assistance and the two nations have enjoyed good relations ever since, particularly regarding the sales of British defence equipment to the Kingdom of Saudi Arabia. During his five-day visit Beetham held talks with officials at the RSAF headquarters in Riyadh, and he also met with RAF personnel working in Riyadh as part of a Ministry of Defence team. He then visited the King Faisal Air Academy and met with representatives of British Aerospace working under contract in Saudi Arabia, after which he visited the King Khalid Air Force Base and King Abdul Aziz Air Force Base, where he was given a tour of the Technical Studies Institute and visited 13 Squadron, which operated Lightnings. Following a farewell lunch at the Intercontinental Hotel he departed Dhahran and on the way back to the UK he made a short stopover in Cyprus, and the following day, he flew a Whirlwind helicopter there to visit RAF personnel serving at Troodos, the United Nations Protected Area in Nicosia and at Episkopi.

The visit to Saudi Arabia had provided Beetham with another welcome break from Whitehall. Having returned to London he was able to spend the next few weeks concentrating on RAF matters rather than political concerns, and he made a number of visits to training bases before the end of the year. However, the political aspect of being the CAS was never far from his mind and these visits coincided with the prime minister's first official visit to Washington in December, as there were still some important military decisions to be made following Callaghan's meeting with President Carter and the other Western European leaders on Guadaloupe earlier in the year. The two main issues, which were essentially interconnected, were the deployment of cruise missiles in Europe and the possible replacement of Polaris with Trident.

Taking the deployment of cruise missiles first, Thatcher informed Carter that missiles could be deployed in Britain, a decision not taken lightly; although the deployment of missiles would not present any financial cost to Britain, the political importance could not be understated as it would make Britain vulnerable to specific attack in the event of any conflict. Furthermore, it would give the opposition party a major issue on which it could fight the next general election. The question of potentially replacing Polaris with Trident was not as straightforward. First there were a number of options to be considered, ranging from the cheapest option – the refurbishment of the Polaris submarines and missiles – to the more expensive options of either developing a submarine-launched cruise missile system or the purchase of Trident I, or indeed the more advanced Trident II (a more sophisticated system than Trident I and with a greater payload), should it be offered to Britain. Ultimately, Republican Ronald Reagan's victory in the US presidential election in November 1980 strengthened the political relationship between Britain and the United States. Reagan accelerated the Trident II programme, which now brought it into Britain's timeframe as a potential replacement for Polaris, and the Thatcher government eventually opted for Trident II D5 missiles, which would be carried by the Royal Navy's Vanguard class SSBN submarines from the mid-1990s to provide Britain's nuclear deterrent.

Thatcher's visit to Washington coincided with the Soviet Union's willingness to use force beyond the NATO area. The Soviet invasion of Afghanistan on 24 December to support the self-declared socialist state of the Democratic Republic of Afghanistan against the local Islamist Mujahideen insurgents marked the beginning of a Soviet–Afghan war that would last for nine years. Elsewhere, a further threat to Western oil supplies from the Middle East was also

emerging as relations between Iran and Iraq continued to deteriorate; this would eventually lead to the Iran–Iraq War following
Iraq's full-scale invasion of Iran in September 1980, a conflict that
lasted eight years.

These events highlighted the global instability faced by Britain,
but Beetham had already noticed a clearer and unambiguous new
attitude by the government towards defence. As prime minister,
Thatcher wanted to gain a thorough understanding of some of the
strategic decisions that she might be asked to make as prime minister,
as was highlighted by her willingness to participate in national
strategic planning exercises so that she could play the part of prime
minister herself. This was quite unusual: normally during these desk-
top exercises someone would stand in for key politicians, such as the
prime minister and secretary of state for defence, but once Thatcher
had learned of the importance of these exercises she was keen to take
part in them herself. In her opinion, if strategically important decisions
had to be made during these exercises then it was best for her to make
them rather than to have someone else make them on her behalf.

Now that pay had been restored to a proper level, and the government had stated its firm intention to keep it there, Beetham was
sure the RAF could face the tasks that lay ahead without further
distraction, although he remained fully aware that the service was
still walking a tightrope when it came to manpower and conditions
of service. The damaging outflow of skilled servicemen had largely
been stemmed, and recruiting was starting to look healthier, but he
was very much aware of the strains that remained, in particular the
long hours that seemed to have become quite normal in parts of the
service. The correctives would take time but the first step, to rebuild
the training system to sufficient strength where it could deliver the
right quantity of suitably trained personnel to an enlarged front line,
was now in place, and among Beetham's first visits in the New Year
were the Yorkshire training bases at Linton-on-Ouse and Church
Fenton. He was also keen to continue pursuing the development
of the reserves, and his schedule included visits to the auxiliary
squadrons. There was also new equipment to look forward to, such
as Tornado, and so the new decade started on a more positive and
strengthening note for the RAF.

Beetham then went on two quite different overseas visits. In January
he went to India on a seven-day goodwill tour of the Indian Air
Force. Accompanied by his wife and his PSO, John Thomson, he flew

by VC10 to New Delhi, where he was welcomed by the IAF's Chief of the Air Staff, Air Chief Marshal Idris Latif. The following day was spent in talks and briefings at Vayu Bhavan, the Air Headquarters, with Latif and the IAF air staff, and there were office calls with Air Marshal Dilbagh Singh (the AOC-in-C Western Air Command), General Om Prakesh Malhotsa (Chief of Army Staff) and Admiral Ronald Peveira (Chief of Naval Staff). Beetham also took time to lay a wreath at India Gate, the national monument that commemorates the ninety thousand soldiers of the British Indian Army who lost their lives fighting for the British Empire during the First World War and Afghan wars.

The following day, 26 January, he attended the Republic Day celebrations in New Delhi, which commemorates the date on which the Constitution of India came into force in 1950 and honours the declaration of independence in 1930. The main parade took place at the Rajpath, the ceremonial boulevard, after which Beetham had afternoon tea with the Maharajah of Jaipur, Sawai Bhawani Singh. In the evening there was an Indian Air Force banquet at the Ashoka Hotel, the most sought-after five-star hotel in the historic capital, in honour of his visit and hosted by Latif. The following day the Beethams flew to Agra, where they enjoyed a private tour of the Taj Mahal and they then visited Agra Fort before flying on to Bangalore, where they were met by the IAF's AOC-in-C Training Command, Air Marshal B. W. Chauhan. In the evening Beetham met with the governor, Govind Narain, and the following day he visited the Institute of Aviation Medicine and Hindustan Aeronautics Limited, India's leading aerospace agency – licensed to manufacture the Jaguar aircraft locally under the name Shamsher. He then visited the IAF Academy in Hyderabad and then the air base at Ambala, where he visited 14 Squadron IAF, which had recently taken delivery of the Jaguar IS. On his final evening he attended a 'beating retreat', an ancient military custom dating from the days when troops disengaged from battle at sunset, which involved the massed bands of the Indian Army, Navy and Air Force, and the pipes and drums from a number of Indian Army units. At the end of the ceremony flares went up, lending their hue to the evening sky. It was a marvellous occasion and brought to an end a truly unforgettable visit.

His next overseas trip, in April, was a five-day visit to Yugoslavia. Under the leadership of the revolutionary and statesman Yosip Broz Tito, Yugoslavia had pursued a policy of neutrality during the Cold War and had been a founder member of the Non-Aligned Movement

– an organisation of international states that considered themselves not aligned with or against any major power – when it had formed in Belgrade in 1961. Accompanied by Thomson, Beetham met with the assistant federal defence secretary for the air force, Lieutenant Colonel General Enver Cemalovic, and the commander of the air force, Lieutenant Colonel General Stevan Roglic. He also visited the aircraft manufacturer Vazduhoplovna Industrija Soko in the beautiful city of Mostar, where he noticed that the commander was greeted with great affection as he had been a local partisan leader there during the Second World War.

In addition to dealing with the many service issues, there were also many social engagements for Beetham to enjoy. One of the more memorable occasions took place in April when he attended a Bomber Command reunion dinner at Grosvenor House, attended by twelve hundred members, to honour the former Chief of Bomber Command, Sir Arthur Harris. Harris had celebrated his eighty-eighth birthday just days before, and evenings such as this were proving tiring and emotional for him. The dinner was chaired by Air Marshal Sir Harold 'Micky' Martin, Guy Gibson's deputy during the Dams Raid in May 1943 and a former air member for personnel, and among the guests was Dame Vera Lynn. As well as honouring Harris the evening also raised funds for the Leonard Cheshire Homes as guests were invited to bid for a painting by Air Vice-Marshal Norman Hoad, director of the Air League, depicting the Lancaster flown by Beetham during his tour with 50 Squadron at Skellingthorpe. Beetham was particularly proud to attend the dinner in his capacity as the CAS as he had always been full of admiration for his former wartime commander.

In July he hosted the Queen Mother, accompanied by Prince Andrew, during a royal visit to Leeming in Yorkshire to mark the sixtieth anniversary of the Central Flying School Association, and he then went to the RAF Benevolent Fund's Duke of Kent School at Woolpit in Surrey. This was the first visit by a CAS in office since the school was founded in 1920 and during the visit he addressed the staff and pupils of the school and his wife presented the school prizes for the year. Events such as these were a welcome diversion from the political and military debates and wrangling, which all came as part of being the Chief, and Beetham always found these additional responsibilities to be most rewarding.

Having now been the Chief for three years, Beetham was able to reflect on RAF activities, particularly during the past year. Of primary importance was the fact that the day-to-day task of intercepting the Soviet aircraft that continued to probe Britain's air defence system had increased from an average of four interceptions per week in 1979 to five per week in 1980. The RAF was also involved in the air resupply and casualty evacuation for the Commonwealth Monitoring Force in Rhodesia as part of Operation Agila, where the role of the multinational force was to keep peace between the guerrilla fighters and the Rhodesian forces during the ceasefire in the run-up to the 1980 elections. Also overseas, RAF helicopters were as busy as ever continuing their work in Hong Kong, Belize and Northern Ireland as well as carrying out search-and-rescue missions back home.

However, it had now become apparent that the government's honeymoon period in office had come to an end. While the government had initially met its commitment to strengthen defence, the economic situation towards the end of 1980 meant that an immediate saving of £200 million in defence expenditure had to be made, followed by further financial limitations that would give the defence budget a below-inflation rise in the coming years and, therefore, give the armed forces a longer-term problem. This meant that the sustainment of Britain's four main defence tasks – BAOR, UK air defence, naval defence of the approaches to the Atlantic and the Polaris/Trident nuclear submarines – were now under threat and one of these tasks would probably have to go. Of the four main military tasks, the Trident programme was probably the most vulnerable. Even though Trident would provide Britain with a national strategic nuclear deterrent, the Treasury wanted the cost of the programme to be met from the Royal Navy's budget at the expense of conventional warships. Alternatively, in the Treasury's view, the nuclear deterrent could be met from the budget for cruise missiles and a strike force of Tornado bombers.

As Beetham saw it, there were two problems for the RAF to manage. First, in the short term, the service had to live within its means. Cost escalation in real terms in areas such as works services and in equipment procurement had markedly exceeded the inflation rates allowed in the cash limits for the programme. The second, and longer-term, problem was posed by actual reductions in planned spending levels and the implications for the future size of the RAF's budget. It was also his view that there was a real need to present a strong case for air power in the national defence priorities. Losing control of the UK's airspace was not an option, not only from a national perspective but also because Britain provided a vital rear base for the entire NATO Alliance. Furthermore, apart from the maintenance of Britain's nuclear deterrence, the other two pillars of the four main military tasks also relied on air power. Beetham was convinced that neither task had the remotest chance of being effective without the prerequisite of adequate air power. Whether the task was sinking submarines in the Eastern Atlantic or holding an armoured thrust across the North German plain, it would be air power that would have the dominant role to play.

The secretary of state for defence, Francis Pym, was in a difficult position, as to opt for a significant reduction in the defence equipment programme would most probably have led to another defence review. This would have been a difficult option for Pym, particularly as there was no military justification for doing so and it would have been time consuming. Therefore, having taken the various options into account, Pym imposed a moratorium on all defence spending not already committed and he imposed a period of severe financial restraint for the rest of the year. Then, together with the other two services, and along similar lines to those seen under the Labour government only a couple of years before, the RAF commenced a period of reduced training activity.

Once again, some started to leave the services as a feeling of déjà vu spread through the armed forces. Six documents demonstrating the concern of the service Chiefs about reduced military spending were leaked to the press and these cast doubts on the government's general election commitment to improve defence. One of the documents was a record of a meeting chaired by the PUS, Sir Frank Cooper, with the three Chiefs of Staff, during which the Chiefs protested at the cuts in defence expenditure. Each of the Chiefs was keen to protect the major equipment programme for his own service. For Beetham it was the planned replacement for the Jaguar and Harrier combat aircraft that was under threat. For the army, Bramall made the point that the financial allocation for the new Challenger main battle tank was inadequate and for the Royal Navy Leach complained about the inclusion of the Trident programme to be procured as a national deterrent from the Royal Navy's own budget.

For some time the prime minister had been concerned about Whitehall leaks, and Thatcher was said to be furious at the latest revelations, which were suspected to have come from senior military officers or high-ranking civil servants. Some politicians were suspicious of the service Chiefs of Staff; the Chiefs were not in fact responsible but, once again, found themselves the subjects of media headlines. On the day the story first hit the papers, 24 October, Beetham was many miles away in Lincolnshire, visiting Coningsby. Although he was very much aware of the media reports, he took the opportunity to enjoy a nostalgic flight in the Lancaster of the Battle of Britain Memorial Flight.

Having returned to Whitehall it was obvious that the planned cuts in defence expenditure were going to go ahead despite the concerns of the Chiefs of Staff. After consulting with senior RAF staff and the other service Chiefs it was decided that the only way to try and prevent such cuts was for the Chiefs of Staff to request a meeting with the prime minister. The request was granted and the meeting, which included Pym, took place at 10 Downing Street on 12 November. The meeting, which lasted two hours, came on the eve of a resumed discussion by the cabinet to discuss where savings could be made during the following year in light of the economic situation. Led by Lewin, the Chiefs made it clear to the prime minister that any further cuts in defence spending would put impossible strains on Britain's commitment to NATO and they urged Thatcher to forestall any cuts in the following year's planned defence spending.

During the meeting Beetham illustrated the effects on the RAF by talking about air defence of the UK in response to the government's last Defence White Paper, which stressed the need for improvements to meet the increased Warsaw Pact capability for conventional air attack, in particular from the Tupolev Tu-22M long-range supersonic swing-wing strategic bomber. Against this threat he reported the RAF could muster a hundred fighters, but the real increase of 3 per cent per year that had been expected after the government had decided on some interim improvements during the previous year would have enabled the RAF to build up its strength to nearly 150 fighters, which both the RAF and NATO had assessed to be the number required to meet the task. However, further cuts now would put the RAF back to where it had started and it would also mean there would be a gap in radar early-warning coverage of two or three years before the Nimrod AEW became operational.

He went on to explain why cuts could not be made elsewhere, such as from the air transport or maritime patrol fleets, and said that improvements, such as they were, were not even keeping pace with the developing threat, and the RAF would be worse placed than when the government had first come to power. He also explained that the planned budget for the following year had originally been £2.954 billion but this had already been reduced by £76 million and, when taking into account committed expenditure on things such as pay and pensions, there was less than £200 million available. It was, of course, possible to cancel existing contracts, but any savings would be offset by the payment of cancellation charges.

The meeting proved to be an honest and frank discussion, something that Thatcher always welcomed from the Chiefs. She fully understood their views and would like to have spent as much as possible on defence but the fact was that she could not ignore the overall economic state of the country. In the end an agreement was made as something of a compromise. The prime minister accepted that the overall reduction of £500 million that was being asked for, or even £400 million, was not attainable, but she believed a reduction of £250 million should be possible and this reduction was very small when compared to the total size of the defence budget. Having all said their piece everyone all then enjoyed a gin and tonic together after the meeting – such was Thatcher's manner and style of leadership, which Beetham respected and admired.

Not surprisingly, the meeting between Thatcher and the Chiefs of Staff was reported in all the national papers the following day. The line taken by the press was how the prime minister had stood firmly against the plea of her service Chiefs, and the man caught in the middle was Pym as the secretary of state for defence. Although Pym always seemed to be worried about finances and expenditure, Beetham found him to be a most delightful man and he fully recognised the difficult and sensitive position that the secretary of state was now in, particularly because Pym was due to fly to Brussels later that day where just fifteen months before he had promised a 3 per cent increase in defence spending. While Pym was committed to NATO's 3 per cent annual increase in spending, he was also committed to the cabinet's programme of retrenchment with a savings target believed to be in the region of between £1.7 billion and £2 billion the following year. Some Conservative MPs feared that if Pym did not win the battle against the Treasury then he and the Chiefs of Staff might resign, and other ministers were reluctant to cut their own budgets unless defence took its share. In the end there would be a contribution to the Treasury's campaign, but nowhere near as much as the chief secretary to the Treasury, John Biffen, had asked for. The defence saving was probably nearer £100–150 million rather than the £500 million asked for, or even the £250 million proposed by Thatcher.

Whether there was any internal wrangling between Thatcher and Pym is unclear, but in the cabinet reshuffle of January 1981 Pym was appointed as the leader of the House of Commons, a political move sideways, and he was replaced as the secretary of state for defence by John Nott. A former army officer with the Gurkha Rifles, Nott had worked in the City before entering Parliament in 1966 as the Member of Parliament for St Ives, a seat he would hold for the next seventeen years; he had then served as a Treasury minister before he sat in Thatcher's first cabinet as secretary of state for trade.

Although Nott had been appointed by Thatcher to take a tougher line than Pym, his appointment as the new secretary of state for defence was well received by the Chiefs. The fact that he was a former banker might have suggested that Nott would concentrate solely on financial matters but he quickly made it clear to the Chiefs that he wanted to look first at the strategic choices for the armed forces and then to match the military resources to the commitments. Given the political commitment to NATO and the lack of finance, Nott soon realised that all that could be achieved in the short term was a force structure to meet the main threat to the UK while trying to ensure that the structure put in place was sufficiently flexible to meet the unexpected.

Nott acquitted himself well in his first task of producing a cleverly constructed and well-timed solution to the cabinet's demand for a cut in the following year's defence budget. The clear-out of old equipment early meant that the re-equipment programme for all three services had remained largely untouched. However, there was no way that the country's likely resources could be stretched effectively to cover all the main military tasks, and so the problems facing the armed forces in the 1980s were no less serious than before. Therefore, Nott's next immediate task was to look realistically at the longer-term defence programmes; this would inevitably result in hard decisions having to be made.

From the Chiefs of Staff's perspective the armed forces were already at a critical level and there was little that could be offered as a potential savings. While in previous years there had usually been an overseas base, or bases, that could be offered up to ministers as a saving, this was not the case any more. At Nott's request the Chiefs met for two days at Greenwich to discuss the options available to them. The event was also attended by Sir Frank Cooper, Sir David Cardwell (chief of defence procurement) and Sir Ronald Mason (chief scientific adviser), and during the two days every aspect of defence policy was covered to answer the question posed by Nott – 'What is the strategy?'

Beetham felt that it was possible to identify the factors that should determine the priorities in the defence programme and policy, some of which were facts and others a matter of judgement, but all needed weighing in the balance. Although an island, the UK was, in every sense, part of Europe. It was, militarily speaking, in a rear area, but the UK was nonetheless vulnerable to attack. As far as strategy was concerned, the UK could no longer be assured of its own security and for this it depended on its membership of the Alliance. Therefore, the UK had to subscribe to the strategy of the Alliance, which was basically one of deterrence, which rested on the possession of nuclear weapons and, whether anyone liked it or not, forward defence. In determining the threat faced by the UK, it was important to identify the Soviet objectives and to determine by what military means they would seek to achieve them. It was also important to assess what warning of attack could be expected and what the duration of any conflict might be.

As far as national considerations were concerned, Beetham knew that the UK's contribution to NATO must be commensurate with its perception of its place in the Alliance, its economic resources, the just expectations of its Allies, and the influence it would wish to exert with them. Its nature should be determined by what the UK considered it was able to provide, by its geographical location, by its industrial and technological base and by the demographic and educational trends. The UK should also assess where the greatest dangers lay and what capabilities contributed most to deter the threats considered most serious. There were also other factors to consider, such as establishing whether there were situations outside NATO where, either alone or with allies, the UK might wish to use military force to protect its interest. The UK should then decide what influence, if any, this should have on its force structure and determine what degree of independence it could realistically seek to maintain.

The answer essentially came down to the difficult choice of either supporting NATO in Europe or adopting a maritime strategy that would effectively ignore the ground situation in Europe. The RAF was in the fortunate position to be able to support either strategy but the Chiefs were divided in their opinions. Beetham and Bramall were both adamant that Britain's contribution to NATO in Europe was paramount, whereas Leach was keen to protect the interests of the Royal Navy by emphasising that in time of war priority should be given to maintaining resupply routes across the Atlantic. To Beetham, Leach's view was countered by the fact that the threat from the Soviet Union could be measured in days rather than weeks, and he felt that it was vital for priority to be given to the immediate threat facing Britain – the Soviet Union in Europe. Even adopting a NATO strategy of 'flexible response', any resupply of Britain from across the Atlantic would take far too long and Beetham believed a nuclear conflict might well have started by the time any resupply could take effect. Furthermore, there was also the political angle to consider and he felt it politically unacceptable to reduce Britain's contribution to NATO in Europe.

While Beetham was certainly not in favour of any cuts, he felt that if something had to go then a reduction in the number of Royal Navy surface ships was logical. However, it was never going to be that simple and the RAF certainly came under scrutiny when Nott posed Beetham some difficult questions on Air Force strategy: What exactly was the RAF doing in Germany? Would it not be more cost effective to retain some forward operating airfields in Germany while withdrawing RAF aircraft back to the UK where they would have more chance of protecting the airfields against a first strike? Why were the German Tornado squadrons tasked to perform a maritime role in the Baltic while the RAF was tasked with carrying out interdiction against the Soviet second echelon in Germany? Would it not be more logical for the RAF to pursue a maritime role and leave the Germans to take responsibility for the central front? Nott was also keen to make savings in the later years of the RAF's equipment programme. In particular he was aware that the cost of the tri-national Tornado programme was more costly than Trident but Beetham was quick to point out that the cost of cancellation would be excessive. Tornado survived and fortunately for the RAF the planned upgrades to the Harrier and Nimrod were also contracted. Furthermore, when it came to assessing the RAF's ability to defend the UK, Nott could see the RAF was short of aircraft and he soon found out there was less room to manoeuvre with the RAF than with the other services.

Lewin, as the CDS, was in a most difficult position. He was a Royal Navy officer with the responsibility as the CDS to represent the collective view of the service Chiefs and could not be seen to be biased towards his own service, nor could he expect Beetham and Bramall to come down on the side of Leach. Lewin wanted the Chiefs of Staff to present a united front but obviously that was not going to happen. To Nott it was clear that the Chiefs could not agree how to share the pain and so he turned to others, including Sir Frank Cooper and Sir Ronald Mason, as well as consulting the

Foreign Office. The Foreign Office clearly saw Britain as a European power, and scientific studies had concluded that the Royal Navy had less of a case when it came to preventing cuts within the armed forces. In the draft paper by the deputy under-secretary (policy), Michael Quinlan, it became apparent to Beetham that the Royal Navy was to suffer the severest cuts, and the army and the RAF would survive relatively unscathed.

Protecting the RAF's long-term capability had always been Beetham's main objective throughout the process of government savings and after Nott's appointment he had been the first to speak publicly on the issue of defence cuts. During an address to the Air Public Relations Association he explained there were no easy pickings left in the defence programme after many years of scrutiny and any economic exercise would lead to unpalatable measures. The measures that would have to be taken to satisfy the cut in the following year's defence budget were unwelcome but just about manageable. There were potential savings in retiring earlier than planned some parts of the front line that had already been scheduled for replacement, and doing this would leave intact the core of the RAF's major re-equipment programme for the 1980s. In the shorter term the first of the Chinook helicopters had been delivered and a number of Nimrods had been upgraded to Mk II standard. Furthermore, the first of the Tornado multi-role combat aircraft were about to enter service and the recent reopening of Chivenor in North Devon had meant the RAF now had a second Hawk Tactical Weapons Unit for advanced training.

In January 1981 Beetham attended the opening of the Tri-National Tornado Training Establishment at RAF Cottesmore in Leicestershire, where British, German and Italian crews would be trained on the supersonic swing-wing multi-role combat aircraft known as the Tornado IDS (Interdictor Strike). Also attending the opening ceremony were the Chief of the West German Air Force, Generalleutnant Friedrich Obleser, the Chief of the Italian Air Force, Generale Lamberto Bartolucci, and the Commander-in-Chief of the German Navy, Vizeadmiral Günter Fromm. Preparatory work had begun at Cottesmore in 1978, and the Memorandum of Understanding between the nations had been signed the following year, and so the base had been steadily working up to a full contingent that would eventually reach more than two thousand personnel, including military personnel from Germany and Italy, as well as civilian personnel, and forty-eight aircraft.

At its peak TTTE would produce 170 Tornado crews per year and the establishment represented an important collaborative venture between the three participating nations, effectively integrating the cost-sharing economics of a tri-national programme with the advantages of interoperability between the three nations. The total cost of the programme to Britain was about £5 billion, which would eventually give the RAF 385 aircraft, of which 220 would be the IDS variant and 165 would be the Tornado F2 Air Defence variant, with training on the F2 being conducted at Coningsby. Germany was due to receive 334 aircraft (212 for the German Air Force and 122 for the German Navy) and the Italian Air Force was due to receive 100 aircraft. Although each aircraft cost about £11 million, Beetham explained to the press that defence capability did not come cheap – a tank cost £1 million and a guided-missile destroyer cost £100 million. He was quick to justify the expense by explaining the versatility and capability of Tornado: it could destroy ships in the Baltic, crater enemy airfields in Central Europe, defend the airspace over the UK and protect a task force at sea. He added that the opening of TTTE not only further strengthened the bonds of NATO friendship but also symbolised another major step forward for the most important aircraft – in terms of numbers and capability – to enter service with the three nations in recent years.

Whatever further economies the service would have to make, Beetham realised that the introduction of the Tornado had helped secure a bright future for the RAF. The service was leaner than he would have liked but he was fully aware that highly effective aircraft and equipment, as well as the serving men and women, were second to none. On the issue of retention, recent figures showed that retention in most categories had improved, and was now at its best in recent years, and as far as recruitment was concerned the figures again showed there had been a significant improvement since the issues of pay and conditions of service had been resolved.

In February John Thomson handed over as Beetham's PSO to Wing Commander David Cousins, who had completed his tour as OC 16 Squadron (Buccaneers) at Laarbruch in Germany and had spent the past six months at the Central Trials and Tactics Organisation at Headquarters Strike Command, High Wycombe, where he had been sent to set up, and then run, a Tactical Leadership School for the RAF. However, Strike Command had then decided that the NATO Tactical Leadership Programme at Jever in Germany served the RAF's needs quite adequately and so decided not to pursue the idea of running its own school. Cousins's stay at CTTO had been cut short and he had needed another challenge. He knew that John Thomson was about to move on and so he was delighted when he found out that Beetham had selected him to become his next PSO.

There was a further change in the outer office when, in March, David Bonner took over as private secretary from Stephen Crew, who had previously succeeded Tony Pawson. Bonner was no stranger to senior RAF officers, because his wife was then the ADC to AOC 11 Group at Bentley Priory, but he initially felt somewhat overawed. He had not worked so closely with a service Chief before, nor had he worked so closely with the RAF, as much of his previous work had been with the Royal Navy. Bonner found Beetham to be a very modest man who was extremely comprehensive and meticulous in everything he did, and thought he was more 'air force' than 'joint services', perhaps more so than he had expected, although Beetham always listened to the views of the other services.

Although this period marked another change of key outer-office personnel, both Cousins and Bonner would remain in their appointments throughout the rest of Beetham's tour as Chief and this would provide him with some much-needed continuity in the difficult months ahead. They had both arrived during the staffing process for the defence review, when there were a number of options and proposals for savings being worked up, and both would act as facilitators to make sure that any briefs from the numerous meetings, or answers from any follow-up work, came back to Beetham in a timely and seamless way. Throughout this process Beetham was most ably supported by his Vice-Chief, Sir David Craig, and his Assistant Chiefs, and he would regularly hold meetings in his office and discuss the options around the table. It proved to be a most slick and effective process with work of extremely high quality coming from some very capable people – most notably from Paddy Hine, who picked up much of the work.

Beetham knew the key point was to get the right inter-service decisions in the first place. While he was not the original thinker, he certainly understood air power and his task was to make sure the RAF case was put forward in a coherent way. This was where he was at his best as he excelled when it came to arguing air power and RAF policy with ministers. He was always diligent when it came to making sure that Nott was well briefed on matters relating to the RAF and Beetham respected the fact that Nott was prepared to think more laterally than other ministers, and for these reasons he found that Nott would often accept the views the RAF put forward.

When Nott's Defence White Paper, 'The Way Forward', was published in June 1981 the four main military tasks remained unchanged but their priorities were more defined. Along with Britain's strategic nuclear deterrent, the air defence of the UK was a top priority, although it was acknowledged that this required strengthening. Britain's contribution to NATO in Europe was given more priority than the Eastern Atlantic, and there was no doubt that the Royal Navy was the hardest hit of the three services.

From Nott's point of view the outcome of the defence review had a logic that was difficult for the Royal Navy to deny. The number of frigates was to be reduced from sixty-five to around fifty and the number of anti-submarine warfare carriers was to be reduced from three to two. Although the number of nuclear-powered submarines was also to be reduced, the planned reduction from twenty to seventeen was seen as a smaller cut in percentage terms than the cut in the number of surface ships. It was also announced that the dockyards at Portsmouth and Chatham were to close, and another of the navy's cuts was the planned withdrawal of the Antarctic patrol ship, *Endurance*, from the South Atlantic, although this measure was strongly opposed by the Foreign Office.

The overall impact of the defence review had reduced the real growth in defence expenditure to about 7 per cent over three years since the Conservatives had come to power. Although this figure would eventually rise to around 8 per cent over the following year, this was still some way short of the 12 per cent figure that had been planned under Britain's commitment to NATO's 3 per cent annual growth.

Beetham was still digesting the detail of the defence review when he visited South America in July. Unlike some of his overseas visits undertaken as the CAS, there had been no great pressure from the Foreign and Commonwealth Office for a visit to South America, but it did provide an ideal opportunity to pull a number of strands together in a part of the world where there were few strong relationships with Britain, such as building industrial and bilateral relations with each of the four nations on his tour – Brazil, Ecuador, Peru and Venezuela – and pursuing defence interests such as the Brazilian Embraer EMB-312 Tucano two-seat turboprop basic training aircraft, which was fast emerging as a potential replacement for the RAF's Jet Provost.

Accompanied by Cousins, Beetham arrived at Rio de Janeiro International Airport in the early evening of 6 July for the start of his five-day visit to Brazil. The Força Aerea Brasileira is the largest air force in Latin America and throughout his visit Beetham was hosted by the air attaché in Brazil, Wing Commander Jeremy Brown, and Brigadeiro Murillo Santos. Santos had been the senior overseas student at the RAF Staff College at Bracknell during Beetham's time as commandant and was now an influential base commander at Natal Air Base, and he had been selected by the FAB to act as the senior hosting officer because of his excellent English and his earlier acquaintance with Beetham.

The following day Beetham flew to Brasilia, where he met with the British ambassador, William Harding, who had only recently taken up his appointment, and he also met with the Brazilian minister of air and the FAB's Chief of the Air Staff. The next morning he visited the Regional Air Command Headquarters and in the afternoon he travelled to the Mirage air base at Anapolis. He then went to São Paulo to visit the Brazilian aerospace company, Empresa Brasileira de Aeronautica (Embraer), the company building the Tucano, and visited the Comando-Geral de Tecnologia Aerospacial at São José dos Campos, the military aviation research centre, where the Tucano was being built and tested. The prototype had flown just the year before and Jeremy Brown would later fly the second prototype, making him the first RAF pilot to fly the Tucano, before the aircraft was later selected by the RAF to replace the Jet Provost in 1989.

Having returned to Rio de Janeiro, Beetham found time to enjoy the sights and took a swim off the side of a boat in Guanabara Bay. On the morning of 11 July he left Rio de Janeiro for Ecuador and during his quick visit to the Fuerza Aérea Ecuatoriana he met with officials of the FAE, which had recently taken delivery of the Jaguar ES aircraft, before he moved on to Peru to meet officials of the Fuerza Aérea del Perú. He visited the air base at Pisco and the Escuela de Oficiales de la Fap, the air academy, at the Las Palmas Air Base.

Beetham left Lima on the long flight to Caracas for his final visit of the tour to Venezuela. Because it was such a long flight the aircraft made a scheduled refuelling stop at Bogotá in Colombia where, unfortunately, the aircraft became unserviceable while on the ground. After a period of no information, just coffee, Cousins telephoned the British embassy to inform the staff they were in the country and delayed at the airport. One of the embassy's officials kindly went to the airport to keep them company and eventually, after sixteen hours in the airport terminal, the flight continued on to Caracas. Beetham's visit to the Fuerza Aérea Venezolana was now behind schedule and it was to be a short stay in Venezuela but, even so, it was clear the FAV had been able to increase its capability during recent years and was soon to become one of the first export customers for the US F-16 fighter. At the end of his stay in Venezuela, Beetham flew by RAF VC10 to Belize for a short stop-over to visit RAF personnel before returning to the UK.

The tour of South America had lasted just over two weeks and the most important gain had been the strong relationships that Beetham had formed with key military and government officials in each country. During each visit he had taken time to brief the host nation on the RAF's equipment programme, the threat it faced and its role within NATO, after which he would ask each nation about its own perceived threat; most interestingly, Argentina was mentioned every time. The tour of South America had been a great success but what no one could have realised at that time was just how important it would prove to be, particularly Beetham's visit to Brazil, where the relationships he had built with key officials in Brasilia during July 1981 – such as with the British ambassador and Brazil's minister of air – might well have played a crucial role during the Falklands conflict less than a year later.

Now back in London, Beetham was honoured and privileged as the CAS to be invited to the marriage of the Prince of Wales with Lady Diana Spencer in St Paul's Cathedral on 29 July. Two days before the wedding the Beethams attended the evening reception at Buckingham Palace, which included a grand buffet in the ball supper room and in the ballroom there was dancing to Kenny Ball and his Jazz Men, Hot Chocolate and the Band of the Welsh Guards. On the day of the wedding an estimated crowd of 600,000 filled the streets of London around the Mall, Trafalgar Square, The Strand, Fleet Street and Ludgate Hill, and a global audience of some 750 million watched the events on television. The Beethams were among the congregation of 3,500 at St Paul's Cathedral and from their seats in the historic dome they were able to enjoy a commanding view of the traditional service led by the Archbishop of Canterbury, Dr Robert Runcie.

Beetham now needed to look ahead to the longer term and decide how best to reshape the equipment programme to make the most effective use of the RAF's limited resources, which would have to be deployed against the background of a volatile world situation and a growing Soviet threat. Soviet bombers armed with long-range missiles able to reach British targets at supersonic speeds posed a significant threat that was far more deadly than anything Britain had faced before. Beetham was also aware that the Soviet Union recognised the vital role of air power in any future conflict and in the previous year had spent more on aircraft than on ships, submarines and land armaments combined.

While always mindful of the continued threat posed by the Soviet Union, Beetham had to remain realistic about the future capability of the RAF, particularly given the outcome of the defence review, but he was reassured by the fact that the RAF's contribution to the defence of the UK and to the NATO Alliance would be significantly enhanced during the 1980s. While the V-force had provided a central bulwark of Britain's defences for more than twenty-five years, the Tornado, with its purpose-built low-level all-weather capability, would undoubtedly be a worthy successor, and its introduction into service would mark a significant step-change in technology and military capability.

Air-to-air refuelling too, for so long the adjunct of defence expenditure, started to get the attention it deserved. Additional VC10s and Super VC10s had been bought from various commercial airlines, including British Airways, for conversion to air refuelling tankers; these aircraft would become the VC10 K2 and K3 variants to enter service from 1984. Furthermore, as a way of supplementing the RAF's air defence capability, the RAF's Hawk jet trainers were to be armed with Sidewinder air-to-air missiles, and the RAF's aerobatic team, the Red Arrows, was retained by re-forming the team as a 'shadow' air defence squadron in times of emergency.

There were also to be improvements to the RAF's airborne early-warning capability. The Soviet Union's ability to launch weapons against UK targets from several hundred miles away meant that it was now essential to extend airborne radar coverage far out to sea. As a replacement for the ageing Shackleton AEW Mk 2, the British government had originally intended to join with NATO in the procurement of the proven Boeing E-3A Sentry Airborne Warning and Control System (AWACS) for a multinational AEW force. However, delays in the member nations agreeing to the conditions of the programme had led the previous Labour government to opt instead for the development of the Nimrod AEW Mk 3 for the RAF.

The concept of using the Nimrod as an AEW platform was new and the Mk 3 was readily distinguishable from its maritime predecessor by the bulbous radomes mounted on the nose and tail, which contained the scanners for the Marconi Avionics radar system. The decision to opt for the Nimrod AEW had been taken before Beetham had become the CAS, but he would have supported the decision had he have been in post at the time; although he was keen for a NATO AEW force, no decision had been forthcoming and so the UK had no choice but to go it alone. Nimrod had certainly been assessed as a sound prospect and, in any case, AWACS was considered to be unaffordable.

In 1981 it seemed there was much to look forward to regarding Nimrod AEW; the outcome was very different, though, and the project would be remembered as one of the great procurement fiascos of its time. The project was soon plagued by severe technical problems and rising costs, and the Ministry of Defence eventually realised that the technical success was looking unlikely and the cost of developing the radar system to achieve the quite demanding specification was unaffordable. Five years later the decision would be made to cancel the Nimrod AEW project in favour of the Boeing E-3D Sentry AEW1, which would eventually enter operational service with the RAF in 1991.

Although Beetham understood the importance of Britain maintaining its aviation and technical industries, he was nonetheless keen to ensure the service had the best equipment available, regardless of whether it was British or not, and one notable example about to enter operational service with the RAF was the US Boeing Chinook HC1 heavy-lift helicopter. An order for the Chinook had been made as early as 1967 but had then been cancelled soon after because of cut-backs in defence spending at the time. Now, several years on, the RAF was to get the helicopter it required. Capable of carrying a payload in excess of 20,000 lb or up to fifty armed troops, at speeds of up to 170 knots, the Chinook represented a huge leap forward in capability and it would prove to be an extremely versatile support helicopter and an outstanding work-horse for the armed forces for many years to come. Capable of being operated in many diverse environments, ranging from arctic conditions to desert warfare operations, the RAF would eventually become the second-largest operator of the Chinook outside the USA.

Beetham was keen to pursue his belief that the RAF's airfields should be protected by the RAF Regiment and where there were insufficient regulars to meet the task the shortfall should be made up using auxiliary squadrons. Under NATO's old strategy of massive retaliation there had been no need for reserve forces but its policy of flexible response was another matter. The RAF's normal manning establishment did not permit any manpower flexibility in a crisis and would mean that the service could not stretch itself for any length of time. He felt the RAF's reserve forces needed building up, starting with the RAF Regiment squadrons, and he supported the proposal for the formation of four auxiliary squadrons for airfield defence, although he was quick to point out to the commandant general of the RAF Regiment, Air Vice-Marshal Henry Reed-Purvis, that this proposal in no way would threaten the existence of the regulars within the regiment.

He was also mindful from conversations with the CGS, Dwin Bramall, that the army was keen to scope the feasibility of taking over from the RAF Regiment the role of protecting the RAF's airfields. Beetham's response was usually along the lines that he was happy to explore this suggestion further provided that at the same time the two services could closer examine the role of the Army Air Corps with a view to the RAF taking over its role – and that was usually the end of the conversation!

Beetham also recognised the dangers in the emerging trend of civilianisation and private contracting in certain areas of the RAF. To keep within the government's arbitrary ceiling on RAF manpower, which was not specifically related to the task, meant that more support and training tasks were being performed by civilians. While this could show economies in purely financial terms, and may have helped keep the RAF within arbitrary manpower ceilings, he was concerned for the effect such changes had on the service's ability to meet its task as it meant the RAF giving up a large part of its flexibility and ability to reinforce the front line. He tried, therefore, to swing the pendulum back towards more service personnel as much as possible and he tried at every opportunity to devise numerous ways of using reserve personnel to save regular manpower and to prevent private contracting.

After the defence review proposals had been made to change the structure for decision making at the highest levels of defence. First, the posts of the three single-service ministers were abolished to ensure that ministerial control within the Ministry of Defence was truly tri-service, and there were to be no more separate single-service responsibilities. Secondly, following general dissatisfaction within Whitehall at the lack of a single defence voice, there were proposed changes to the role and responsibilities of the CDS. The formation of the post of CDS in 1958, and the creation of a unified Ministry of Defence in 1964, had led to the role and responsibilities of the CDS being defined in 1963, during the Mountbatten era, but it was now felt within the government that the single-service Chiefs and their departments had gradually taken back control during the past eighteen years; particularly so during the last two or three years. To some in government, there were simply too many Chiefs. Lewin, as the current CDS, did not disagree. He felt the Chiefs of Staff had failed to agree a single and united view for the recent defence review, and so he proposed to his colleagues a strengthening of the powers to ensure that the CDS was the pre-eminent member of the Chiefs of Staff.

The proposal was based on five principles. First, the CDS would become the principal military adviser to the secretary of state and the government. This was significantly different to the current situation, where it was the collective advice of the Chiefs of Staff Committee that would be tendered by the CDS. When there was divergence of view between the Chiefs of Staff, the CDS would submit the alternatives and the CDS, as the principal military adviser to the secretary of state, would tender his own advice to the minister in the light of the views expressed.

Second, the Chiefs of Staff Committee, chaired by the CDS, would be the forum where the CDS would seek the views of his single-service colleagues. This was not a significant change because there was already a Chiefs of Staff Committee, but it was a change regarding the responsibility of the CDS as the current situation was that the Chiefs of Staff were collectively responsible to the government for professional advice on strategy and military operations of defence policy. The composition of the Chiefs of Staff Committee was revised to be: the CDS as the chairman; the single-service Chiefs as members; the Chiefs of Staff Secretariat; the secretary of the committee and Vice-Chief of the Defence Staff (Personnel and Logistics) in attendance when personnel, logistics and joint training issues were to be discussed. Others would be invited to attend as required from the central staffs, the service departments, defence secretariat, defence scientific staff, the procurement executive and other government departments.

The third principle was that the single-service Chiefs of Staff would continue to be the professional heads of their own services, responsible for the morale and efficiency of their service, and the conduct of single-service operations. As heads of their own service they would continue to give advice on strategy, military operations and the military implications of defence policy and they would also continue to have right of access to the secretary of state and the prime minister. This was effectively no different from the current situation.

The fourth principle was that the central defence staffs would be accountable to the CDS, who would be responsible for directing their work. They would provide support for the CDS to enable him to proffer independent military advice but they would also consult with the single-service departments to ensure that matters discussed in the Chiefs of Staff Committee had been fully staffed. To this end it should be recognised that there should be direct freedom of access at all levels between staffs throughout the department. Again this marked a significant change as the current situation was that the naval, general and air staffs, with the joint-service staffs of the MOD, constituted the defence staff and were responsible to the Chiefs of Staff Committee, with the committee collectively directing the work of the central defence staff.

The fifth principle was that the CDS would chair a Senior Appointments Committee, approximately every four months, with the single-service Chiefs of Staff as members to make future recommendations to the secretary of state on the appointments and promotions of all three- and four-star officers, as well as key two-star appointments who were accountable to, or directly responsible to, the CDS. Up to now the career of an officer up to the highest ranks was in the hands of his own service and the single-service Chiefs of Staff made the recommendations, even for key central staff and rotational appointments. While this principle worked for each service, there was a feeling among others external to the services, particularly ministers, that the rotation system might not always be in the national interest.

Lewin had some, but not total, support from the Chiefs of Staff. The main opposition to his views came from Leach and to a lesser extent from Beetham, who had for some time been reflecting on the collective responsibilities of the Chiefs of Staff. The most important thing in peacetime, and at the same time the most difficult, was to decide the allocation of resources to provide the best possible military capability within resource constraints. Some months earlier, Beetham had written to the other Chiefs, expressing his concern at the long-standing and widely held view in Whitehall that they did not face up to the issues involved in resource allocation and, regrettably, he believed it was with some justification. He felt the

Chiefs of Staff had not been seen and accepted as a body capable of rising above single-service interests and put the overall interest of defence first. While the mechanism for taking such decisions had proved adequate, and the Chiefs should be tolerably content with the review of defence policy, the basis in logic for the decisions was weak, to say the least, and many of the more difficult decisions had simply been deferred to be faced in LTC 81.

As a single-service Chief, Beetham was only too aware of how difficult it was to take the broader view when it could mean transferring resources away from one's own service, but the Chiefs should be prepared to do so. He felt the Chiefs needed to be more positive in their collective approach if they were to have real influence as a committee, and they needed to be prepared to examine positively the optimum force mixes to meet individual threats; this was an area where they always seemed to get bogged down, yet it was one of the keys to resource allocation. He did not feel it needed a major change, but the Chiefs could look at some aspects of how they did their job and he believed more use could be made of the Vice-Chiefs of Staff, particularly to sort out some of the more detailed issues sometimes dealt with by the Chiefs. The Chiefs should always strive to reach a united collective view, but they should not shirk from occasionally spelling out different views. Indeed, a united front on every issue would be scarcely credible to the outside world.

Fundamentally, Beetham believed there was a need for a change of approach. Decisions should be made more analytically and in the wider interests of defence. Failing this, he could only see that their position and influence as a committee would erode further, as it had done over previous months. Nonetheless, he firmly believed that the Chiefs of Staff had a much greater voice as a body of four rather than the CDS offering a voice of one. Essentially, if the CDS was ever opposed by the permanent under-secretary of state for defence, the top civil servant at the Ministry of Defence, then it would give the Chiefs of Staff an advantage of four voices to one, rather then there being parity in terms of the military opinion versus the Civil Service opinion. Furthermore, the sight of the four Chiefs of Staff marching across from Main Building to 10 Downing Street in their uniforms had always had quite an impact during their previous battles against the politicians and civil servants.

Bramall, on the other hand, had been a member of Mountbatten's team during the 1960s and was himself the front-runner to be the next CDS, and so, unsurprisingly, he was more supportive of

Lewin's proposal. He did not disagree with Beetham's thoughts but he was more optimistic about the way in which the Chiefs conducted their business. Nott did not overtly take Lewin's side against the opposition of Leach and Beetham, but he nonetheless agreed to his proposal. From the secretary of state's perspective, this was a vital reform and the proposal was subsequently endorsed by Thatcher. In January 1982, while Beetham was in Australia conducting airman-to-airman talks, the new principles were implemented, but the change stopped short of the full integration of the naval, general and air staffs. Lewin did not have the full support of the other Chiefs of Staff and the services were not yet ready for a fully functional defence staff but, although no one could have imagined it at the time, these reforms would soon be put to the severest test of all.

CHAPTER 12

The Falklands

———

At the beginning of April 1982 Beetham was finalising the programme for his final six months as the Chief when Argentina suddenly invaded the Falkland Islands. Largely unknown to much of the population of the United Kingdom at the time because of their location just three hundred miles from the coast of mainland South America, the Falkland Islands consist of two main islands, East Falkland and West Falkland, and more than seven hundred smaller islands making up the archipelago in the South Atlantic. The islands, which in 1982 had approximately eighteen hundred inhabitants, are a self-governing territory of the United Kingdom but ever since the re-establishment of British rule in 1833 Argentina had claimed sovereignty.

Leading up to the invasion there had been a period of economic crisis and large civil unrest in Argentina, which at the end of 1981 had witnessed a change in the Argentine military regime and had brought to office a new junta led by its president, General Leopoldo Galtieri. The junta decided to opt for a military solution to resolve Argentina's long-standing claim to the Falkland Islands and by doing so hoped to divert public attention at home away from the country's severe economic situation and the regime's continuing violation of human rights. The decisions announced in John Nott's Defence Review the year before might well have led the Argentine junta to believe that Britain was either not capable or not prepared to mount a military response to an Argentine invasion. But the junta's decision to land a group of Argentine scrap-metal merchants on the island of the British Dependent Territory of South Georgia, some six hundred miles to the east of the Falklands on 19 March 1982, followed by the invasion of the Falkland Islands on 2 April, in the belief that Britain would not respond with military force, proved to be a grave error of judgement.

In Britain there seems to have been little firm evidence that an Argentine invasion was about to take place. The defence review had raised some concerns within the Royal Navy about the planned withdrawal of HMS *Endurance* from the South Atlantic, as it was the only naval presence in the region at the time, and the option to extend the existing runway at Stanley on East Falkland, estimated to cost around £3 million, had been explored by the RAF but had not been fully supported by the other services because it was not a NATO commitment.

The Foreign Office had recently expressed concerns about the Argentine junta's reaction to talks on the future of the Falkland Islands. A Chiefs of Staff note circulated on 19 March, updating a paper produced six months earlier, identified a number of options available to Argentina – including a full-scale military invasion – but, even though Argentine scrap-metal workers had landed on South Georgia, the Chiefs of Staff were still unaware of any hard intelligence to suggest that an Argentine invasion of the Falkland Islands was a strong possibility.

HMS *Endurance* sailed from Port Stanley for South Georgia on 21 March with a contingent of Royal Marines, in case the British government might wish to remove the Argentine scrap-metal workers by force, but it was not until 29 March that the cabinet decided to send a nuclear submarine to the South Atlantic. Then, on 31 March, Henry Leach received intelligence reports about movements of the Argentine Navy that suggested that an invasion was now imminent, and he met with John Nott in the House of Commons to advise him that he was assembling a naval task force should it be required.

Only now did Beetham become aware that something serious was developing. At the time he was the acting Chief of the Defence Staff, as Lewin was away in New Zealand. Bramall, too, was away on a visit to Northern Ireland, which left Beetham and Leach as the only Chiefs in London that day. Early the following morning Beetham chaired a meeting at the Ministry of Defence, attended by Nott and other senior military and civilian personnel, to discuss the situation and the options available. That evening he attended a meeting with the prime minister, Nott, Leach and the deputy prime minister, Willie Whitelaw, and by then he had prepared a full minute laying out all the military options available. It was evident very early on that Nott and Leach both favoured sending a task force rather than just submarines, and Beetham was insistent that the RAF should contribute as much as possible to the operation and was keen to ensure that his service was properly represented at the various levels of command.

Friday 2 April was a day of confusion. In the morning Beetham attended a cabinet meeting but there did not seem to be too much new information to report. An invasion was now thought to be imminent but at that time no confirmation had been received. The government had planned to make a statement to the House of Commons later that morning, but there had been no further communication with the Falkland Islands and there had been no corroborative information at all. Because the foreign secretary, Lord Carrington, sat in the House of Lords, it was the Lord Privy Seal, Humphrey Atkins, who acted as the chief government spokesman in the House of Commons for foreign and Commonwealth affairs. In his statement Atkins said that the government was unable to confirm that an invasion had taken place but he did say that the governor of the Falkland Islands, Rex Hunt, had been in touch with the Foreign Office some hours earlier, although this later proved to be incorrect.

It was around midday London time that news filtered through from a British Antarctic Survey vessel that the Falkland Islands had been occupied, and the BBC and other radio stations were starting to broadcast from Buenos Aires that an invasion had taken place. With a significant numerical advantage, the Argentine forces had managed to overwhelm the small British garrison on the Falkland Islands, which consisted of just sixty-five Royal Marines, with some ease. That afternoon there was a meeting between the Chiefs of Staff and in the evening Beetham attended a further cabinet meeting, during which the decision was made to send a task force to the South Atlantic. At that stage it was not known whether a landing on the Falkland Islands was a practical military option but it was obvious to him that the government now needed to do something urgently as Thatcher was concerned that to do nothing risked the fall of the government. Beetham immediately put in place a daily Chiefs of Staff meeting so that he could get the most up-to-date information and review what action should be taken; the first of these meetings took place the following day, Saturday 3 April.

The invasion of the Falkland Islands had certainly taken the British public by surprise. The day after the invasion, one national newspaper reported that the government was reeling amid the wreckage of Britain's biggest disaster since Suez; another reported that the British government had failed to deter the invasion and went on to add that it had been a day of deeply embarrassing confusion for the government and that the islands were almost certainly beyond military recovery. Many MPs felt that the government had been too casual in its handling of the situation, which led to opposition MPs calling for two of Thatcher's senior ministers, Nott and Lord Carrington, to be sacked.

Following an emergency meeting in the House of Commons on 3 April, the first Saturday emergency session since Suez in 1956, the prime minister announced that a naval task force was to immediately sail for the South Atlantic to take back the islands, by force if necessary. This was the start of Operation Corporate. Leach's earlier preparations meant that two days later, on 5 April, the task force, consisting of more than a hundred ships, many of which had been commandeered from the shipping trade, and with 28,000 men embarked, set sail from their home ports at the start of their long voyage south where they would join up with Royal Navy ships already dispatched from a fleet exercise that had been taking place off Gibraltar. At the heart of the task force were the two aircraft carriers, HMS *Hermes* and HMS *Invincible*, with the task force commander, Rear Admiral Sandy Woodward, in *Hermes*, and two assault ships, HMS *Fearless* and HMS *Intrepid*. The air component consisted of twenty Sea Harrier FRS1s embarked in *Hermes* and *Invincible*, and more than fifty helicopters of different types.

It was, without doubt, a fantastic national effort. Not only was it a great effort from the many servicemen involved but also from the civilians at the dockyards who had prepared and modified the ships ready for war. It would take nearly four weeks for the task force to get within striking distance of the Falkland Islands and this would prove to be an important period for military preparation, as well as providing valuable time for the politicians to try and resolve the issue without the use of force.

With the task force now on its way, attention turned to the command of the operation. Because the initial phases were to be almost entirely naval, command of the overall operation was given to C-in-C Fleet, Sir John Fieldhouse, at his joint maritime headquarters at Northwood. Apart from the nuclear submarines, which would remain under the command of Northwood, Fieldhouse delegated command of the task force to Sandy Woodward and in the event that a landing was to be made, command of the land war would be the responsibility of the land force commander, Major-General Jeremy Moore.

Lewin returned to London on the day the task force sailed for the South Atlantic and Beetham immediately brought him up to date on the course of events so far and the actions that had been taken. The following evening the Chiefs of Staff met with the prime minister, the secretary of state and the permanent under-secretary at the House of Commons. Initially Nott had only planned to take Lewin and Leach with him to meet with the prime minister but Beetham pointed out to the secretary of state that it was important for all the Chiefs to be fully aware of the developing situation and the military options available. The reluctance of Lewin to involve all the Chiefs in the early discussions and decisions did not go away and it was only after another meeting between Lewin and Nott that Beetham first learned of the decision to announce an exclusion zone around the Falklands and that the decision to recapture South Georgia had been agreed.

On 12 April, Easter Monday, Britain declared an exclusion zone of 200 miles from the centre of the Falkland Islands, which meant that any Argentine naval or auxiliary ship entering the zone could be attacked by a British nuclear submarine. That same day Beetham had an early meeting with the secretary of state before Nott's meeting with the prime minister and the US secretary of state, General Alexander Haig, later that morning. During his meeting with Nott, Beetham reviewed the military situation and, in particular, the sustainability of holding the task force in the South Atlantic for any length of time. While this was unlikely to prove too difficult in the short term, any lengthy campaign would make maintaining the task force difficult after a period of two or three months.

With the task force sailing further southwards, any hopes of a diplomatic solution with Argentina rested with the United Nations and USA under the auspices of Haig and the personal intervention of the US president, Ronald Reagan. Should there be no diplomatic solution it was important to establish the rules of engagement and any restraints that needed to apply. Although the Argentine junta had committed an act of aggression, they had achieved their aim without a single British casualty. Therefore the British government was reluctant to start hostilities as long as a diplomatic solution remained an option, and one consideration, although it was not a serious option, was for the task force to return to the UK with the Falkland Islands still in Argentine hands.

For now, Beetham concentrated on ensuring that the RAF provided full support to the task force but he was disappointed there had been little discussion at the highest level about the possible role of land-based air power. He was very much aware that the RAF options were limited due to the distance of the Falkland Islands from the nearest British territory, Ascension Island, but he was also mindful that the navy's initial request for air transport, which amounted to just three C-130 Hercules aircraft, was way off the mark and he rightly believed an operation of this size would require all the air transport support the RAF could provide.

Beetham and his staff had already been exploring a number of possible options using mainland South American bases for aircraft such as the Nimrod maritime patrol aircraft, Canberra reconnaissance aircraft, Victor air-to-air refuelling tanker, and also for the deployment of aircraft such as the Phantom, Buccaneer, Harrier and Jaguar for offensive missions. Consequently, various options using airfields in Chile were hastily considered by the air staff. Chile still had a long-standing dispute with Argentina over access to the Beagle Channel, which made the chance of military co-operation with Chile a distinct possibility. Although there were considerable misgivings on both sides about any political or military co-operation between the two nations, the use of airfields in Chile would bring Argentina and the Falkland Islands within closer range.

While the South American options were explored further, the focus turned to Ascension Island. This small isolated volcanic island in the South Atlantic Ocean, just to the south of the Equator and roughly mid-way between Africa and South America, and approximately half-way between the UK and the Falklands, was about to become a strategically important staging post for the task force, without which the entire Falklands operation would have had to be conducted quite differently, certainly as far as the RAF was concerned. The runway at Wideawake Airfield was long enough for use as an emergency airfield for America's space shuttle, which meant that it was ideal for the air resupply of the task force. Wideawake was about to become one of the busiest airfields in the world as men and supplies were ferried to Ascension Island by a constant stream of RAF transport aircraft, and the ships of the task force were replenished by its fleet of helicopters and landing craft. There was also the opportunity at Ascension to use the helicopters to help redistribute some of the equipment that had been hastily loaded on board the ships in the rush to sail from the UK.

When assessing the offensive options available to the RAF, Beetham was aware that Vulcans operating from Ascension Island could attack Argentine cities or ships with 1,000-lb bombs but, because the Vulcan no longer had an air-to-air refuelling capability, this option would require the use of airfields somewhere in South America. Similarly, Buccaneers could be used to attack enemy shipping but they would also suffer from limited range even with air-to-air refuelling. When it came to assessing whether the Buccaneer could reach the Falkland Islands, the amount of air-to-air refuelling required for just one aircraft meant that this was not a viable option.

With the Buccaneer not an option, the Assistant Chief of the Air Staff (Operations), Air Vice-Marshal Ken Hayr, who would be Beetham's right-hand man throughout the campaign, was quick to request the preparation of three Vulcans at Waddington. The flight refuelling system was reactivated and the crews commenced training to refuel from Victor tankers. The Vulcans were also modified back to their pre-nuclear weapon days so that each aircraft could carry a conventional bomb load of twenty-one 1,000-lb bombs, and at Marham a number of Victors were fitted with long-range navigation systems and improved camera installations that meant that, in addition to its air refuelling role, the aircraft could be used for long-range reconnaissance missions if required.

Without an air-to-air refuelling capability, the role of the Nimrod maritime patrol aircraft was limited. Even if it was deemed politically acceptable to operate from mainland South America, the Nimrod would still suffer from a limited radius of action. While the feasibility of modifying the Nimrod for air refuelling operations and to carry the Sting Ray torpedo was being considered, along with the political options for its possible deployment to South American bases, two Nimrod Mk Is were quickly deployed to Ascension to provide communication links with the navy's nuclear submarines en route to the South Atlantic and to provide the task force with surface surveillance. Beetham was later briefed on the air refuelling modification programme for the Nimrod, which was to be completed within a month, and the plan to deploy air refuelling-capable Nimrods to Ascension Island in early May.

In addition to the fixed-wing assets available there were also the RAF's heavy-lift Chinook helicopters that had been used extensively in loading the ships of the task force before it sailed from the UK. Although the first request for Chinooks to be deployed to the South Atlantic was not made until a week after the task force had sailed, Beetham had already asked for some preliminary measures to be looked into and the preferred method was to send them by sea. The British Merchant Navy container ship *Atlantic Conveyor* had been requisitioned by the Ministry of Defence and was identified as suitable to deploy two Chinooks to Ascension Island. There was a further request from the task force for more Chinooks, but it was a balance of providing as much heavy-lift capability as possible for the limited amount of deck space available and, eventually, there would be four Chinooks on board the *Atlantic Conveyor* when it sailed from Ascension Island for the Falkland Islands in early May.

While the Air Staff considered the options available, the RAF immediately set up a resupply route to Ascension Island using C-130 Hercules transport aircraft, staging through Gibraltar and Africa. The airlift between the UK and Ascension had begun on 3 April, with the first eight Hercules landing at Wideawake Airfield the following day. The Hercules would be required to conduct the additional task of dropping supplies to ships at sea and so Marshalls of Cambridge were instructed to proceed with the design, manufacture and installation of an in-flight refuelling probe. As with the modification to the Nimrod, this could not be done overnight but the first modified aircraft was completed by the end of April and deployed to Ascension in early May. From then on the Hercules operated regularly to deliver supplies and mail to ships of the task force, thereby placing further demands on the Victor refuelling tankers operating from Ascension Island and thus complicating the planning of tanker operations.

Beetham was very much aware that the Argentine Air Force would provide a considerable threat. It was estimated to have in excess of 150 combat aircraft available, consisting of Skyhawks, Mirage IIIs, Daggers (an Israeli copy of the Mirage V ground-attack version of the Mirage III), Canberras and Super Etendards with the capability of carrying the French-built Exocet anti-ship missile; the Super Etendard and Exocet combination, in particular, would provide the task force with the biggest threat of all. In addition to the main combat aircraft available, the Argentine Air Force had more than a hundred Pucaras and Macchi light-attack aircraft, which would also provide a threat to the task force if its ships ever ventured within their range, or once British ground forces had gone ashore. This gave the Argentine Air Force an estimated strength of nearly three hundred aircraft and, while some of the aircraft might have been considered obsolete and lacked modern navigation equipment, as well as suffering from the lack of spares and high-quality maintenance, the size of the force and the skill and courage of the pilots could not be underestimated.

This meant the task force's twenty Sea Harriers would be significantly outnumbered should an air war start and, if so, there would be the need to replace attrition losses once hostilities had commenced. Beetham was briefed by the air staff on the availability of the RAF's own Harriers – specifically the GR3s at Wittering – to complement the task force's Sea Harriers. However, before any RAF GR3s could be deployed to the task force, the pilots would need ski-jump and deck practice at Yeovilton as well as air combat training, and the aircraft would require modifications, including the fitting of Sidewinder air-to-air missiles. Furthermore, since neither *Hermes* nor *Invincible* could take more Harriers at that time, three contingency plans were examined: to deploy up to six aircraft to Ascension Island using in-flight refuelling; to deploy twelve aircraft on the third navy carrier *Illustrious*; to deploy twelve aircraft aboard the *Atlantic Conveyor* for transit to the South Atlantic and then to transfer the Harriers to one of the carriers or ashore.

Of the three options, the use of the *Illustrious* would take the longest and it soon became apparent that the other options would become more likely if the RAF GR3s were to be used in the recapture of the Falklands. Plans were, therefore, put in place for a detachment of GR3s from 1 Squadron, led by Wing Commander Peter Squire, to deploy to Ascension Island, from where the Harriers could eventually join the task force to carry out either ground attack or reconnaissance missions, or to provide a limited air defence capability in the event of any Sea Harrier losses. This would provide the GR3 detachment with a significant challenge. While the Argentine Air Force would be able to operate from the Falkland Islands or from home bases on mainland Argentina, with all the support needed to conduct operations, the RAF's Harrier GR3s would be operating from carriers at the end of a lengthy supply line stretching over eight thousand miles.

In addition to the air threat faced by the task force there was also the airfield at Stanley to consider. The runway was just over 4,000 feet long and 150 feet wide, which meant that it was capable of handling a small number of fighters as well as transport aircraft. Discussions took place within the task force and in the UK on how to deny the runway at Stanley to the Argentine Air Force using Sea Harriers but, although this was certainly an option, it would require taking the task force within striking range of the airfield before an attack could be carried out and there was also the rapidly deteriorating weather in the South Atlantic to consider as the Southern Hemisphere entered its winter months.

Attention now turned back to the Vulcan, and it was calculated that one Vulcan operating from Ascension Island, with air-to-air refuelling provided by several Victor tankers, could attack the airfield at Stanley. A number of attacking options were assessed, using varying bomb loads and release heights, and an assessment was made on what was considered to be the best angle to attack the runway. Using the technique of bombing at an angle of thirty degrees off the direction of the runway heading, rather than trying to bomb along the length of the runway, would be more likely to result in success, and the probability of getting one, or even two, bombs to crater the runway in one attack was estimated to be 75 per cent or better.

Preparation of the three Vulcans at Waddington was going well and the aircraft could now be deployed to Ascension within a matter of days. Beetham knew the Vulcans would pose a real threat to Argentina, particularly if the Argentines believed there was a will to use them, and, as well as the Falkland Islands, it would also bring Argentina's capital of Buenos Aires within range as well. He briefed the secretary of state on the Vulcan option, with an attack taking place at night and using airfields in Brazil as an emergency diversion.

While it was considered essential to deny the airfield at Stanley to the Argentine Air Force, the use of a Vulcan rather than Sea Harriers would increase the risk of civilian casualties – as Beetham was quick to point out during a number of meetings that followed. However, the Vulcan option certainly offered the element of surprise, as it would be able to carry out a raid before the task force was even within range to launch its Sea Harriers against the airfield, and an early raid would prevent further Argentine air resupply to the Falklands that much sooner.

The decision was made to deploy the three Vulcans to Ascension Island, although Beetham knew that the key to long-range bombing operations in the South Atlantic would ultimately rest with the Victor tanker. The Victor was now also capable of carrying out maritime radar reconnaissance operations, but to put just one Victor on task for one hour around the Falklands would require several more Victors in support. There was an initial reluctance to use the Victor in this role, because of the lack of time on task and the inability to identify any surface contacts, but Beetham would eventually seek the approval of the secretary of state to use the Victor in support of Operation Paraquet, the military operation to retake the island of South Georgia, given that the task force had no other way of performing this task.

Six Victors were deployed to Ascension Island on 18 April and the first MRR operation was flown in the vicinity of South

Georgia two days later. During a working lunch with Nott that same day, Beetham was able to update the secretary of state on the Victor operation, as well as other key areas such as Nimrod operations in the South Atlantic, the resupply of Ascension Island and the Vulcan and Harrier GR3 options. Beetham also felt it right that the Chiefs of Staff should examine the plans of the task force commander and expressed his frustration at the navy's planned use of the Sea Harriers or, indeed, the apparent lack of any air plan. There was little point in using the Sea Harriers just for air defence and, provided the two carriers remained east of the Falklands and therefore out of range of the land-based Argentine combat aircraft, the Sea Harriers could be used effectively for offensive operations; what else were aircraft carriers for?

On the morning of 22 April Beetham and the other Chiefs of Staff attended a cabinet office briefing room, known as COBR, a committee to co-ordinate the actions of bodies within the government in response to a national crisis, which was chaired by the prime minister. During the meeting the Chiefs briefed Thatcher and her senior ministers on the current military situation and the preparations being put in place. The Chiefs remained cautious, pointing out the problems caused by the long lines of communication, and Beetham was quick to emphasise the closeness of the Argentine Air Force and the significant threat it presented, particularly if allowed to operate from the airfield at Stanley.

Thatcher was particularly interested in the option to use the Vulcan to bomb the airfield, which came as pleasing news to Beetham. While he knew the other Service Chiefs were in support of the Vulcan option, he was not altogether convinced that Lewin, the only military representative on Thatcher's war cabinet, felt the same way. Beetham also brought the ministers up to date with all the other key RAF activity. As he explained to them, there were a lot of balls in the air. In addition to the Vulcan option, there were the Victor operations in the South Atlantic – another was planned for the next day – the Harrier GR3s were being prepared for dispatch to the task force and the Nimrods were being modified for air-to-air refuelling.

He came away from the meeting fully satisfied with the way the RAF preparations were going and full of confidence in his team, particularly the unwavering efforts of the air staff and of those in the headquarters of the various commands and groups. Two days later he noticed a distinct change in Lewin's attitude towards the Vulcan option after Lewin had accompanied the prime minister on a short-notice visit to Northwood. With it now looking increasingly likely that the Vulcan would soon be required to carry out an attack against Stanley Airfield, Beetham met with the AOC-in-C Strike Command, Sir Keith Williamson, on 24 April to discuss how the training and preparations were going. Beetham was due to go to Chequers the following morning and he felt that everything had fallen into place. It was now time for decisive military action and all that was needed was the decision to commence.

Beetham did not have to wait long. He woke the next morning to find the meeting at Chequers was delayed until the afternoon so that ministers could be briefed at Northwood. Once again the single-service Chiefs had not been invited to the briefing but Beetham, Leach and Bramall decided to go anyway. The situation in South Georgia was that Special Forces and Royal Marines had landed and were in the process of recapturing the island, and the Argentine submarine *Santa Fe* had been taken out of action. This came as great news.

The afternoon at Chequers was an enjoyable occasion, with drinks on the terrace and an informal lunch during which the conversation understandably focused on the success at South Georgia that day and on what was to happen next. There was a general consensus that the airfield at Stanley needed to be bombed soon and there was much discussion over whether or not the Argentine aircraft carrier, *Veinticinco de Mayo* (formerly the Royal Navy's HMS *Venerable*), should be sunk. The afternoon session at Chequers ended with the news that the Argentinians at Grytviken had surrendered and South Georgia was once again in British hands.

The following day Beetham attended a Chiefs of Staff meeting in the morning before he travelled to Waddington in the afternoon with Williamson to meet the Vulcan crews and to discuss the likely course of events over the coming days. The crews were a little tired after all their hard preparations and training but were now ready. Beetham discussed with them the merits of bombing at different heights, but he would obviously leave any final decisions to them. The next day he briefed the prime minister that the Vulcan crews were ready and proposed that the Vulcans should now deploy to Ascension Island, with a final decision on whether to bomb or not being made in two days' time.

That evening, the foreign secretary, Francis Pym, asked for a meeting with Beetham to discuss the Vulcan option. During the meeting Beetham could sense that Pym was worried but he made it clear to the foreign secretary that the task force needed the air blockade of the Falklands to start soonest. With the decision of whether to bomb or not to be made in just two days, Beetham was a little concerned that the raid might receive some late ministerial opposition. However, he need not have worried. The following day, 28 April, he learned that his proposal to deploy the Vulcans had been approved and that a total exclusion zone around the Falkland Islands would be effective in just forty-eight hours' time.

Any hope of a diplomatic solution effectively came to an end on 29 April when the junta rejected the Haig peace proposals. Political clearance was now given to the task force to commence military action to demonstrate Britain's intent and on 30 April the total exclusion zone came into effect as the task force sailed within range of the Falklands and authority was given for the Vulcan to attack the airfield at Stanley.

Later that evening, just before 11 p.m. Ascension time (8 p.m. Stanley time), two Vulcans took off from Wideawake Airfield under the code name Black Buck. The Vulcans were accompanied by eleven Victors and the plan was for one Vulcan to continue all the way to the Falkland Islands and bomb the airfield at Stanley. Not long after take-off the crew of the lead Vulcan discovered their cabin would not pressurise and so it was the second Vulcan, XM607 captained by Flight Lieutenant Martin Withers, that continued southwards with its supporting Victor tankers.

It was a long transit south, during which the crew of XM607 carried out in-flight refuelling five times. Within three hundred miles of the target Withers commenced a descent to low level to ensure the Vulcan was safely beneath the cover of any Argentine early-warning radars, and once within fifty miles of the airfield he pulled up to the attack height of 10,000 feet and set the attack heading of 235 degrees. At 4.46 a.m. (Stanley time) on 1 May the crew of XM607 carried out their attack against the runway at Stanley. Having released their bombs, Withers turned hard to the north and climbed away for the long transit back, making the final rendezvous with a Victor off the coast of Rio de Janeiro before landing back at Ascension. The round trip of nearly eight thousand miles was completed in nearly sixteen hours, making it the longest-range air attack in the history of air warfare.

The Vulcan attack against the airfield at Stanley took the Argentinians completely by surprise and it was followed up soon after by a further raid on the airfield by Sea Harriers from the task force while other Sea Harriers attacked the air strip at Goose Green. In London it was 9.30 a.m. when Ken Hayr informed Beetham of the Vulcan raid and then there was the long wait until it had been confirmed that the Vulcan had returned safely to Ascension.

In Beetham's opinion it had been a great day for the RAF. That evening he attended a Bomber Command reunion dinner in London, which was also attended by Bomber Harris, and understandably Beetham received a great reception. During his speech he first paid tribute to Bomber Harris, who had celebrated his ninetieth birthday less than three weeks before, and he was able to confirm that the attack on the airfield at Stanley had been carried out by a Vulcan and that initial intelligence had reported the runway had been cratered. He was also able to update those attending the dinner on the vital role being played by the RAF during operations in the South Atlantic and explained that inter-service co-operation was at its best. Over and above the Falklands, he was also pleased to report a Royal Air Force in good and thriving shape. There was a confidence that stemmed from a government demonstrating its belief in defence, and there was now a re-equipment programme in train that would give the service a quantum leap in its operational capability. He also predicted that the Tornado would win a notable place in the affections of the RAF, as the Lancaster and Mosquito had done in their day, and he finished off by telling the former members of Bomber Command that they had helped forge the traditions of the service and that their exploits were the yardstick by which the RAF today set its standards – standards that had been so dramatically demonstrated by the Vulcan crew the previous night.

The following day there were more congratulations at Chequers, in particular from the prime minister, and much of the talk over lunch was about the Vulcan raid. An aerial photograph later showed that Withers and the crew of XM607 had carried out a perfect attack, especially given the Vulcan's ageing technology. The attack heading of 235 degrees had proved to be correct as the stick of bombs had cut a line of destruction south-west from the centre of the airfield, with the first bomb landing almost in the centre of the runway, where it had created a large crater, and the second had caused similar damage to the southern edge of the runway. The attack height of 10,000 feet had been sufficiently high to provide protection from any anti-aircraft guns or surface-to-air missiles, but was not so high to cause inaccuracy in the bombing and there had been sufficient height for the bombs to have enough vertical momentum to penetrate the runway and then detonate beneath the surface to cause maximum destruction.

Three nights after the first Black Buck raid, Black Buck 2 took place. This involved the same Vulcan aircraft, but a different crew, and was almost identical in detail to the first. It was some days before Beetham knew the extent of the damage but on this occasion the western end of the airfield was heavily cratered, which prevented any possible extension of the airfield for high-performance combat aircraft.

Not only did the two Black Buck raids make the airfield at Stanley unusable by aircraft such as the Super Etendard, they also demonstrated the far-reaching capability of the RAF and provided the junta with evidence that the Vulcan also posed a real threat to mainland Argentina, something that would have had a significant psychological effect. However, although the Argentine combat aircraft would be restricted to operate from mainland bases in Argentina, it did not remove the threat to the task force altogether. Nonetheless, while the Argentine Air Force would continue to use the airfield at Stanley for some air resupply, it did not deploy its main combat aircraft to the islands and this would have a significant impact on its capability.

In the eyes of the world Britain and Argentina were now at war. In the four days spanning the first Black Buck missions, the Argentine cruiser *Belgrano* had been sunk by the Royal Navy's nuclear submarine *Conquerer* on 2 May, with the loss of three hundred lives, and then two days later an Exocet missile, fired by an Argentine Super Etendard, had crippled the destroyer HMS *Sheffield* with the loss of twenty lives. *Sheffield* had been on radar picket duty about twenty miles to the west of the main task force, which was operating about a hundred miles to the south of Stanley and well within the total exclusion zone as Woodward started to deploy his ships closer to the islands to land and support reconnaissance parties ashore by helicopter. The attack was carried out by two Super Etendards from Rio Grande and each fired an Exocet at the task force. Only one of the Exocets hit the *Sheffield* and it is unlikely that the warhead detonated fully but the impact of the missile and the subsequent fire caused significant damage and loss of life on board; the other Exocet went into the sea.

This news came as a great disappointment to Beetham. The most tragic factor was the loss of life on the *Sheffield* but he had warned many times before about the threat posed by the Argentine Air Force. He was keen to know why the task force was continuing to operate so close to the Falklands, well within striking range of the Super Etendards, and he wondered why the task force, in particular the carriers, were so close to the radar picket ship. It was a bit late to answer these questions now that the *Sheffield* had been hit, but he was convinced that the task force could still operate as effectively further to the east, where the main ships would be outside the range of the Argentine Air Force.

Beetham felt the Royal Navy was just starting to learn the harsh lessons of how effective air power could be. He made his points known at the next meeting of the Chiefs of Staff and also during a meeting with Nott the following day, when he reinforced the fact that surface ships were vulnerable to land-based aircraft and he further made the point that any landing of ground forces could prove to be a hazardous operation. Following the loss of *Sheffield*, the task force moved well to the east of the Falklands and never again during the conflict would the aircraft carriers spend any length of time so close to the islands. Then, on 7 May, the total exclusion zone was extended to within twelve miles of the Argentine coast.

The Falklands campaign understandably received much media attention and during a controversial BBC *Panorama* programme on the crisis that was broadcast on 10 May, the Labour politician, Tam Dalyell, suggested that some of the Chiefs of Staff, and he named Beetham in particular, had advised against the dispatch of the task force to the Falkland Islands. The impression given in the programme was that the BBC believed there was substance to Dalyell's remarks and this was heightened by the way in which a picture of Beetham was shown. Beetham was watching the programme at home and was appalled by the comments made. The accepted convention was that the Chiefs of Staff did not comment publicly on the advice they gave to the government and so, not surprisingly, the programme was the subject of discussion at the Chiefs of Staff meeting the following day.

Having read the transcript, the Chiefs asked the secretary of state to write to Tam Dalyell to let him know there was no truth whatsoever to the assertion. Conservative MPs also protested about imputing these views to Beetham and about the suggestion that the Chiefs of Staff were at loggerheads over the issue. Nott then wrote to Dalyell and also to the chairman of the BBC, George Howard, asking the BBC to confirm that the impression they may have given on the programme was without foundation. The following day Howard wrote a letter of apology to Beetham, regretting that unsubstantiated reference was made to his views in the *Panorama* programme and this should not have been done, particularly since Beetham was in no position to confirm, deny or comment in any way upon the suggestion. Beetham also received a letter of apology from the BBC director general, Sir Ian Trethowan. While the whole episode proved to be an unwelcome distraction for Beetham, his main concern was how members of the task force, let alone their families, would feel as they headed towards conflict, believing that a member or members of the Chiefs of Staff had advised against sending them. He was grateful, therefore, when Sir Ian Trethowan's remarks were published in the *Daily Telegraph* to put the record straight.

The Argentine success against the *Sheffield* was followed with moderate success against HMS *Glasgow* on 12 May when Skyhawks attacked the ship off Stanley and a 1,000-lb bomb passed clean through the ship's hull and clear before it went off. In some quarters the capability of the Argentine Air Force and the courage of its pilots came as a revelation; Beetham was not surprised, and he remained frustrated at the navy's apparent lack of appreciation of what air power could do. On this matter he found Nott and the CGS, Dwin Bramall, to be strong allies when it came to assessing the additional resources required for the campaign and how much air power should be made available.

The main military option was now pointing more and more towards an invasion of the islands since a total blockade of the Falklands could not realistically be enforced without the constant risk of losing ships, either from the air or from the two Argentine submarines still thought to be operating in the area. It was quite understandable that more ground forces were being asked for but Beetham also felt there was a need to balance the ground forces deployed with the logistic support required; he felt at that time the balance was not quite right. He also felt that greater use could be made of the Sea Harriers and, while he knew the task force had lost three Sea Harriers, he also knew that at least two of these had not been lost to enemy action – and possibly not the third. He had waited several days for a reconnaissance of the airfield at Stanley to take place and when he found out the reconnaissance was to be carried out at 15,000 feet he sensed that there was a reluctance to take any risks. He also felt that if an invasion was to have any chance of success then the Argentine forces on the ground would have to be softened up first.

Although reconnaissance photographs did slowly find their way back to London during the course of the next few days, the intelligence analysis was extremely limited and it made it difficult for Beetham to understand the true state of the airfield at Stanley. Again, he found this most frustrating and during a meeting of the Chiefs of Staff on 17 May he stated that the information being provided was simply not good enough; this, as far as he was concerned, was further evidence of the lack of appreciation of the importance of aerial reconnaissance and the understanding of air power.

The Chiefs of Staff had now been informed of the details of the landing operation. On the positive side, the task force was certainly in a position to invade the islands and the ground had been prepared by constant shelling of strategic points around Stanley and by gathering intelligence to work out the disposition of the Argentine garrison. Six RAF Harrier GR3s, along with eight additional Sea Harriers, had now made the long journey south and had joined the task force. This brought the total number of Sea Harriers available to the task force to twenty-five, and during the forthcoming invasion they would provide vital air cover over the landing area, and the GR3s would provide air support for the troops on the ground. However, on the negative side, the Argentine air threat had not been contained.

One of the most important meetings of the Falklands conflict took place on 18 May. During the meeting the Chiefs of Staff briefed the prime minister and ministers on the risks attached to a proposed landing at San Carlos Bay, on the west side of East Falkland, which had been identified as a suitable landing site because the terrain provided visual and electronic cover from the Argentine forces. There were no other suitably protected landing areas further east and the beaches around Stanley were known to be heavily mined. Each Chief spoke in turn about his own particular aspect of the proposed landing. Beetham was in full support of an immediate landing, but he believed it was not the time to deliver words that politicians might wish to hear. It was the time to tell the truth and deliver the facts and concerns as they were.

In John Nott's book *Here Today Gone Tomorrow*, he describes Beetham's briefing as the most striking of all four presentations. Nott better describes the meeting in his book, but he states that Beetham made the point very graphically that the Argentine Air Force had not been neutralised as had been hoped. Furthermore, the Argentine Air Force had already succeeded in locating the ships of the task force and during the landing the ships would be close together and within range of the land-based fighters, which would make them even more exposed than they had been up to now. Beetham went on to add that the Argentine Air Force still had a substantial force of Skyhawks, Mirages and Super Etendards and that the air threat was still significant. Some aircraft would inevitably get through the defensive shield and he felt that some ships might well be lost during the landing. Nonetheless, he took the view, as did all the other Chiefs, that the risks were substantial and that a blockade of the islands made no sense at all given the weather and that any further delay would only further increase the risks. The point was also confirmed by Bramall, who said that it was an established principle of warfare that a hazardous amphibious landing should not normally take place without air superiority. Furthermore, because of the distance between San Carlos and Stanley, there was a risk that the advance across East Falkland could get bogged down if faced by determined Argentine resistance.

The war cabinet was understandably concerned about how an invasion could be achieved without a great loss of life, and Thatcher in particular expressed her concerns about the air threat that still remained. Then, on 19 May, the prime minister and the war cabinet gave permission to go ahead with the landings, which took place just two days later. Supported by nine supply ships, and escorted by one destroyer and six frigates, the landing ships *Fearless* and *Intrepid* and the luxury cruise liner *Canberra* landed some five thousand troops at San Carlos during the early hours of 21 May with scarcely any casualties. There were, however, subsequent losses once the Argentine Air Force located the landing site. One destroyer (*Coventry*), two frigates (*Ardent* and *Antelope*) and the container ship (*Atlantic Conveyor*) were all sunk in the aftermath of the landings and many more ships were damaged. Beetham remained concerned about how long the Argentine Air Force would keep coming back and he also wondered just how many more Exocet missiles were left.

Despite the losses, the most difficult part of the operation was over by 26 May and the British troops advanced towards Stanley. The RAF continued to provide valuable support to the land campaign but there remained a lack of good intelligence analysis finding its way back to London; not only of the situation on the islands but also in establishing the state of the Argentine Air Force. This proved to be a constant source of frustration for Beetham but the campaign was now entering its latter stages.

On 31 May a Vulcan carried out an attack against an Argentine long-range early-warning radar near Stanley using Shrike radiation-homing missiles mounted on improvised pylons under the wings, which achieved some success and restricted the way the Argentines operated their radars on the islands. This was Black Buck 5, but it was only the third raid to reach the Falklands as the two previous raids had been cancelled: Black Buck 3 (13 May) was cancelled because of strong headwinds and Black Buck 4 (28 May), which was to be the first use of Shrike, was cancelled because of an unserviceable Victor within the formation and resulted in the Vulcan having to return to Ascension.

A further Vulcan attack, Black Buck 6, was carried out three days later against the Argentine early-warning radars around Stanley. The radar operators were now more aware of the threat and had detected the Vulcan as it approached the islands. The radars were turned off but the pilot, Squadron Leader Neil McDougall, descended in an effort to tempt the radar operators to turn the radars back on. The plan worked and two Shrikes were launched against the radar site, resulting in its destruction. Some hours later, as the Vulcan attempted its final refuelling with a Victor tanker, its refuelling probe broke, leaving the Vulcan in serious trouble. For all the Black Buck missions the Vulcan and Victor crews had the option to use Brazilian airfields in an emergency and so McDougall headed for Rio de Janeiro. He needed all of his experience and flying skills to nurse the aircraft towards safety and after the crew had discarded the secret documents on board the Vulcan eventually landed at Rio de Janeiro.

The crew members were treated well in Brazil but, for now, the Vulcan was impounded. Beetham was kept informed of developments as Brazil was under pressure from Argentina not to release the aircraft but, from his point of view, it was now time for the diplomats to earn their money and to get the aircraft back. The outcome was that the diplomats did their part and the Vulcan eventually flew back to Ascension on 11 June – ten days after it had taken off. Although Beetham was thousands of miles away in London at the time and played no part in the successful diplomatic conclusion, it is likely that his visit to Brazil the year before had forged friendly relations in Brazil that had helped make the diplomatic negotiations considerably smoother and enabled an early release of the aircraft.

As the land campaign in the Falklands entered its final phase, the weather over the islands was poor and this limited the air operations flown. However, by 7 June the weather had improved enough to enable the first Harrier operations to be flown from a new airstrip prepared at Port San Carlos. For Beetham the period leading up to the final assault on Stanley was in the hands of others and for now he was able to turn his attention to what was going to happen after the Falklands had been recaptured, such as repairing the airfield at Stanley and extending the runway with matting to allow C-130 operations, as well as making it possible for a detachment of Phantoms and perhaps Buccaneers to operate from Stanley.

As British forces were preparing for the final assault, the president of the USA, Ronald Reagan, visited London on an official visit to the Queen at Windsor Castle. Accompanied by the secretary of state, Alexander Haig, the president arrived at Heathrow Airport on 7 June and Beetham and the other Chiefs of Staff were included in the prime minister's welcoming party. The following day the president was entertained at lunch by the prime minister and in the evening Beetham attended a banquet given by the Queen and the Duke of Edinburgh at Windsor Castle in honour of the president's visit, and after dinner he was pleased to have the opportunity to discuss the Falklands campaign with Reagan.

The following day came news from the Falklands of an air attack against the landing ships *Sir Galahad* and *Sir Tristram* at Bluff Cove, which proved to be another harsh reminder that the Argentine Air Force still posed a significant threat. During the final assaults on the high ground overlooking Stanley, which commenced on the night of 11/12 June, many army units fought distinguished actions. RAF support to these operations included the seventh, and final, Black Buck mission on 12 June, which was flown against Argentine troop positions close to Stanley. With the high ground won, the British then descended on Stanley and the Argentine forces laid down their arms. Beetham received the good news on the final day of the conflict, 14 June – the battle for the Falklands was over.

While the conflict had, once again, demonstrated the professionalism and inter-operability of the armed forces, and the islands had quickly been restored to British sovereignty, it had come at a cost, with 255 killed and more than 700 wounded from across the services. Argentine losses, depending on source, were recorded as 649 killed, and three Falkland Islanders were also killed during the campaign.

The Royal Navy had suffered the heaviest equipment losses. In addition to the loss of its two destroyers and two frigates, a further three destroyers, six frigates and four Royal Fleet auxiliaries had been damaged; one of these, *Sir Galahad*, was eventually scuttled. As far as the air war was concerned, the RAF's losses were modest at four Harrier GR3s and three Chinooks. Three of the Harriers were shot down by anti-aircraft fire, although all three pilots ejected safely, and one was written off after suffering a partial engine failure while landing at the airstrip at Port San Carlos; the pilot was unhurt. All three Chinooks were lost on board the *Atlantic Conveyor*. The Royal Navy lost six Sea Harriers, with four pilots killed, and twenty-one helicopters, including seven on the *Atlantic Conveyor*. Argentine aircraft losses, depending on source, were recorded as 102 with many more probably destroyed and captured on the ground.

There were several reasons why Beetham felt enormously proud of the RAF's contribution to Operation Corporate. The modification of some aircraft to conduct air-to-air refuelling, which had been completed in a remarkably quick time, meant the RAF had significantly increased its long-range operational capability. There were no better examples of this than the Vulcan Black Buck missions and the long-range Nimrod reconnaissance sorties lasting over nineteen hours. The conflict had also seen a significant step forward in joint operations, which had emphasised the importance of air transport when supporting operations thousands of miles from the UK. Furthermore, the Harrier GR3s and Nimrod maritime patrol aircraft had proved to be a significant addition to the task force.

With hostilities over, Beetham became increasingly concerned of what he considered to be the 'Dark Blue Lobby' in the immediate aftermath of the conflict. The Royal Navy sought replacements for the ships that had been lost during the conflict and the naval staff were quick to make the point that some of the surface ships it had used had been identified for the scrapheap under John Nott's defence review just a few months earlier, and so would not have been available if the Falklands conflict had happened much later. These ships included the carriers *Hermes* and *Invincible*, the assault ships *Fearless* and *Intrepid*, and some of the navy's destroyers and frigates that had been deployed to the South Atlantic. Not surprisingly, the Royal Navy now saw its opportunity to reverse some of the decisions that had been made in the defence review. Leach, quite openly as the CNS, and Lewin, rather less overtly as the CDS, wasted no time at all in trying to seize their chance as the

Chiefs worked on establishing the force levels required to maintain a military presence in the Falklands.

The proposals being staffed through the CDS all had high navy force levels and showed the Royal Navy retaining command and control of all military forces. The line taken by the Royal Navy was fully understandable, and no doubt the other services would have done the same in similar circumstances, but both Beetham and Bramall were keen to establish an appropriate mix of forces in the South Atlantic and there were many other matters that needed to be resolved. In the short term the task force needed to be returned home, the airfield at Stanley needed to be repaired and then prepared for use by British forces, and there were many Argentine prisoners being held on the islands who needed dealing with. In the longer term it was important for both the government and the armed forces to identify the lessons learned from the campaign, to make sure that such a thing never happened again, and it was important that the government reviewed Britain's overseas and defence policy.

While it was still too early to draw together all the detailed lessons learned from the Falklands campaign, Beetham was keen to make sure that the wrong lessons were not drawn from the conflict, certainly as far as Britain's support to NATO was concerned. There were already articles and letters in the national press that seemed to lend support to the erroneous conclusions for British defence policy based on the Falklands campaign. In particular, those lobbying opposition to the changes in emphasis for the fleet, which had stemmed from the previous year's defence review, had jumped on the Falklands bandwagon and appeared to have taken some of the national press and a number of politicians with them.

Beetham and others were quick to point out that the first priority of Britain's defence remained with the strengthening of its conventional forces to meet the principal threat of the Soviet Union and that an adequate force, land and air, was a much better assurance of defence than an operation to recapture what had been lost through absence. Furthermore, the UK had just witnessed near-obsolete technology doing fatal damage to its naval and other forces. It was essential when making future plans to remember that the air threat to NATO was not posed by aircraft such as the Skyhawk, and that the dramatic improvement in the quality of Soviet combat aircraft represented a major development in Soviet air power. He also felt the threat of a land and air offensive in NATO's Central Region was more serious than the threat at sea, and outside the NATO area the importance to the West of the Gulf oilfields demanded priority attention.

On 22 June a Defence White Paper was published in the aftermath of the Falklands campaign as a holding statement while the lessons of the conflict were identified. Nott's task was to determine the most cost-effective balance for the UK's future conventional forces and, having examined the relative threats to NATO, it was obvious that the balance in Central Europe was very much in favour of the Warsaw Pact. The decision was made to maintain a strong land and air capability in Germany, which Beetham felt was based on sound political, military and financial logic. Nott took some criticism from the 'Dark Blue Lobby' for failing to recognise the importance of maintaining powerful maritime forces, using the recent losses in the South Atlantic as the peg on which to impale his misguided policy, but Beetham felt the secretary of state deserved credit for tackling the problem head-on rather than following the path of compromise, which had so often been the case with his predecessors. Nott would go one better at the end of 1982 in his Defence White Paper 'The Falklands Campaign: The Lessons', which concluded that the government would devote substantially more resources to defence than had previously been planned, specifically by taking measures that would increase the flexibility, mobility and readiness of all three services for operations in support of NATO and elsewhere if necessary.

The Falklands conflict and its immediate aftermath had dominated Beetham's life for the past three months, which meant that all his other commitments and engagements had been put to one side. While discussions on the Falklands conflict and the Defence White Paper would continue long after he had handed over as the CAS, he was at least able to return to his other duties and enjoyed three royal engagements in less than two weeks.

First, on 21 June, he joined the commandant-general of the RAF Regiment, Air Vice-Marshal Henry Reed-Purvis, at Wittering for the Royal Review of the RAF Regiment to mark its fortieth anniversary, which was attended by the Queen, as Air Commodore-in-Chief, accompanied by the Duke of Edinburgh. After the review there was a flypast by aircraft of Strike Command, followed by a tour of an exhibition covering the history and roles of the RAF Regiment, and after lunch in the officers' mess there was a tactical demonstration. During the day Beetham had taken the opportunity to inform the Queen and the Duke of Edinburgh of the RAF's role during

Operation Corporate, although it soon became apparent to him just how well-informed the Queen seemed to be.

Three days later he was at Bentley Priory to welcome a visit by the Queen Mother to perpetuate her association with the priory and to mark the formal reopening of the restored building following a fire three years earlier. During the visit the Queen Mother was briefed in the Dowding Room on the restoration work to the Clock Tower, main entrance and front rooms on the first floor, after which she unveiled a commemorative plaque and toured the public rooms. The visit aroused many nostalgic memories for the Queen Mother and she was greatly impressed by the restoration. Then, on 1 July, Beetham was invited to take the Queen's Royal Review at the RAF College Cranwell.

The period in between Beetham's royal engagements had also been very busy. On 22 June he first met with the secretary of state to discuss his views of the lessons of Operation Corporate and its implications for the defence programme, and he then attended a Chiefs of Staff meeting, during which the Chiefs discussed the force levels for the Falklands garrison. During the meeting Ken Hayr gave a briefing on the development of Stanley Airfield and made it clear that a C-130 Hercules would land as soon as the land forces commander gave permission; this would counter some recent press criticism that the RAF was reluctant to land at the airfield. Beetham had also found time for a quick trip to Ascension Island to meet the RAF personnel who had been involved with the Falklands conflict. He flew down overnight in a VC10 and was met on arrival by the Commander British Forces Support Unit, Group Captain Jeremy Price, who had been the senior air-to-air refuelling officer in the operations room during the conflict. Beetham was extremely impressed by what he saw and heard during his visit, although he was not surprised by the extreme professionalism shown by the RAF and its people when conducting operations during the campaign.

The Falklands conflict continued to come under scrutiny and by now there had been increasing speculation about the relationship between the UK and Chile during the campaign. This led to a question in the House of Commons on 5 July, when a Foreign Office minister was asked whether or not there had been any bilateral agreements between the two countries during the past twelve months. The minister answered the question by saying there had been none but there has been speculation ever since about the use of air bases in southern Chile by RAF aircraft and Royal Navy helicopters, and that Britain gained access to material gathered by Chilean intelligence. It has been speculated that in return Chile gained delivery of three Canberras and twelve Hunters, and also benefitted from the dropping of British restrictions on arms sales to Chile and received Britain's support in undermining United Nations investigations into Chilean human rights abuses.

While some politicians have since been reported to have hinted that Chile had been helpful to Britain during the conflict, the military speculation remains. What is known, however, is that a Sea King from the task force made a forced landing near Punta Arenas during the early hours of 20 May where it was then destroyed by its crew before they handed themselves over to Chilean authorities; the purpose of the helicopter's mission has also been the subject of speculation. As far as the delivery of Canberras and Hunters to the Chilean Air Force, the Fuerza Aerea de Chile, was concerned, the Ministry of Defence stated that these were not given or sold to Chile as a result of agreements during the Falklands conflict but an agreement had previously been made between the two countries before hostilities had commenced. During his final weeks as the CAS Beetham was invited to Chile by its Chief of the Air Staff but the Foreign Office would not approve the visit and so he did not go.

As Beetham entered his final months as the CAS, attention turned to his successor. After discussions with the CDS, and having consulted with the air secretary on other senior RAF appointments, Beetham proposed Sir Keith Williamson, then AOC-in-C Strike Command, to the secretary of state as the next CAS. Then, on 14 July, it was officially announced that Beetham was to be promoted to the rank of marshal of the Royal Air Force on 15 October and he was to be succeeded as the CAS by Sir Keith Williamson.

Beetham felt there was still much to be done before handing over to his successor and he was keen, once again, to look towards the future. In an address titled 'Air Power and the RAF: Today and the Future', he informed the Royal United Services Institute for Defence Studies that the RAF wanted a ground-attack aircraft with a good air combat capability, preferably British, to replace the Jaguar. Air Staff Target 403 had initially called for a short take-off and vertical-landing aircraft to replace the Harrier and Jaguar but the AST had then been split in two; AST 409 for a straight Harrier replacement and AST 414 for an agile fighter aircraft with more emphasis on the air combat role.

British Aerospace, the UK's largest aircraft, munitions and defence systems manufacturer, was quick to try and persuade the government to back its P110 proposal, which was to be a smaller version of the Tornado and designed as a twin-finned delta canard aircraft to be powered by two Rolls-Royce engines. The company was keen to build the aircraft for the international market and was looking to receive an order from the RAF, but in the event there should be no international interest or government support then the company was prepared to build the aircraft as a private venture. The P110 design eventually morphed into the Experimental Aircraft Programme, which British Aerospace did build and fly in 1986, and this, in turn, led to the Eurofighter and subsequently the Typhoon, the multi-role combat aircraft that was first delivered to the RAF in 2003.

At the end of July Beetham attended a Falkland Islands service of thanksgiving and remembrance at St Paul's Cathedral, after which he paid his last visit to RAF Germany. In August he visited Honington and flew in a Tornado GR1 of the Tornado Weapons Conversion Unit, his last flight in a combat aircraft. The visit also gave him the chance to catch up on former times with the station commander, Group Captain Peter Harding, his first PSO while he was the C-in-C RAF Germany.

The last few weeks as the CAS were particularly busy for Beetham. In early September he hosted two visits by senior officers from overseas, first from Air Chief Marshal Dilbagh Singh on the fiftieth anniversary of the Indian Air Force and then from the New Zealand CDS, Vice-Admiral Sir Neil Anderson. Later in the month Beetham attended a service of thanksgiving for the Battle of Britain at Westminster Abbey before he flew to Akrotiri in Cyprus for his final visit as the Chief. Then, on 11 October, Beetham was among sixty guests invited by the prime minister to a formal dinner at 10 Downing Street to celebrate the success of the Falklands campaign. The following day there was a victory parade through the City of London and a flypast over St Paul's Cathedral by Harriers and Victors, followed by luncheon at the Guildhall hosted by the Lord Mayor, Sir Christopher Leaver, in honour of the South Atlantic Task Force.

As Beetham was now in his last few days in office he was able to reflect on his time as the CAS. The RAF had certainly become more capable and flexible in the past five years, and there was no better example of this than the recent Falklands campaign. However, he felt that it was a pity there were now fewer opportunities for servicemen and their families to enjoy the benefits of serving abroad

15. Leaving Akrotiri in Cyprus for the last time as the CAS, 29 September 1982

as the number of RAF bases overseas had dwindled over the past few years. He always believed the RAF comprised people first and then equipment, and not the other way around, and ultimately it has always been the quality and standards of the people that has made the difference between success and failure. After many difficulties, the RAF's manning was now more or less in balance, recruiting was generally buoyant and retention was at its best level for many years. He was also pleased that the pay crisis, which had been the root cause of manpower problems just a few years before, now seemed to be well and truly in the past; he still felt, however, there was room for improvement when it came to quality of life.

As far as equipment was concerned, Beetham was pleased that he had managed to sustain largely intact the major re-equipment programme throughout the period of the defence review and the economic pressures faced during the past few years. He always felt the key for the longer term was to get the national economy right so that it would be easier for the government to allocate to defence the resources it needed. Now, with the recent financial difficulties apparently in the past, things were looking much better for the future. In particular, he was immensely satisfied with the way the Tornado programme was progressing. The GR1, optimised for strike attack, was proving a great success and the RAF now had its full complement of aircraft at both the Tri-National Tornado Training Establishment at Cottesmore and at the Tornado Weapons Conversion Unit at Honington. The first squadron had formed at Honington a few months earlier and the build-up would eventually see eleven GR1 squadrons in service, eight of which would be based in Germany. The aircraft was proving reliable and easy to fly, and the crews liked its performance, handling qualities and blind-bombing accuracies. Beetham also knew the Tornado would soon bring a major improvement to the RAF's capability by delivering the new range of air-to-ground weapons about to enter service, such as the JP233, with great accuracy at night and in bad weather. Furthermore, trials of the air defence variant, the Tornado ADV, which would eventually replace the Lightning and Phantom, were going well and there was every indication it would be a first-class fighter for the air defence of the UK.

Beetham was also convinced that the introduction of the Chinook was a significant addition to the RAF's support helicopter force; how right he would prove to be. There was also the increase in air-to-air refuelling capability with the modification of an additional squadron's worth of VC10 transport aircraft into tankers, which would vastly increase the time on task for aircraft on air defence missions or longer-range offensive operations, and in the maritime role all the Nimrods were being upgraded to Mk 2 standard. This would give a quantum step forward in anti-submarine warfare capability, and the Nimrod was now equipped for air-to-air refuelling, which would immeasurably increase the cover provided to the fleet wherever it operated in the future. The Nimrod was also now capable of carrying the Harpoon anti-ship missile, giving the aircraft an offensive capability. For now the maritime strike/attack capability still remained with the Buccaneer, although it would eventually be replaced by the Tornado, and the Buccaneer was due to receive an avionics upgrade that would soon see Martel replaced by the new anti-ship missile, the Sea Eagle.

There were also improvements to all elements of the air defence ground environment, including new radars, improved communications and refurbished sector operations centres. The RAF could look forward to the Nimrod AEW, which would greatly extend radar coverage and significantly improve the RAF's fighter-control capability, and there were other significant modification programmes such as the Hercules stretch programme, which increased the aircraft's volume lift by 30 per cent, and the Harrier would soon have an increased range and payload with the advent of the new GR5 programme.

There was no doubt that Beetham's greatest challenge as the CAS was the Falklands conflict and this was understandably the most satisfying aspect of his term in office. As far as non-operational matters were concerned, his biggest challenge was the pay review soon after he had taken up his appointment, and his subsequent success ranked among his most rewarding achievements. While he had clearly achieved so much during his time at the helm, he was unable to introduce all the changes that he would have liked. For example, much as he wanted to revive the Cranwell cadet scheme he was unable to do so. He was convinced that the RAF was losing some high-quality young people to universities and he would have liked to have reintroduced a degree course for officers, along similar lines to that carried out during the inter-war years, but the reintroduction of such a scheme would have required significant changes at Cranwell, including the establishment of a number of academic lecturers and tutors. Because of other priorities at the time, Beetham knew this idea would have to remain on the sidelines.

Although he could have had an Air Force Board formal dinner to mark his departure, Beetham instead wanted a dinner at Bracknell; a place that meant so much to him. On 13 October, the Beethams were invited to join the air marshals of the RAF and their ladies at a formal dinner held at the RAF Staff College to mark his retirement as the CAS. The dinner was presided over by the air member for personnel, Air Marshal Sir Charles Ness, and music was provided by the Central Band of the Royal Air Force. It was a wonderful occasion.

Beetham's last day in office was 15 October and, after handing over to Sir Keith Williamson, it was time to leave. A large gathering of colleagues were assembled on the front steps of MOD's Main Building to say their goodbye and to wish him well. Beetham was extremely gratified to see so many of his friends and colleagues there. The car waiting for him now had a fifth star on its star-plate and thus Beetham left Whitehall for the last time. It was an emotional day.

Laudatory letters followed from all over the world. One of note was a personal letter from the prime minister, Margaret Thatcher, in which she thanked him for all his hard work as the CAS and in particular for the splendid contribution made by the Royal Air Force during the Falklands campaign. Many letters recognised the work he had done to project air power in such a way that even the most devious politicians could not ignore the issues presented to them for decision. Others commented on the change in the relationship between the service at large and the RAF hierarchy during his term as the CAS, and another commented on the previous lack of communication within the Air Force Department in Whitehall and that the tone of some of the interdivisional correspondence, even between Air Force Board members, was now so different, despite the continuing pressures for economies. There were other compliments regarding Beetham's continuous policy of communication through the senior commanders' conferences at Cranwell and the station commanders' conferences at Bracknell that had brought the Air Force Board to the people of the RAF.

The change in the CAS appointment was not the only change among the Chiefs of Staff at that time; it was also in October that Lewin, who had been elevated to the House of Lords, handed over as the CDS to Dwin Bramall, and Henry Leach handed over as the First Sea Lord to Sir John Fieldhouse. John Nott would continue as secretary of state for defence until the following year when he was replaced by Michael Heseltine in the lead up to the 1983 general election which, just a year after the success in the Falkland Islands, saw Margaret Thatcher win the most decisive election victory since 1945.

On leaving London for the family home in Norfolk, Beetham could only start to reflect on all that he had achieved. He was the last CAS to have operational service in the Second World War and having served for more than five years he had been the longest-serving Chief since Lord Trenchard.

CHAPTER 13

What Retirement?

———————

The supreme rank of marshal of the Royal Air Force is the highest rank in the RAF and, as a five-star rank, is equivalent to the Royal Navy's rank of admiral of the fleet and the army's rank of field marshal. Since the formation of the RAF in 1918 only twenty-five men have held the rank of marshal, including four members of the royal family who have held honorary rank. The first marshal was Sir Hugh Trenchard in 1927 and in peacetime the rank was reserved for former Chiefs of the Air Staff, who were promoted to the rank on their last day of service. There were also two wartime appointments to men who had not previously served as the CAS: Sir Arthur Harris and Lord Douglas of Kirtleside. However, defence cuts during the 1990s meant that general service promotions to the rank ceased and Beetham, the twenty-second marshal of the Royal Air Force, is now one of only four men still holding the rank, including the Duke of Edinburgh, with Beetham the most senior (in terms of seniority in rank) of the three former Chiefs of the Air Staff.

Beetham's first weeks as a marshal were not spent in any grand setting but at Catterick army barracks, where he exchanged his gold braid for overalls to spend four weeks on a household maintenance course learning how to paint, decorate, lay bricks and carry out plumbing as part of his resettlement. Unlike most people in the armed forces, who complete their resettlement prior to leaving the services, Beetham had not had the time to do so. Not surprisingly, he was the most senior member of the course by some margin – the next highest rank was a sergeant. He not only found the course useful, because at last he was taught how to paint and hang wallpaper properly, he also found it a thoroughly enjoyable change of lifestyle.

With his resettlement complete, Beetham was again invited to Buckingham Palace for an audience with the Queen on relinquishing the appointment of Chief of the Air Staff and Air ADC. His first formal function since handing over as the CAS was the Guild of Air Pilots and Air Navigators Awards Dinner, when he accepted the Brackley Trophy on behalf of the Royal Air Force for its success during the Falklands conflict. In his acceptance speech Beetham paid tribute to the considerable skill and courage of those who had served in the South Atlantic, and at the same time he recognised the vital supporting role of those back home, as well as the support of the guild and other influential city guilds and companies.

The Beethams were now able to settle in their home in the quiet rural village of South Creake in northern Norfolk, which they had bought in 1978. Having lived in service accommodation throughout his career, Beetham had wanted somewhere away from London for his family to go to relax, particularly during the children's school holidays. While his initial thoughts were that the family might eventually settle in the West Country – maybe Devon or Dorset – the Beethams had not had any success in finding somewhere and so they decided to buy in Norfolk after a weekend visit to friends. Having seen the house – and the local golf club, of course – his initial idea was to use the house as a holiday home while continuing to look for somewhere else, but more than thirty years later the Beethams are still there!

As a former Chief of the Air Staff, Beetham was always going to be in demand. For example, during May 1983 he was invited to speak at four formal dinners in the space of just ten days – the fiftieth annual dinner of the Cambridge University Air Squadron, the Bomber Command annual reunion at Grosvenor House, the Pathfinder annual dinner at Wyton and the 617 Squadron Association dinner at Marham. He was pleased to attend them all, particularly as he had been unable to attend three of the functions the year before because they had taken place during the Falklands conflict. The success of the Falklands campaign was still fresh in everyone's minds and Beetham was able to pay tribute to the RAF as well as to update those attending the dinners on the RAF's re-equipment programme and to continue promoting his own personal belief in the capability and future potential of air power.

Everything was going as he had initially planned on leaving the service. When he had first moved to Norfolk his plan had been to do nothing for six months, certainly as far as work was concerned, but he was now approaching his sixtieth birthday and was wondering what to do next. He felt ready to work again, at least part time, and he was prepared to listen to any offers, but he was also mindful of the fact that he was not obliged to commit to anything unless it fitted in with his own personal plans, and he certainly did not want any stress or hassle; he had endured his fair share of that in recent years!

As a former military Chief of Staff there was no shortage of offers and he would spend the next ten years working part time for two quite different companies. The first attractive offer that came his way was from the property investment company, Brixton Estate, who offered him a position as a non-executive director. The company had always had a former Chief of Staff on its board and Sir John Grandy had been in the position when Beetham had been the CAS. It was Grandy who approached him during a lunch meeting to ask if he would be interested in taking the position over. Beetham accepted the offer and in addition to attending the board meetings he also toured many properties in the UK, Europe and America to gain a full understanding of the company's business.

Soon after joining Brixton Estate, Beetham also became a non-executive director of GEC Avionics at Rochester to help project the company through his military knowledge and network. This proved to be another most enjoyable position and he made a number of overseas visits, primarily to America, where there was much business connected with the F-16 fighter, and also to the Far East. During these visits he would talk to the various air force Chiefs and their staffs to lobby interest in the company and its technologies and capabilities, particularly regarding head-up displays and weapon-aiming systems. After a year he was offered a full-time position with an extremely tempting salary, but he declined as he felt he did not need to work full time and he did not want to take on the extra commitment. He was then asked to become the company's chairman, which he accepted.

Beetham thoroughly enjoyed his time with GEC Avionics and was struck by the similarities between the company and the Royal Air Force, rather than the differences, and he was impressed at how the company strived to produce the best possible equipment for the armed forces. In particular he was impressed with the people who designed and built the equipment, and by the great importance placed on its training of people to achieve standards of the highest quality. During one speech at an apprentice awards ceremony he highlighted the problem that existed with matching the country's educational system with the job market and, in particular, matching the skill requirements of industry. To him this was a worrying state of affairs given the nation's high unemployment figures of more than three million, and that the wealth of the country depended on a healthy manufacturing industry. He was pleased that GEC Avionics placed great emphasis on training and sponsored the wide variety of training schemes that were necessary to ensure young people gained the technical skills that were needed in the age of increasingly high technology.

In addition to joining the companies of Brixton Estate and GEC Avionics, Beetham was invited to join the Cheltenham College Council in 1983 as a governor. Beetham found Cheltenham to be a very good school, and very much enjoyed his time there, but after seven years the long drive from his home and the overnight stay became too demanding. He had very much enjoyed his time as a governor, as it was something he had always wanted to do, and so he was delighted when he was then invited to become a governor at Wymondham College in Norfolk. Wymondham was built on the site of a former Second World War US military hospital and had been the largest state boarding school in Europe when it had first opened but the old Nissen huts had now been replaced by some excellent facilities and it was much closer to home. Beetham was delighted to accept the offer and he spent the next seven years as a governor at Wymondham. He found the contrast between the two schools most interesting; Cheltenham was a very good public school, and the first of its type of the Victorian period, and Wymondham was an excellent state school and one of only a few of its type. Beetham thoroughly enjoyed his time at Wymondham and was always impressed with the staff. Such was the standard of the school that some of the boys were former pupils of the excellent Gresham's School nearby that had moved to Wymondham to complete their A level studies.

While Beetham continued to work with Brixton Estate and GEC Avionics until the age of seventy, it was his contribution to raising awareness of the Royal Air Force and preserving its legacy that would continue to dominate his life. Early in 1983 he took over as the chairman of the Trustees of the RAF Museum at Hendon from Sir Neil Cameron. At the time the museum had a debt of around £1.8 million. The Battle of Britain extension had cost a significant amount of money, as had the Bomber Command Hall, which was opened in April 1983 by the Queen Mother. The Bomber Command Hall, in particular, had proved difficult to secure funding for because of the controversy which always seemed to be associated with any project relating to the Bomber Command campaign. However, the museum had been keen to trace and preserve all the great bombers used during the RAF's history to depict the history of bombing offensives from 1914 until the present day. The timing of its creation had been in no small part dictated by a message that had come up through the ranks of many who had served with Bomber Command. The message had been simple: if the Trustees would take the risk of building the Bomber Command Hall and opening it in time for Arthur Harris's ninety-first birthday, then there would be a spontaneous donation of generosity that should raise the £2 million required.

Despite the great efforts of all those involved in trying to raise the money, unfortunately the funding did not materialise. The museum's annual income was barely covering the interest on the debt, which was nearly £200,000 per year, and so Beetham immediately had to address just how the museum would get back on its feet financially. He looked at various options, such as trying to get the interest rate lowered, and in the end he gained valuable support from the second PUS, John Blelloch, which resulted in the Treasury making an interest-free grant to the museum of £1.8 million to clear the debt, which had to be paid back within five years. For the museum this was a financial turning point as it would no longer have to pay interest to the bank; for Beetham it was a mark of personal success.

In April 1984 Sir Arthur Harris died at his home in Goring-on-Thames, just eight days before his ninety-second birthday. His funeral took place with full military honours in the nearby parish church and in May there was a memorial service at Westminster Abbey. Beetham was extremely honoured to be asked by Harris's family to give the address. During his address Beetham described Harris as a great commander, such was his high regard for the man that had led Bomber Command during the final decisive years of the Second World War. He described Harris as imaginative, far-sighted and inventive. While Harris could be blunt and outspoken in forcefully expressing his views, he was held in deep respect and affection by his staff and all who served with him. He was a compassionate man who had inspired his bomber crews; they all knew that he cared and would not hazard them unnecessarily. This was a remarkable feat of leadership on his part when he never had time personally to visit his stations but his personality had reverberated through his staff and commanders at all levels.

Beetham felt that Harris had not been well treated by the nation after the war as he had not, at the immediate post-war stage, been offered the peerage given to many whose contribution to victory had been far smaller. Winston Churchill later tried to correct the injustice done, but the fact that Harris did not accept the peerage offered was, perhaps, deeply regretted. The nation had lost a very great man and a very great gentleman, and Arthur Harris would live on in the memory of not only this country but all over the free world.

Beetham continued to work towards making the RAF Museum a success and, having secured the interest-free grant, the museum could struggle on for the next few years until it became more financially viable. Slowly and surely, through various fund-raising efforts and personal donations, the debt started to decrease. An example of the generosity of the public, particularly among former members of the RAF, was during a Bomber Command annual reunion dinner in 1984, soon after the death of Harris, when a whip-round of the tables, instigated by Beetham during his after-dinner speech, raised £3,500.

In the late 1980s the Ministry of Defence decided that the land of RAF Hendon was to be sold off. The total amount of land to be sold was around thirty-five acres but the museum was keen to remain at its location and needed about five acres of the site. Furthermore, the Grahame White hangar was a listed building and would need to be moved to within the museum's site.

The affair became drawn out over two years as there were delays while the Ministry of Defence had the land valued, and then further delays because of the legal processes involved. Beetham found this whole period frustrating and costly to the taxpayer as the MOD hired valuers and lawyers to value the site. In the end the MOD valued the land at £30 million and the museum was asked to pay £5 million to purchase its site. There was a time when one property company made a slightly reduced offer for the land, and was prepared to move the hangar, but the MOD was determined to hold out for its full asking price. Gradually the delay in the whole process of valuation, negotiation and legal processes resulted in fewer companies remaining interested and in the end the whole site was sold off for around £6 million. The museum was not in a position to pay anything towards the purchase of its own site. As Beetham put it during discussions, it made no difference whether the MOD wanted the museum to pay £1 or £1 million and he made it clear that any costs would have to be met by the MOD.

In 1989, following a meeting of a group of trustees and the armed forces minister, 3.5 acres of land was allocated to the museum by the MOD, but the Grahame White group of buildings remained, in a derelict state, on the old RAF Hendon site. Many years later, and after protracted negotiations with the developer and English Heritage, the property company agreed to move the hangar, followed by the watch office and control tower, which means that all the surviving buildings are retained on the Hendon site.

Now its financial future was stable, Beetham saw the museum's future task as three-fold – to enlighten, to educate and to entertain – and he could now help take the museum forward. By now there was a new director general of the RAF Museum, Michael Fopp, the son of the Australian Battle of Britain pilot, Desmond Fopp, and under Beetham's and Fopp's leadership the RAF Museum went from strength to strength. The opening of the Battle of Britain Experience in 1990 to mark the fiftieth anniversary of the battle demonstrated the intent of the museum to appeal to the more recent generation. Modern audio-visual aids, with rather clever 'talking heads' and careful inter-pretation of the objects on display were all tools used by the museum staff to tell the story in a more dynamic way. Furthermore, the cost of the exhibition had been met from fund-raising efforts and the commercial enterprise of the museum itself. Beetham's three elements – enlighten, educate and entertain – were all used in full measure and there was something for everyone, young or old, male or female, to enjoy. The modern RAF Museum was no longer the dusty, dark, solitary place which had characterised the word 'museum' in the past.

How long Beetham expected to remain as chairman of the trustees was not something he had particularly considered when he took over the position but he became so immersed in the work of the museum, just like everything else he ever became involved with, and he remained as chairman until 1999. One of the last projects he was involved with followed the MOD's decision to close RAF Cardington, near Bedford, and to sell off the land. This meant the closure of the aircraft restoration centre at Cardington and it was decided to move the centre to Cosford.

The move was successfully completed and Beetham was delighted and honoured when he was approached by the trustees of the museum for permission to name the centre after him. The Michael Beetham Conservation Centre at Cosford was officially opened by Beetham in 2002 and it quickly became one of the world's centres of excellence in aircraft conservation, restoring aircraft and artifacts for display at both of the RAF museums at Cosford and Hendon. The centre remains committed to preserving aviation heritage through its conservation of aircraft and associated exhibits, as well as recognising the need to ensure that unique skills are retained, nurtured and developed among the younger generation in respect of fostering ongoing aircraft conservation efforts for the future. The museum's unique apprentice programme takes in two young people each year for a four-year course that is becoming well regarded internationally, and the work of the centre, and the dedicated team of staff and volunteers, ensure that unique and historic aircraft are preserved for future generations; without them Britain's aviation heritage would be much poorer.

Having handed over as the chairman of the trustees, Beetham later became the president of the Society of Friends of the RAF Museum, which keeps him in regular contact with the museum. Michael Fopp remained as director general until February 2010, when he handed over his responsibilities to the deputy director general, Air Vice-Marshal Peter Dye, bringing to an end a period of twenty-two years during which he had led the museum with a commitment and extreme energy to all aspects of curatorship, and he could take enormous personal credit for making the museum the success it had become. Some of the major projects in recent years have included the museum's computerised collections' management system, which has made millions of objects held by the museum available to the public through the internet, the 'Milestones of Flight', the Grahame White factory buildings and, at Cosford, the opening of the immensely successful National Cold War Exhibition, which recently welcomed its one-millionth visitor.

Alongside his commitment to the RAF Museum, it has also been the Bomber Command Association that has become a significant part of Beetham's life for the past twenty-five years. The association was formed in 1985 as a way of continuing the strong comradeship and indomitable spirit of its members, and to perpetuate the command's history. In 1987 Beetham became its president after the death of Air Vice-Marshal Don Bennett, the legendary leader of the Pathfinder force.

Two years later, and five years after the death of Harris, as Beetham was leaving a service at the RAF Church of St Clement Danes in London, the chairman of the Bomber Command Association, Group Captain Ken Batchelor, suggested to him that it was time there was a statue of Sir Arthur Harris alongside that of Lord Dowding outside the church. Batchelor felt that Bomber Command should be represented in the same way that Fighter Command had been, with a statue of their leader, and the statues of two of the RAF's greatest wartime leaders would represent those men of Fighter Command that had saved the nation during the Battle of Britain and those of Bomber Command who had paved the way for victory. Beetham thought it a good idea and soon gained the support of the Chief of the Air Staff and the Air Force Board, after which more detailed planning took place, although at that time there was little or no publicity outside Bomber Command.

In March 1991 Beetham formally wrote to the Queen Mother, as patron of the Bomber Command Association, inviting her to perform the unveiling ceremony and asked her to nominate a date when the ceremony could take place. The date was set for 31 May the following year and there was some public controversy later in 1991 when the appeal went public and the press in both Britain and Germany seized upon the opportunity to resurrect the debate about the wartime bombing strategy of Harris. Some national papers went so far as to call for the project to be abandoned, whereas others showed great national support. There was certainly opposition to the project, not least from the peace activist Canon Paul Oestreicher, who continually seemed to stir up feeling; from the Mayor of Cologne, who said that the timing of the unveiling was extremely insensitive given that the date marked the fiftieth anniversary of the thousand-bomber raid against his city; and from the Mayor of Dresden.

Despite the opposition, the project continued without the use of public money. In fact, much of the negativity and opposition to the campaign in the national press had the opposite effect of bringing in more donations, enough to raise the £100,000 required, and the unveiling ceremony was planned as a private RAF occasion with the Queen Mother invited because of her own personal admiration for Harris.

The service of reconciliation and remembrance took place at St Clement Danes, as planned, on 31 May 1992. Only a few days before, protesters had put red paint on the base of the statue, but this was easily cleaned. On the day of the service the church was full and afterwards the Queen Mother unveiled the statue commemorating Harris and the crews of Bomber Command who had lost their lives in the service of the nation. Soon after starting her speech, the Queen Mother was interrupted by some heckling in the crowd. She turned to Beetham next to her and suggested that she should carry on. Beetham strongly agreed and the Queen

Mother continued to deliver an excellent speech, during which she spoke of Harris's inspiration as a leader and of the heavy burden he had carried during the last three years of the war. She went on to add that there was nowhere more fitting to honour Harris and the brave crews who died defending freedom than outside the Church of St Clement Danes, and beside Lord Dowding whose statue she had unveiled four years earlier.

Rather emotively, the day after the unveiling had taken place a wreath was laid at the memorial, which said 'From the people of East London with gratitude'. The statue of Harris was a major achievement for the Bomber Command Association but Beetham always felt that a permanent memorial to Bomber Command in London, along the same idea as the Fighter Command memorial on the Embankment, was long overdue. In 2008 the Bomber Command Association joined forces with the Heritage Foundation, which has commissioned more than a hundred memorials and plaques to famous Britons, to provide a permanent national memorial for the 55,573 men of Bomber Command who lost their lives during the Second World War. These losses were from a force of 125,000 volunteers and, in addition to those killed while serving with Bomber Command, a further 8,403 were wounded and 9,838 were taken as prisoners of war; the Command had suffered the highest casualty rate of any British organisation during the war. Former Bomber Command aircrew felt they never received any public recognition because of the controversy surrounding bombing raids against German cities such as Dresden, but Beetham has always been adamant that Harris and Bomber Command had done everything they had been ordered to do and there was no other way of hitting directly back at Germany other than bombing.

To discuss the proposal, the first meeting between the Bomber Command Association, led by Beetham, and the Heritage Foundation, led by its chairman, David Graham, was held at the RAF Club in London. The campaign soon gathered strong support from the leaders of all three main political parties and huge public support following an appeal in the *Daily Telegraph*. The memorial, which is of seven bronze statues of crew members in flying clothing and standing facing outwards in a circle, is to be situated in Green Park and is currently planned to be unveiled in the spring of 2012.

Among his many other commitments, Beetham is president of the RAF Historical Society. He was involved in its formation in 1986, the result of the labour of a small committee led by Air Marshal Sir Freddie Sowrey, as a public institution dedicated to examining the history of the RAF and to provide a forum at which it can be discussed. Sowrey was the society's first chairman and Beetham its president; in 1996 Sowrey handed over to Air Vice-Marshal Nigel Baldwin. The society has charitable status and, although it is entirely self-funding, has the support of the Air Force Board, with the aim of advancing the education of the public in the history of the Royal Air Force. Beetham remains a regular attendee at the seminars, usually at the RAF Museum Hendon, with each seminar exploring a specific theme and taking the form of papers read by interested parties, ranging from academic historians to veterans recalling their own personal experiences.

Since 1982 Beetham has held many other appointments including: Honourary Air Commodore of 2620 Squadron Royal Auxiliary Air Force Regiment between 1983 and 2001; he was made a fellow of the Royal Aeronautical Society in 1982; he was awarded the Poland Order of Merit in 1998 by the Polish president, Aleksander Kwaśniewski, for his work as a vice-president of the Polish Air Force Association in the UK; he was president of the RAF Club in Piccadilly for ten years during the 1990s and he is now a vice-patron; he is president of the 50 and 61 Squadrons' Association, president of the 214 Squadron Association and he also remains closely associated with the 57 and 630 Squadrons' Association at East Kirkby, where he opened the Heritage Centre in 1989 and then ten years later he opened the extension to the centre. There is also a classroom named after Beetham at the Defence Intelligence and Security Centre at Chicksands, which he opened in October 2009.

Whenever possible, Beetham also attends the annual dinner of the Old Philologians Association, which was formed for the former pupils and staff of St Marylebone Grammar School. The school was closed in 1981 after a history dating back nearly two hundred years, but Beetham is pleased to see the Old Philologians thriving as an association as he owed a great debt to the teaching received at the school, not only the academic content but also the more general education for life; this, he felt, had stood him in good stead throughout his career in the Royal Air Force.

Since first moving to Norfolk, Beetham has also been a member of the Royal West Norfolk Golf Club at Brancaster, where for many years he enjoyed playing golf once or twice a week and, not surprisingly, he soon joined the committee. He chaired the club's centenary committee from 1989 until the club's centenary year of 1992, and was honoured to be the club captain between April 1991 and April 1992. Beetham and his wife have always enjoyed living in the country, particularly walking in the forest nearby and along the sandy beaches of north-west Norfolk. Beetham immersed himself into the Norfolk lifestyle of country pursuits, in particular shooting, and his other main interests have remained reading about military history, something he has enjoyed throughout his life, and he always enjoyed spending time in his garden, although he readily admits that he was the brawn and his wife the brain!

Quite simply, there has been no retirement. For a marshal of the Royal Air Force, there was never likely to be a retirement and Beetham has continually been invited to perform many duties – presenting squadron standards, opening museums and other buildings, attending and speaking at public events, attending numerous lunches and dinners, many of which he is asked to speak at, attending committee meetings in his many different capacities and attending the annual reunions. While his diary may not be quite as full today as it was in the 1980s and 1990s, he remains extremely busy as he continues to strive for excellence in preserving the legacy of the service he so dearly loves.

CHAPTER 14

On Reflection

Sitting in his garden room at home, Beetham is able to reflect on the past. What a career it has been. He looks back to the summer of 1940, when he was just seventeen years old; there was no way he could have imagined just how things would turn out. During that long hard summer, when the future of the nation had hung in the balance, the heroics of the young men of Fighter Command had inspired him to join the RAF rather than to follow in his father's footsteps into the army.

Not surprisingly, he often reflects on his experiences during the Second World War. His training under the US Arnold Scheme had been good in terms of the quality and quantity of the flying training received, as well as fun, but the ground school left much to be desired and the 'honour system' had provided evidence of the difference in attitudes between the US and RAF cadets.

His operational tour as a young Lancaster pilot with 50 Squadron provided him with experiences that he would never forget – the excitement, the trauma, the tension, the fear, the pride, the elation and, of course, the sadness at the loss of comrades. Not that the losses were something he reflected on during the hard winter of 1943–4 – that came later. At the time he only looked as far as his next operational sortie but in his own mind he had always believed that he would survive.

There are still those who find it difficult to understand the impact of air warfare, and there are still those who criticise the bombing campaign on moral grounds; Beetham feels that these people completely fail to understand the feelings and emotions at the time, and the desire of the British public to hit back. What other way was there of hitting back? The strategic bomber offensive was unique and will remain so because the advent of nuclear weapons and the changing political world mean that there could never be such a sustained campaign ever again.

Beetham would like to have played a part in D-Day but he had only just finished his tour of operations and was an instructor at the time. Then, while everyone was celebrating the end of the war in Europe, he had fully expected to go to the Far East as part of Tiger Force to continue the war against Japan, but the dropping of the atomic bombs, on Hiroshima and Nagasaki had brought the Second World War to an abrupt end.

After the war Beetham had to decide what to do next in his life. He was still only twenty-two years old and enjoyed his flying. He also liked the people and took much pleasure in the RAF way of life, and so what else was there for him to do? There was a time when he wondered if he might go into law, but that thought never developed any further. He knew that he had been lucky to get a permanent commission in the post-war RAF and from that moment on he never looked back. His flying tours with 35 Squadron and then 82 Squadron were a memorable and unforgettable part of his life. In particular, his experiences as a young detachment commander with 82 Squadron in Africa, with the responsibility for the welfare and discipline of his detachment, proved to be a good test of his personal leadership skills, and his occasionally unorthodox style of leadership seemed to work well. Beetham also considered it to be the best tour in his career for developing his man management skills.

Beetham's time at Staff College provided him with his first opportunity to widen his thinking beyond Bomber Command, and his following tour in Operational Requirements at the Air Ministry opened his eyes to a completely new world. He experienced the problems of bringing the RAF's new V-bombers into service and has always believed that the decision to cancel the TSR2 was a great mistake as it left a capability gap that would take the RAF years to fill.

Beetham's memories of Operation Buffalo, the nuclear tests at Maralinga in Australia, and the four mighty explosions with the blinding flash and mushroom cloud, have remained with him ever since. Witnessing the tests undoubtedly had a major influence on all his strategic thinking later in his career, particularly regarding NATO's policy on the employment of nuclear weapons, and it certainly convinced him that it would not have been practicable to impose limits on any nuclear conflict.

Not surprisingly, the highlight of his peacetime flying tours was commanding 214 Squadron and Beetham was particularly pleased to have been one of the RAF's early tactical pioneers of air-to-air refuelling, which he felt the RAF had not grasped particularly well up until then. His record-breaking flight to Cape Town in July 1959 had proved to be one of the high points of his career, and the experience and knowledge he had personally gained during his tour, particularly in terms of the potential of in-flight refuelling as a capability, would be of great benefit to him later on in his career when he was Chief of the Air Staff during the Falklands conflict.

He had then enjoyed being at the centre of Bomber Command affairs during the early 1960s, but the introduction of nuclear weapons had taken warfare to a new level and the Cuban Missile Crisis of October 1962 had been a close-run thing. Beetham has always felt that it is a sad fact that man is an aggressive beast and if war cannot be prevented entirely then it is essential that a major war never recurs, and this can only be assured if defences are kept strong and the nuclear deterrent is kept intact and credible. Freedom comes at a cost.

Beetham realises that he had been fortunate throughout his career to have a number of overseas postings but none was better than his tour as the station commander at Khormaksar in Aden during the mid-1960s. It marked another high point of his career because it was the biggest of the RAF's overseas bases and operated many different types of aircraft, providing the RAF with a strong presence in the region as well as a vital staging post to Africa and the Far East. His arrival had virtually coincided with the start of a major terrorist campaign, which meant that much of his time was devoted to dealing with matters of security of the base, but they were great days and he no doubt benefitted from having Johnnie Johnson as his AOC. During his tour as station commander he had managed to fly with all of his units, and this gave him the most varied flying of his career. He had always been told that being a station commander was the best job anyone could ever have and Beetham could now confirm that, although being Chief of the Air Staff would be special too!

His time at the Imperial Defence College was a very pleasant sabbatical after a hard tour as a station commander that further broadened his experience into a wider sphere than just defence. In terms of training value, it was not in the same league as Staff College, but it was a most useful experience and he learned so much from his colleagues in the other services and from overseas that he found useful in subsequent years when he met up again with fellow graduates.

At the end of the 1960s, as director Operational Requirements 3 and then as director Strike Operations, he was able to see for himself the changes that had resulted from having a central

Ministry of Defence compared to his previous experience at the Air Ministry. Because of the central staff system a range of committees had emerged to get projects through the system. It was a laudable aim to make sure there was no duplication between the services but it could be carried too far. While he understood the need to have a central staff, for overall co-ordination and policy setting, Beetham always felt that more flexibility should be given to the service departments to get on with their own projects.

Although Beetham was perhaps disappointed not to have been given command of a group, this in no way held him back and he thoroughly enjoyed his time as commandant of the RAF Staff College at Bracknell. It had confirmed his feelings that staff training was a vital part of an officer's career development and from his own experience later on, in various headquarters within the service and NATO he saw the quality of the RAF's staff training had shone through in the calibre of work done in all headquarters, which was a great tribute to the service's staff training.

His NATO tour as Assistant Chief of Staff (Plans and Policy) at SHAPE had been most rewarding but occasionally frustrating. He had been the first British officer to fill this important post and thanks to his particularly close access to SACEUR he had gained a valuable insight into the daily workings of the Alliance at the very highest level. For nearly three years he took part in all the NATO planning and, even though most nations tried to push their own national interests, he still considered that it worked well. All the nations had wanted to be represented in the key areas of policy but, because of the language issues, the quality of the staff was often variable and progress at times was slow. This was inevitable, albeit frustrating, when agreement on major matters of policy was being sought from so many different nations. However, the NATO Alliance had proved to be a splendid example of international co-operation of fourteen nations working well and amicably together. While there had been the unavoidable differences and difficulties among the member nations, the measure of NATO's success was that there had been peace in Europe since the Second World War. Beetham has always been unsure of what those who call for the UK's withdrawal from NATO or the abandonment of the national nuclear deterrent really want. They say they want peace but the instability and chaos created would bring an appalling risk of conflict. Nuclear weapons alone cannot guarantee the nation's security and if the deterrent is to be credible then it must be backed by a meaningful conventional capability.

His time as Deputy Commander-in-Chief Strike Command was a relatively quiet period for the RAF; there still seemed plenty to do, but it was over all too quickly. Beetham had, however, been there long enough to recognise the need for a command headquarters that could oversee all of the operational roles of the RAF and to co-ordinate them. Many people were critical of the Strike Command organisation over the years, saying there had been too many layers and it was too centralised, but its work could not be done by the Ministry of Defence. Beetham also believes there remains a need for groups because the task, if left to one command headquarters, would be covering too wide a field; in wartime in particular, when the group commander needs to concentrate on his own tasks and represent any problems to a higher level. The different levels of command did not matter that much, as long as they avoided unnecessary duplication, but there had been too many bites over the years at revising the organisation which had been set up.

As he was already conversant with much of the German scene during his time at SHAPE, Beetham's time in command of RAF Germany and the Second Allied Tactical Air Force, one of NATO's main air forces, was yet another career high point. It was the height of the Cold War and the RAF Germany squadrons had an enviable reputation as second to no other force in NATO. As a member of the NATO Alliance it was essential that the RAF was represented on the continent with a significant physical presence that could be seen every day, and Europe was the forward deployment of the service – as near to the enemy as possible – and provided an essential buffer to protect the UK. The Joint Headquarters at Rheindahlen, with the army and RAF working side by side on a day-to-day basis, both nationally and in NATO, was a shining example of how an organisation should be run, with tactical forces working together; the co-operation and working relationship with 4 ATAF, too, had much improved since his previous days at SHAPE.

The loss of Andrew Humphrey, then Chief of the Defence Staff and his personal friend for many years, had come as devastating news. While he was somewhat surprised to learn that he was to become the next Chief of the Air Staff, Beetham was naturally delighted and felt extremely honoured, although he was sorry to leave his post in Germany earlier than expected. The consequence of his early selection as the CAS meant that Beetham then provided great continuity over a period of more than five years, although it was an extremely difficult period when he first took over. The RAF was still bearing the scars of manpower and pay problems, and – although he was particularly pleased with his success on the pay issue – he never liked the fact that the government put an arbitrary ceiling on RAF manpower not specifically related to the task.

The new Thatcher government in 1979 had provided a welcome change and a major step forward but it was not long before there were financial problems and a defence review, although the RAF did come out better than the other two services. What had concerned Beetham most, however, was the weakness of the UK's air defences, and this was at a time when the Soviet Union recognised the dominant influence air power had on modern warfare.

Beetham hoped he had got the balance right between the military and political aspects of being the Chief of the Air Staff. There had been many challenges working with two different governments, such as foreign policy, but all governments need to cut back. The Labour government did not like to preach the importance of defence but recognised its significance because of jobs. The Conservative government, on the other hand, liked to preach the importance of defence but did not always come up with the money. There were also problems with the turnover of politicians. When a minister was first appointed the armed forces would go to great lengths to brief the new minister and take him round on visits, only to find that the minister soon changed and they needed to start all over again. There was also the fact that some ministers thought they knew more than they actually did and were a menace, whereas others were prepared to listen and take advice.

Rarely has a Chief of the Air Staff had the opportunity to preside over the Royal Air Force during a significant military conflict, though all have to be ready for it; for Beetham the possibility became a reality in April 1982 when Argentina invaded the Falkland Islands. As the last CAS to have flown in the face of the enemy in the Second World War he could well appreciate the possible consequences of the decisions that had to be made. The Falklands conflict had come out of the blue and it provided the service with many challenges but it was another career success for Beetham. Whichever way he looked he was so proud of the RAF's contribution to the success of the campaign; he has always felt the Royal Navy has never truly acknowledged the RAF's outstanding contribution.

In many ways it was easier to be the CAS during the Falklands conflict than it had been during the defence review. During the Falklands campaign everyone was working together with one objective in mind. The services worked splendidly together, there was no bureaucracy, there was no shortage of money, rapid decisions had to be made and rapid action transpired, and, of course, there were great achievements. It had all been very stimulating when compared to peacetime, particularly during a period of a defence review when cuts were in prospect and it was vital for him to deploy the arguments with ministers and the other Chiefs of Staff to preserve the long-term future of the RAF.

While equipment procurement had often been compromised because of highly complicated and very expensive programmes, and collaborative projects had often been procured at the expense of capability, Beetham has always believed that it is the people who make the RAF what it is. The people are more important than the equipment; they have ensured that the service has always met the challenges it has faced. As the CAS he worked hard on communication and visiting RAF stations, and he felt that he was known around the RAF, although being popular was never essential as far as he was concerned. Nonetheless, he was satisfied that the RAF was in a better state in 1982 when he left than it was in 1977 when he had taken over as the CAS. It was certainly bigger, despite the defence review, and although he would have liked even more resources the service was 98,000 strong when he left, compared to 94,000 when he arrived.

Since then, the RAF has continued to reduce in size, in terms of manpower, and is now considerably less than half the size it was in 1982 and yet it has been asked to take on an increasing number of commitments. The world has changed radically since the last major defence review of 1998 and Beetham is only too aware that recent operations in Iraq and Afghanistan have shown how difficult it can be to run two campaigns concurrently. The fact that the RAF now remains actively involved in support of NATO operations in Afghanistan is proof that air power is not a luxury but is the essential foundation for any military operation.

What does the future hold for the RAF? Defence planners must look ahead ten to twenty years and whatever threat they may predict now is almost certain to be wrong; experience has shown that the threat seen now will almost certainly be very different in the future. It is the unexpected that happens, but planners need to make sure that the RAF has a balanced capability and a basic infrastructure of airfields to support whatever challenges it faces in the future.

Throughout his distinguished career Beetham has enjoyed exceptionally strong support and backing from his family: from his wife, who has worked tirelessly for him, to his two children and five grandchildren. He is enormously grateful to them all. Meanwhile there are more meetings to attend, particularly regarding the Bomber Command Memorial, and more letters to write. He remains, as ever, in demand and when he speaks everyone listens. His opinion is always valued and he is held in the highest respect by everyone who knows him. On reflection, and looking all the way back to 1941, was it the right decision to join the Royal Air Force? Unquestionably it was!

Summary of Promotions, Awards and Appointments

———

Date	Promotion	Award/Appointment
6 October 1941	U/T Pilot	Initial Training + Pilot Training (USA)
13 December 1942	Pilot Officer	
12 March 1943		7 Elementary Flying Training School, Desford
6 April 1943		18 Advanced Flying Unit, Church Lawford
1 June 1943		14 Operational Training Unit, Cottesmore
13 June 1943	Flying Officer	
14 September 1943		1654 Heavy Conversion Unit, Wigsley
26 October 1943		50 Squadron, Skellingthorpe
15 January 1944	Acting Flight Lieutenant	
6 June 1944		Awarded Distinguished Flying Cross
20 June 1944		Lancaster Finishing School, Syerston
1 April 1945		57 Squadron, East Kirkby
24 June 1945	Acting Squadron Leader	
1 September 1945		Permanent Commission
25 November 1945		35 Squadron, Graveley
24 February 1947	Flight Lieutenant	Personnel Staff, HQ Bomber Command, High Wycombe
20 May 1949		82 Squadron, Eastleigh, Kenya
5 November 1951		205 Advanced Flying School, Middleton St George
1 December 1951		231 Operational Conversion Unit, Bassingbourn
1 January 1952	Squadron Leader	Awarded King's Commendation

Date	Promotion	Award/Appointment
28 April 1952		RAF Staff College, Andover
15 April 1953		Operational Requirements 1a, Air Ministry
7 May 1956		Operation Buffalo, Maralinga, Australia
10 February 1957		3 All-Weather Jet Squadron, Manby
24 April 1957		231 Operational Conversion Unit, Bassingbourn
22 July 1957		Valiant Course, Gaydon
1 January 1958	Wing Commander	
10 February 1958		OC 214 Squadron, Marham
1 January 1960		Awarded Air Force Cross
7 June 1960		HQ 3 Group, Mildenhall (Ops Staff)
4 October 1961	Group Captain	HQ Bomber Command (Trg Staff), High Wycombe
9 July 1962		HQ Bomber Command (Ops Staff), High Wycombe
23 October 1964		OC RAF Khormaksar, Aden
1 July 1966	Air Commodore	
1 January 1967		Companion of the Order of the British Empire
10 January 1967		Imperial Defence College, London
4 January 1968		Director Operational Requirements 3, Ministry of Defence
11 November 1968		Director Strike Operations, Ministry of Defence
27 September 1970	Air Vice-Marshal	Commandant RAF Staff College, Bracknell
14 August 1972		Assistant Chief of Staff (Policy & Plans), SHAPE, Belgium
7 June 1975	Air Marshal	Deputy C-in-C Strike Command, High Wycombe
1 January 1976		Knight Commander of the Order of the Bath
19 January 1976		Commander 2 ATAF & C-in-C RAF Germany
21 May 1977	Air Chief Marshal	
1 August 1977		Chief of the Air Staff
1 January 1978		Grand Cross of the Order of the Bath
14 October 1982	Marshal of the Royal Air Force	

Select Bibliography

Air Force List, various years.

Arnold, Lorna, *A Very Special Relationship* (HMSO Publication Centre, London, 1987)

Bowyer, Chaz, *History of the RAF* (Hamlyn, 1977).

—— , *For Valour, the Air VCs* (William Kimber & Co., 1978).

Ethell, Jeffrey and Alfred Price, *Air War South Atlantic* (Sidgwick & Jackson, 1983).

Gander, Terry, *Encyclopedia of the Modern RAF* (Patrick Stephens, 1984).

Guinn, Gilbert S., *The Arnold Scheme* (History Press, Charleston SC, 2007).

Halley, James J., *The Squadrons of the RAF and Commonwealth* (Air-Britain, 1988).

Jackson, Bill and Dwin Bramall, *The Chiefs* (Brassey's UK, London, 1992).

Jacobs, Peter, *The Lancaster Story* (Arms & Armour Press, 1996).

—— , *Bomb Aimer Over Berlin* (Pen & Sword Aviation, 2007).

Lee, David, *Flight from the Middle East* (Air Historical Branch (RAF), 1978).

Mason, R. A., *British Air Power in the 1980s* (Ian Allan, 1984).

Middlebrook, Martin and Chris Everitt, *The Bomber Command War Diaries* (Penguin Books, 1985).

NATO Information Service, *NATO Facts and Figures* (Brussels, NIS, 1976).

Nott, John, *Here Today Gone Tomorrow* (Politico's Publishing, London, 2002).

Operational Record Books, various (Air Historical Board).

Probert, Henry, *High Commanders of the Royal Air Force* (HMSO, 1991).

—— , *Bomber Harris: His Life and Times* (Greenhill Books, 2003).

RAF Historical Society, various journals, (Brighton, Hastings, Oxford, 1993 onwards), including: 'RAF Reserve and Auxiliary Forces', 'The Birth of Tornado', 'The Cuban Missile Crisis', 'The Direction of the Air Policy in the 1950s and 1960s', 'The Royal Air Force in Germany 1945–1993'

Temple Press, *The History of the Royal Air Force* (Aerospace Publishing Ltd, 1984)

Tillotson, Michael, *Dwin Bramall* (Sutton Publishing, Stroud, 2005).

Tevenen James, A. G., *The RAF: The Past 30 Years* (Macdonald and Jane's Publishers, 1976).

Wynn, Humphrey, *RAF Nuclear Deterrent Forces* (Air Historical Branch, 1991).

Index

Ranks are shown in the index as correct at the time of inclusion in the book. Where more than one reference to an individual is made, the most senior rank attained is shown.